THE
ASSEMBLY
HANDBOOK

THE
ASSEMBLY
HANDBOOK

David Self

HUTCHINSON
London Melbourne Sydney Auckland Johannesburg

Hutchinson and Co. (Publishers) Ltd
An imprint of the Hutchinson Publishing Group
17–21 Conway Street, London W1P 6JD

Hutchinson Publishing Group (Australia) Pty Ltd
PO Box 496, 16–22 Church Street, Hawthorn, Melbourne, Victoria 3122

Hutchinson Group (NZ) Ltd
32–34 View Road, PO Box 40-086, Glenfield, Auckland 10

Hutchinson Group (SA) (Pty) Ltd
PO Box 337, Bergvlei 2012, South Africa

First published 1984
Reprinted 1985
© Selection and commentary David Self 1984

Set in VIP Palatino by
D. P. Media Limited, Hitchin, Hertfordshire

Printed and bound in Great Britain by
Anchor Brendon Ltd, Tiptree, Essex

British Library Cataloguing in Publication Data
The Assembly handbook.
    1. Schools—Exercises and recreations
    I. Self, David
    377'.1   LB3015

ISBN 0 09 159240 2

Contents

Contents

Contents

7

Contents

INTRODUCTION

Suppose you become a headteacher at the age of forty-five. Suppose you decide that you personally will conduct no more than one school assembly a week. By the time your retire, you will have conducted about 800 separate assemblies. Each pupil in your school will have been present for at least 150 of those assemblies.

Or suppose you are a willing deputy head, a head of house or year, or a member of staff who admits a readiness to lead assembly. You will be responsible for devising an even greater number of assemblies during your career.

This *Assembly Handbook* has been compiled to help those whose responsibility it is to provide a succession of memorable, educational and possibly spiritual experiences for groups of pupils, often of widely differing ages, gathered together in a far from suitable hall. As an anthology of passages suitable for reading in such circumstances, it is complete in itself. It is also complementary to an earlier and similar book, *Anthology for Assembly*, the gratifying success of which has led in part to the compilation of this present collection of passages. Should a user fail to find a passage on a particular theme or for a specific season in this book, then he or she may well find it in *Anthology for Assembly*.

Of course, once upon a time, when assembly consisted of a story, a hymn and a prayer, everything was very much easier. According to a strict rota, the school prefects read their way through St Mark's Gospel, the Acts of the Apostles and selected chunks of the Old Testament. Everyone sang a well-known Christian hymn with some measure of conviction and more or less in unison. The teacher on duty could then enlist the power of prayer in a drive towards better behaviour, tidy corridors and thorough revision.

There are many schools where assembly is still an act of Christian worship and frequently it is one that is very much more inspiring and uplifting than the one painted above. For such schools, I hope this *Handbook* will provide a variety of religious and secular readings that will illuminate and enrich such acts of worship.

In many secondary schools the picture is very different. The lack of a suitable hall may mean there can never be an assembly of the whole school in one place. Shortage of time in the school day, cost of suitable materials, problems relating to the provision of music, and pupil (and staff) apathy all contribute to the great 'assembly problem'. So great are these practical problems that reports abound of schools where assembly occurs 'only twice a decade', 'never', 'just for fire drill and bomb hoaxes' or 'when a member of staff dies'.

These harsh practicalities are not the only reasons the 1944 Education Act's requirement that each school day 'shall begin with collective worship on the part of all pupils in attendance at the school' is neglected. As that Act was being drafted and debated, news of Nazi atrocities was becoming public, as was the bleakness of Stalin's God-less state. Then it seemed natural to build an educational system upon Christian practice.

Much has changed in the intervening forty years. Britain has become a multi-cultural society. It has also become much more secular and (many would say) more materialistic. Perhaps even more importantly, so far as the assembly is concerned, our educational philosophies have matured and deepened and assemblies are now assessed by educational as well as religious standards. This places great strains on those charged with their planning and conduct. An assembly leader may anguish over the presentation of anything too explicitly Christian and the danger of involving the non-religious in a hypocritical exercise, yet still wish to present standards and values which have passed the test of time.

However, even committed bodies like the Free Churches Federal Council have stated (in a discussion document published in 1976) that 'the time has clearly come for a distinction to be drawn between Christian worship (or even religious worship) and school assemblies'; while, in 1983, the Christian Education Movement welcomed the suggestion that there should be discussion about the nature of assemblies.

Problems and the continuing debate aside, the assembly (whether it be of the whole school, upper or lower school, house or year) remains a unique and precious opportunity to nurture an awareness of standards and values, to develop a sense of community, to widen emotional responses and to create a sense of wonder, mystery and joy.

The passages included in this book have been selected with those opportunities in mind. They will not all work in every circumstance but they have all worked successfully in varying conditions. In selecting them, I have drawn on my experience over ten years as a teacher responsible for school assembly, my continuing work on BBC School Radio religious education and assembly programmes and on my other work in education and religious broadcasting.

I have chosen passages which have a wide and immediate appeal and which read aloud naturally, even in large assemblies. I have not included anything I would be embarrassed to stand up and read aloud myself. I have let the writers' voices be heard unadapted, rather than rewriting them in some kind of bland prose.

Rehearsal is advised before any reading, and some thought should be given as to who is the best available reader (or readers) for any particular passage. Brief introductions are provided where necessary. These should be adapted to meet local needs.

Sixty of the passages have been grouped thematically and a sequence of such readings can be used within one assembly or during a series of assemblies. Also included are series of single and seasonal readings for individual assemblies, together with notes on the various religious calendars and the occurrence of festivals and special occasions.

In many of the secondary schools in Britain, it now appears to be quite common to include a semi-dramatized presentation by two or more readers or performers. In some schools this format is used almost daily. To help them and those who would like to initiate such presentations, a series of simple scripts has been provided at the end of the *Handbook*. (See page 237.)

I hope that this new collection of ideas and material for assembly will be of help and inspiration to those who carry the responsibility of organizing assemblies. Despite all the problems, school assembly remains an event of considerable educational, social and spiritual potential.

CALENDARS

The Christian calendar

The Christian calendar is a mixture of fixed dates (e.g. Christmas Day and most saints' days) and movable feasts.

The churches' year begins traditionally with Advent Sunday (the fourth Sunday before Christmas). Advent is a period of preparation leading up to the coming (or advent) of Jesus on Christmas Day. After the twelve days of the Christmas festival, Epiphany (6 January) marks the visit of the wise men to the infant Jesus.

The calendar dates of the spring festivals are governed by the date of Easter. Easter Sunday is the first Sunday after the full moon that occurs on the day of the spring equinox (21 March) or on any of the next twenty-eight days. Easter Sunday can therefore fall on any date between and including 22 March to 25 April. Easter in the Orthodox Church (e.g. in Greece) is calculated by another method.

Lent is a period of forty days, beginning with Ash Wednesday, which leads up to Easter. Traditionally a period of fasting of various degrees of severity, it is now seen more as a time of penitence and thoughtful preparation for Easter.

Holy Week is the week before Easter. It begins with Palm Sunday (the entry of Jesus into Jerusalem), goes through Maundy Thursday (the Last Supper), Good Friday (the Crucifixion) and so to Easter. The first Easter occurred at the Jewish Passover (see pages 215–16). As Passover is always on the 14th of the Jewish month of Nisan, the two festivals do not always coincide.

The end of the life of Jesus on earth is marked by Ascension Day (forty days after Easter, and always on a Thursday), and the coming of the Holy Spirit to the apostles at Whitsun or Pentecost (see pages 229–31) is commemorated ten days later.

15

The Western world numbers years from the supposed year of the birth of Jesus. AD means *Anno Domini*, the year of our Lord. An alternative term for AD is CE (Common Era).

The Jewish calendar

The Jewish calendar is based on both lunar and solar movements. Because the lunar and solar years are of different lengths, an extra or 'leap' month is added to the calendar seven times in each nineteen years. This keeps the months (and festivals) in harmony with the seasons of the year but results in minor variations when compared with the Western calendar. Precise dates can be found at the front of most desk or office diaries. Note that Jewish holy days begin at dusk on the day before given dates.

Jewish tradition calculates that the world was created in 3760 BC (or BCE: Before the Common Era). To calculate the Jewish year from the Western year, one therefore adds 3760 to the year. For example, 1986 is 5746 in the Jewish calendar. (Although all Jews use this system, they do not believe the world is only 5000 years old.)

The Muslim calendar

The Quran decrees the use of the lunar year, which is eleven days shorter than the solar year. In relation to the Western year, the Muslim year therefore starts 'earlier' each year and so, for example, the month of Ramadan can occur in any season.

The precise timing of a Muslim holy day can be calculated only a few days before its occurrence, and takes account of local sunrise and sunset times.

Muslim years are numbered from the *Hegira* when the Prophet and his companions left Mecca for Medina (622 in the Common Era, i.e. AD 622). They are described as AH (Anno Hegirae). New Year's Day 1405 AH coincided with 27 September 1984. See pages 235–6.

The Hindu calendar

The Hindu calendar evolved in ancient India. It has twelve months linked to the phases of the moon. Hinduism has many holidays. Some are celebrated by the majority of Hindus, others only in certain communities or areas, and dates may differ from area to area. See also pages 54–5.

Sikh festivals

Sikhs have two kinds of festivals: 'melas' (meetings or fairs) which re-interpret Hindu festivals, and 'gurpurds' which mark the anniversaries of the gurus (see page 222).

Three of the major 'melas' are Hola Mohalla (the Sikh 'holi', a spring festival which occurs in February or March), Baisakhi (the anniversary of the khalsa, see page 222), and Divali (see pages 190–1) when Sikhs celebrate the release of Guru Hargobind from captivity in 1620.

The most important gurpurds are the birthdays of Guru Nanak and Guru Gobind Singh and the martyrdoms of Guru Arjan and Guru Tegh Bahadur.

Sikhs usually defer the celebration of a feast to the weekend closest to the actual anniversary.

The Chinese calendar

The Western calendar has been used in China since 1911, though it was not fully adopted until 1949.

The Chinese calendar was a lunar calendar, following the phases of the moon, and calendars printed today still show the dates in the lunar calendar, underneath the Western-style dates. So, while 1 January is recognized as New Year's Day, it is not a holiday, for the celebrations come with the beginning of the lunar year, which may fall in either January or February.

Another way of marking the years in traditional China was according to the twelve-year cycle, represented by a series of twelve animals. The animal of your birth year was one of the points considered by fortune-tellers. In simple terms, it was not a good idea for a man born in the year of the rat to marry a lady born in the year of the tiger or the snake.

1984	Rat	1990	Horse
1985	Ox	1991	Goat
1986	Tiger	1992	Monkey
1987	Hare	1993	Cock
1988	Dragon	1994	Dog
1989	Snake	1995	Pig

A CALENDAR OF READINGS

Autumn Term
(Page numbers appear in *italics*.)

11   Alexander Solzhenitsyn born 1918   *(163)*
End of term: Christmas

Spring Term
January
4   Louis Braille born 1809   *(136)*
6   Epiphany, Twelfth Night   *(204)*
17   Wassailing   *(207–8)*
18–25 Week of Prayer for Christian Unity   *(111, 182)*
26   Australia Day   *(104)*
Also: Chinese New Year (late January-early February)   *(206–7)*
February
2   Candlemas   *(208–9)*
7   Sir Thomas More born 1478   *(181–5)*
11   First Lourdes Miracle 1858   *(92–4)*
14   St Valentine's Day   *(136, 154, 156)*
20   Archbishop Luwum (memorial service 1977)   *(60–2)*
23   John Keats died 1821   *(121)*
Also: Shrove Tuesday   *(209–11)*
       Ash Wednesday   *(15, 209–10)*
       Lent   *(15, 209–10, 273)*
       Purim (February–March)   *(211–13)*
March
8   International Women's Day   *(32–6)*
17   St Patrick   *(213–15)*
25   Lady Day (quarter day); Feast of the Annunciation (day commemorating visit of the angel to Mary)
29   Start of the Crimean War 1854   *(45–7)*
Also: Mothering Sunday (mid-Lent Sunday)   *(163)*
       Passover (late March–early April)   *(215–16)*
       Palm Sunday   *(15)*
       Maundy Thursday   *(217–18)*
       Good Friday   *(218, 264)*
       Easter   *(220)*
April
5   End of financial/tax year   *(254, 255)*
7   World Health Day   *(261, 270)*
12   Yuri Gagarin in space 1961   *(48)*
13   Baisakhi   *(222–4)*

Summer Term

April
26   Daniel Defoe died 1730   *(133–5)*
28   Lord Shaftesbury born 1801   *(58–60)*
30   Iranian Embassy siege 1980   *(141)*

May
1   May Day, Labour Day   *(224–5)*
8   Mother Julian of Norwich   *(56–8)*
12   Florence Nightingale born 1820   *(45–7)*
        Christian Aid Week (third week in May)   *(275–8)*
29   Oak Apple Day   *(231)*
Also: Rogationtide   *(226–7)*
        Ascension Day (forty days after Easter)   *(226)*
        Pentecost   *(229–31)*
        Wesak (May full moon)   *(227–9)*

June
15   World Children's Day   *(102–3)*
24   Midsummer Day, St John the Baptist   *(232–4)*
27   Helen Keller born 1880   *(135–6)*
Also: Hindu pilgrimages   *(234–5)*

July
7   Sir Thomas More died 1535   *(81–5)*
15   St Swithin   *(138)*
21   First moon walk 1969   *(48–9)*
Also: Summer holidays   *(278)*

Precise dates for the festivals of all the world faiths for any given year are available in the *Calendar of Religious Festivals*, published annually by the Commission for Racial Equality, Elliott House, 10–12 Allington Street, London SW1E 5EH; distributed by the Shap Working Party, 7 Alderbrook Road, Solihull, West Midlands B91 1NH.

THEMES

1
Cautionary tales

Three tales, not to be taken too seriously, but each making a point.

1: A CHEWING GUM STORY

Though every thoughtful man agrees
That one good way to clean with ease
Your teeth and their interstices
   Is by consistent chewing,
'Twill harm you not to muse upon
This history of little John,
And mark how chewing led him on
   And on to his undoing.

When first he joined the chewing corps
The years of John were only four,
Or possibly a trifle more,
   To be precisely truthful,
And there can be but slight excuse
For parents who would introduce
The chewing-gum-tree's tempting juice
   To one so very youthful.

For lo! without an interlude
Through all the years that next ensued
Young Johnny chewed and chewed and chewed
   With sedulous devotion,
And up and down would go his jaws,
And round and round without a pause,
In flat defiance of the laws
   Against perpetual motion.

When one recalls what people say
Of stones that dripping wears away,
Or thinks of how each washing-day
   Reduces mangle rollers,
'Tis hardly to be wondered at,
As Johnny went on chewing, that
He gradually bevelled flat
   His whole supply of molars.

No sooner had they sunk from sight
Than his bicuspids, left and right,
Were called upon to do their bite,
   And did it for a little,
But as bicuspids are not meant
To grind away to that extent,
They very naturally went
   And crumbled, being brittle.

In vain his mother shrieked, 'My son,
What have you been and gone and done?'
He wore the rest out one by one,
   Till at the age of twenty,
Whene'er his mouth was opened wide,
As when he yawned at eventide,
You saw no teeth at all inside,
   Instead of seeing plenty.

                               H. A. Field

2: IF YOU ONLY STOPPED TO THINK

Dear Sir,

   By the time I arrived at the house where you sent me to make repairs, the storm had torn a good fifty bricks from the roof. So I set up on the roof of the building, a beam and a pulley and I hoisted up a couple of baskets of bricks. When I had finished repairing the building there were a lot of bricks left over since I had brought up more than I needed and also because there were some bad, reject bricks that I still had left to bring down. I hoisted the basket back up again and hitched up the line at the bottom. Then I climbed back up again and filled up the basket with the extra bricks. Then I went down to the bottom and untied the line. Unfortunately, the basket of bricks was much heavier than I was and before I knew what was happening, the basket started to plunge down, lifting me suddenly off the ground. I decided to keep my grip and hang on, realizing that to let go would end in disaster – but half-way up I ran into the basket coming down and received a severe blow on the shoulder.

I then continued to the top, banging my head against the beam and getting my fingers jammed in the pulley. When the basket hit the ground it burst its bottom, allowing all the bricks to spill out. Since I was now heavier than the basket I started back down again at high speed. Halfway down I met the basket coming up, and received several severe injuries on my shins. When I hit the ground, I landed on the bricks, getting several more painful cuts and bruises from the sharp edges.

At this moment I must have lost my presence of mind, because I let go of the line. The basket came down again, giving me another heavy blow on the head, and putting me in the hospital.

I respectfully request sick leave.

Jean L'Anselme
(Translated from the French by Michael Benedikt)

3: WHEN DEATH CAME TO BAGHDAD

This story from the Middle East illustrates a widespread Eastern belief that you cannot 'cheat' death. Whatever you do, the Angel of Death will come for you at an appointed time.

Sufism is a sect of Islam. Sufis seek to come close to God through self-denial, prayer and also through spiritual exercises which include the dances that made them known as 'Whirling Dervishes'. Many Sufis were (and still are) famous teachers and have groups of students or disciples. *(See also page 174.)*

The disciple of a Sufi of Baghdad was sitting in the corner of an inn one day when he heard two figures talking. From what they said he realized that one of them was the Angel of Death.

'I have several calls to make in this city during the next three weeks,' the Angel was saying to his companion.

Terrified, the disciple concealed himself until the two had left. Then, applying his intelligence to the problem of how to cheat the possible call from death, he decided that if he kept away from Baghdad he should not be touched. From this reasoning it was but a short step to hiring the fastest horse available and spurring it night and day towards the distant town of Samarkand.

Meanwhile Death met the Sufi teacher and they talked about various people. 'And where is your disciple so-and-so?' asked Death.

'He should be somewhere in this city, spending his time in contemplation, perhaps in a caravanserai,' said the teacher.

'Surprising,' said the Angel, 'because he is on my list. Yes, here it is: I have to collect him in four weeks' time at Samarkand, of all places.'

Idries Shah

2
The human zoo

In any organized group of mammals, no matter how co-operative, there is always a struggle for social dominance. As he pursues this struggle, each adult individual acquires a particular social rank, giving him his position, or status, in the group hierarchy. The situation never remains stable for very long, largely because all the status strugglers are growing older. When the overlords, or 'top-dogs', become senile, their seniority is challenged and they are overthrown by their immediate subordinates. There is then renewed dominance squabbling as everyone moves a little farther up the social ladder. At the other end of the scale, the younger members of the group are maturing rapidly, keeping up the pressure from below.

That is the start of the chapter on 'Status and Super-status' in Desmond Morris's famous book The Human Zoo.
   In the book, he aims to help us to understand our own behaviour by comparing it to that of animals. In this particular chapter he is concerned to show how leaders control their followers. The excerpts that follow refer mainly to national leaders and may be used to provide a commentary on news items or historical incidents.
   Alternatively, with subtle introductions (which must be devised to suit local circumstances), they could be used to provide a commentary on 'gang' or group leaders.

If you are to rule your group and to be successful in holding your position of power, there are ten golden rules you must obey. They apply to all leaders, from baboons to modern presidents and prime ministers. . . . These are four of those rules.

1: DOMINATION

You must clearly display the trappings, postures and gestures of dominance.

For the baboon this means a sleek, beautifully groomed, luxuriant coat of hair; a calm, relaxed posture when not engaged in disputes; a deliberate and purposeful gait when active. There must be no outward signs of anxiety, indecision or hesitancy.

With a few superficial modifications, the same holds true for the human leader. The luxuriant coat of fur becomes the rich and elaborate costume of the ruler, dramatically excelling those of his subordinates. He assumes postures unique to his dominant role. When he is relaxing, he may recline or sit, while others must stand until given permission to follow suit. This is also typical of the dominant baboon, who may sprawl out lazily while his anxious subordinates hold themselves in more alert postures near by. The situation changes once the leader stirs into aggressive action and begins to assert himself. Then, be he baboon or prince, he must rise into a more impressive position than that of his followers. He must literally rise above them, matching his psychological status with his physical posture.

For the baboon boss this is easy: a dominant monkey is nearly always much larger than his underlings. He has only to hold himself erect and his greater body size does the rest. The situation is enhanced by cringing and crouching on the part of his more fearful subordinates. For the human leader, artificial aids may be necessary. He can magnify his size by wearing large cloaks or tall headgear. His height can be increased by mounting a throne, a platform, an animal, or a vehicle of some kind, or by being carried aloft by his followers. The crouching of the weaker baboons becomes stylized in various ways: subordinate humans lower their height by bowing, curtsying, kneeling, kowtowing, salaaming or prostrating.

The ingenuity of our species permits the human leader to have it both ways. By sitting on a throne on a raised platform, he can enjoy both the relaxed position of the passive dominant and the heightened position of the active dominant at one and the same time, thus providing himself with a doubly powerful display posture.

The dignified displays of leadership that the human animal shares with the baboon are still with us in many forms today.

They can be seen in their most primitive and obvious conditions in generals, judges, high priests and surviving royalty. They tend to be more limited to special occasions than they once were, but when they do occur they are as ostentatious as ever. Not even the most learned academics are immune to the demands of pomp and finery on their more ceremonial occasions.

2: RIVALRY

In moments of active rivalry you must threaten your subordinates aggressively.

At the slightest sign of any challenge from a subordinate baboon, the group leader immediately responds with an impressive display of threatening behaviour. There is a whole range of threat displays available, varying from those motivated by a lot of aggression tinged with a little fear to those motivated by a lot of fear and only a little aggression. The latter – the 'scared threats' of weak-but-hostile individuals – are never shown by a dominant animal unless his leadership is tottering. When his position is secure he shows only the most aggressive threat displays. He can be so secure that all he needs to do is to indicate that he is about to threaten, without actually bothering to carry it through. A mere jerk of his massive head in the direction of the unruly subordinate may be sufficient to subdue the inferior individual. These actions are called 'intention movements', and they operate in precisely the same way in the human species. A powerful human leader, irritated by the actions of a subordinate, need only jerk his head in the latter's direction and fix him with a hard stare, to assert his dominance successfully. If he has to raise his voice or repeat an order, his dominance is slightly less secure, and he will, on eventually regaining control, have to re-establish his status by administering a rebuke or a symbolic punishment of some kind.

The act of raising his voice, or raging, is only a weak sign in a leader when it occurs as a reaction to an immediate threat. It may also be used spontaneously or deliberately by a strong ruler as a general device for reaffirming his position. A dominant baboon may behave in the same way, suddenly charging at his subordinates and terrorizing them, reminding them of his powers. It enables him to chalk up a few points, and after that he can more easily get his own way with the merest nod of his head. Human leaders perform in this manner from time to time, issuing stern edicts, making lightning inspections or haranguing the group with vigorous speeches.

3: PROTECTION

You must protect the weaker members of the group from undue persecution.

Females with young tend to cluster round the dominant male baboon. He meets any attack on these females or on unprotected infants with a savage onslaught. As a defender of the weak he is ensuring the survival of the future adults of the group. Human leaders have increasingly extended their protection of the weak to include also the old, the sick and the disabled. This is because efficient rulers not only need to defend the growing children, who will one day swell the ranks of their followers, but also need to reduce the anxieties of the active adults, all of whom are threatened with eventual senility, sudden sickness or possible disability. With most people the urge to give aid in such cases is a natural development of their biologically co-operative nature. But for the leaders it is also a question of making people work more efficiently by taking a serious weight off their minds.

4: DECISION-MAKING

You must make decisions concerning the social activities of your group.

When the baboon leader decides to move, the whole group moves. When he rests, the group rests. When he feeds, the group feeds. Direct control of this kind is, of course, lost to the leader of a human super-tribe, but he can nevertheless play a vital role in encouraging the more abstract directions his group takes. He may foster the sciences or push towards a greater military emphasis. As with the other golden rules of leadership, it is important for him to exercise this one even when it does not appear to be strictly necessary. Even if a society is cruising happily along on a set and satisfactory course, it is vital for him to change that course in certain ways in order to make his impact felt. It is not enough simply to alter it as a reaction to something that is going wrong. He must spontaneously, of his own volition, insist on new lines of development, or he will be considered weak and colourless. If he has no ready-made preferences and enthusiasms, he must invent them. If he is seen to have what appear to be strong convictions on certain matters, he will be taken more seriously on *all* matters. Many modern leaders seem to overlook this and their political 'platforms' are desperately lacking in originality. If they win the battle for leadership it is not because they are more inspiring than their rivals but simply because they are less uninspiring.

Desmond Morris

3

Woman's role

1: IN THE SEVENTEENTH CENTURY

This description of the ideal English housewife and of her duties was written in 1615.

She ought, above all things, to be of an upright and sincere religion, and in the same both zealous and constant; giving by her example, an incitement and spur unto all her family to pursue the same steps, and to utter forth by the instruction of her life, those virtuous fruits of good living, which shall be pleasing both to God and his creatures. Next unto this sanctity and holiness of life, it is meet that our English housewife be a woman of great modesty and temperance as well inwardly as outwardly. Inwardly, as in her behaviour and carriage towards her husband, wherein she shall shun all violence of rage, passion and humour, coveting less to direct than to be directed, appearing ever unto him pleasant, amiable and delightful; and though occasion, mishaps or the misgovernment of his will may induce her to contrary thoughts, yet virtuously to suppress them, and with a mild sufference rather to call him home from his error, than with the strength of anger to abate the least spark of his evil, calling into her mind that evil and uncomely language is deformed though uttered even to servants, but most monstrous and ugly when it appears before the presence of a husband. To conclude, our English housewife must be of chaste thought, stout courage, patient, untired, watchful, diligent, witty, pleasant, constant in friendship, full of good neighbourhood, wise in discourse, but not frequent therein, sharp and quick of speech, but not bitter or talkative, secret in her affairs, comfortable in her counsels, and generally skilful in all the worthy knowledge which do belong to her vocation. *Gervase Markham*

2: IN BANGLADESH

A Christian Aid worker in Bangladesh describes the role of women in that country.

Women's Lib is a concept usually connected with the urban North, not with the poorest regions of the South. Yet in out-of-the-way villages of Bangladesh the fight for women's rights is as much a live issue as anywhere else. And the struggle of its campaigners can be a lonely one.

Some of these campaigners belong to the organization Nijera Kori, which means 'help yourself'. Its aim in a largely Muslim society is not women's emancipation as normally understood in magazine columns, but the support of women who are working to free themselves from the basic restraint of poverty and oppression.

Women in rural communities in Bangladesh are often the victims of a family life in which they play the leading role. As in any traditional societies, they are expected to provide for husbands and children first and foremost, leaving very little room for their own needs. In some families, even a bid for independence as innocent as a mothers' meeting or family planning session is a potential threat to marriage and family unity.

An organization which supports small-scale women's activities such as literacy schemes, co-operative groups or vocational training must approach with caution. Only if the confidence of the community has been won, and if a women's group has expressed a particular need, is it possible for outsiders to offer help.

Mina Sarkar, a woman worker with Nijera Kori, is one person making contact with such groups. Mina visits most villages without any previous introduction, by simply informing the village leaders that she is there.

'Are you a family planning worker?' people ask her. 'No, I have just come to help women who are in need.'

Mina wins the trust of village women by asking simple questions and taking an interest in their problems. 'I ask questions like "Why is the child ill?" or "Why is your roof broken?" Gradually,' Mina says, 'ideas come up and after a time – it might take a week or up to a year, depending on the group – meetings can be held and a *samiti*, or co-operative society, can be formed.'

33

However, at this point, when regular meetings start to be held, the group is likely to meet stiff resistance. Many women find it difficult to attend meetings and have to sneak out of their houses to avoid detection. In one village Mina was abused by louts who shouted 'CIA' and 'missionary' at her and hurled insults during their meetings.

In another village some members of the group were beaten up on their return home by their husbands, one of whom demanded some of the samiti savings and slashed his wife's hand with a knife. In most cases, opposition from the family fades after a certain time; but sometimes women are prohibited from joining the group altogether.

Another source of discontent, according to Mina, can be the *gramsharkar*, or village council, which sometimes feels the group is in competition with it and tries to take it over. However, one gramsharkar, seeing the success of a group, offered the use of the village fish-pond in return for a share of the samiti's income.

Nijera Kori, which receives some of its funds from Christian Aid and Oxfam, is now in contact with about forty women's groups in one area of Bangladesh. It also supports men's landless groups.

Nijera Kori does not automatically lend money to these groups, but insists that savings have to be made by the groups themselves. It does, however, make small loans for specific purposes, such as the purchase of a sewing machine. It has found that, as a result of this principle of self-reliance, most groups have a very fast repayment rate.

In another area of Bangladesh, an organization called Gono Unnayan Prochesta – which means 'people's efforts towards development' – is giving help to three women's jute workshops. The aim is to provide women and girls who have no other source of income with a basic training in jute handicrafts. The products are sold through a factory, which also gives some of the women further training.

Ambia Begum is a fifteen-year-old farm labourer's daughter. Her father fell sick and she found she had to support a family of five. She took a short course at one of the workshops and now keeps the family on her earnings of 450 taka (£12.50) a month.

Chearun Nessa is the third wife of an earth-carrier who used to maltreat her and at first refused to allow her to go out to work. Now she earns two-thirds of the family income at the workshops and has bought herself a new sari. Her husband's attitude has changed.

Hanu Begum has been less fortunate. Her husband originally married her because of the savings she earned at the workshop but he changed his mind and kicked her out. Hanu still comes to the workshop; she now brings a six-month-old baby with her.

GUP, who have been working in western Bangladesh since the floods of 1974, say that at that time it was difficult for a Muslim girl even to approach them. Now that their activities among the landless and destitute are better known, they hope, like Nijera Kori, to be able to offer help and training to a greater variety of women's groups.

John Montagu

3: IN HINDUISM

This is a description of the role of women in Hindu society. As the writers say, the practices of Hinduism vary and it may be useful to compare this passage with 'The Indian woman in Britain' (pages 52–4).

God is everywhere. God is not male or female. God is as much She, the Mother of the Universe, as He, the Father of the Universe. Since God may be called as much She as He, women are very much respected. The goddess of knowledge and wisdom is Sarasvati; the goddess of wealth is Lakshmi; and so on. Every girl is called *kanya devi*, the girl-goddess of the home. The title of a married woman might, for instance, be Shrimati Sunila Devi. *Sunila* is the name. *Shrimati* is the equivalent of Mrs and means 'graceful lady'; *devi* means 'goddess'. So every Hindu woman is referred to as a goddess; and, since *ji* is a further term of respect, she is also addressed as Deviji.

The woman runs the home and controls it completely; an average Hindu man has no say in the home at all. Moreover the woman is not given an allowance; the man gets an allowance from his wife, because, at the end of the day or month, he hands to his mother or his wife all the money he has earned, and she apportions it.

Throughout the ages, India has had thousands of queens, women poets, women philosophers, women authors and women warriors. In some Indian villages the entire village council consists only of women members, duly elected. No candidate of any political party in India ever hopes to win an election against a woman candidate; in one state, some years ago, a third of the members of the Legislative Assembly were women.

Purdah, the practice of keeping women behind closed doors, started with the Muslim invaders. At that time women were not safe, and so the Muslims introduced this practice. In those parts of India where Muslims never ruled, *purdah* is unknown. In some parts of South India the property is handed down to the daughters, not to the sons. There, a bride does not go to the husband's home; the husband comes to live with her.

India is a vast country, with a population equal to that of Europe without Russia. So the Hindus have many languages, many denominations, many practices (both good and bad, as with people everywhere), and many forms of diet. The customs in one part of India may not be known to a person from another part, as an Englishman may not know all the customs of someone from Iceland or Poland or even from France.

Marriage

Most marriages are very happy. A Hindu believes that, according to his previous *karma* [actions in this or past lives having inescapable moral consequences], a special person is destined for him or her. The parents must seek out that special person; they compare the age, temperament, education, and other qualities of the prospective partners, and then make a decision. A Hindu boy or girl is always romantically waiting for the day when he or she will see this 'mate of the soul'. Nowadays most young people are allowed to meet their future partners, but they are too shy to say no to the parents' choice. 'After all, our parents have given us birth, nourishment, and education; we owe them our very life. They will do whatever is best for us, whereas we, being young, cannot in the heat of our passions take an objective view. If we chose for ourselves, we might end up with a divorce after a few years – and then what would happen to our children?'

This is what the young people say. Divorce and juvenile delinquency hardly exist among Hindus.

Pandit Usharbudh and Yorke Crompton

4

Disability

---·••·---

A sequence of readings for use in assemblies planned to encourage awareness of the problems of the disabled – particularly those suffering from the commoner and less dramatic disabilities.

It might be possible to ask a speaker (say, a doctor specializing in chest diseases, or a social worker) to talk about their experience of these and related problems such as hay fever, etc.

1: ASTHMA

'Aren't you going to swim?'
Piggy shook his head.
'I can't swim. I wasn't allowed. My asthma –'
'Sucks to your ass-mar!'

That is Ralph's unthinking response to Piggy's disability in William Golding's Lord of the Flies.

Many people are inclined to underrate the problem of people suffering from asthma. 'He's putting it on,' 'She's only trying to get out of the work.' In fact asthma is the most common reason for long absence from school and no genuine sufferer is likely to 'invent' an attack.

Asthma is an allergy.

Asthma is the most frequent and can be the most handicapping of the allergies in childhood. It has been estimated that there are about 150,000 children in the United Kingdom who will have asthma at some time during their childhood. As many as one in ten have a wheezy attack at some time before the age of ten years, but many of them grow out of it after this age. A child who has had frequent attacks of wheezing before the age of three years, particularly if these attacks are not all associated with a cold, is more likely to have to learn to live with asthma for a longer time. He is certainly more likely to have asthma after the age of ten years. It has been estimated that 4 per cent of all children will remain asthmatics, so that it is a very common cause of childish ill-health. For some unknown reason boys are twice as likely as girls to be asthmatics.

Asthma has more emotional results than emotional causes. It may cause a great deal of frustration in limiting a person's activities, especially if he is ambitious. Both his business and his social activities may have to be curbed, and the sufferer may have to put up with bouts of incapacitating illness. The long-term outlook for the severe adult asthmatic is, it must be said, beset with difficulties. Frequent attacks of asthma cause much disturbance to sleep, and possibly chronic tiredness . . .

An attack of asthma usually comes on suddenly. Normally breathing in is an active process when the muscles between the ribs contract and the diaphragm moves downwards. Breathing out is passive, and the muscles and diaphragm relax. In asthma, breathing out is the problem because of the blocked tubes. It needs a positive effort on the part of the patient to get air out of the lung, and the passage of the air may be accompanied by a wheezing sound which can be heard easily from some distance. The muscles in the neck which are called the accessory muscles of respiration will probably contract in an effort to force air out of the lungs. The patient is usually more comfortable sitting up and this may make breathing out easier. At the beginning of the attack there may be coughing with no sputum, but towards the end of the attack mucoid sputum may usually be coughed up.

For a mother it is much more anxiety-making for her child to have asthma than to have asthma herself. It is very easy for a doctor to say that a mother becomes overprotective and over-anxious, but it is difficult to see how any conscientious parent could avoid doing just this.

It is very difficult to accept that a child with so many years ahead of him may have a handicapping illness to live with. Many allergies do improve with time, but nevertheless it may be many years before the child is free, and the tendency remains.

It is very important that a child should get the best possible investigation and treatment so that he may have a good chance of recovering before he leaves school, otherwise a child with asthma enters adult life as a handicapped person if the asthma is at all severe. Sometimes vaccines are used, but usually unscientifically and with few beneficial results. This is partly because of the shortage of doctors with a special knowledge of allergy in the United Kingdom. It is reckoned that with proper investigation and treatment more than 70 per cent of children with asthma could be cleared of the problem by the time they leave school.

Elizabeth Forsythe

2: COLOUR BLINDNESS

Colour blindness is the popular but incorrect term for the very common condition of being unable to distinguish between certain colours. Literal colour blindness (seeing everything in shades of grey) is rare. The most common defect is an inability to distinguish between red and green. Eight per cent of males (but only 0.5 per cent of females) are affected by one type or other of colour blindness.

Uncle Edward's Affliction

Uncle Edward was colour-blind;
We grew accustomed to the fact.
When he asked some-one to hand him
The green book from the window seat
And we observed its bright red cover
Either apathy or tact
Stifled comment. We passed it over.
Much later, I began to wonder
What curious world he wandered in,
Down streets where pea-green pillar-boxes
Grinned at a fire-engine as green;
How Uncle Edward's sky at dawn
And sunset flooded marshy green.
Did he ken John Peel with his coat so green
And Robin Hood in Lincoln red?
On country walks avoid being stung
By nettles hot as witch's tongue?
What meals he savoured with his eyes:
Green strawberries and fresh red peas,
Green beef and greener burgundy.
All unscientific, so it seems:

His world was not at all like that,
So those who claim to know have said.
Yet, I believe in war-smashed France
He must have crawled from neutral mud
To lie in pastures dark and red
And seen, appalled, on every blade
The rain of innocent green blood.

Vernon Scannell

3: LONELINESS

The rock musician Ian Dury was crippled in childhood by polio. In a radio programme he talked about loneliness, something that many disabled people feel very intensely.

Disabled is not a word that people like me use. It's not a word that people like me think about. You don't think about categorizing yourself by your limitations. You think about not having those limitations, or you think about the areas where you're not limited and you live through those areas and for me to talk about loneliness as a disabled person – I really haven't experienced it. But I know of many, many – probably at least a million people, I should think, in this country – who are very lonely because of their disablement. Loneliness did occur for me though from being a celebrity. It's quite lonely out on the street now 'cos I don't feel like I'm part of the street any more. I feel like I'm being witnessed and observed on the street and I don't like that much, it's quite lonely. Where I used to go down the street – I would be flash Harry, you know, I'd be a real noisy little brat stomping around and being vociferous – in the last five years I've not done that because in a way I've been forced to adopt a persona.

Loneliness and depression are very similar . . . and loneliness is part of depression. I read of a guy who'd been in the nick – whenever he got really brought down by the fact that he'd got another seven years to do, he'd go and run round the football pitch until he fell down with exhaustion and that at least revived his spirit. Depression of any kind feeds off itself, it's one of those kind of cancerous things that devours itself, it devours the body. I wrote a song called 'Lonely Town' which weren't a terribly good song, but it was like trying to put oneself into the situation.

There's an Eddie Cochran record called 'Dark Lonely Street'. It was on the B-side of 'Twenty Flight Rock', I think, but I've never seen it since, I couldn't find it anywhere. But that was a good record. That felt lonely.

Probably the only time I do feel very lonely is when I'm on the road, in strange hotels every night, with people that, as much as we love each other, really after a couple of months or so on the road, you don't really . . . You get lonely then. You get lonely for home. We were in New Zealand a year ago and blimey that is a long, long way from home; and I went to America once and I don't really think I'd go there again to tour because it's just too far away from where I feel like a human being, and I don't really feel much of a human being when I'm trudging through Europe really, or America or Australia.

I remember once we were playing in Clarence's Club in Halifax – we weren't supposed to go on stage until about 12 o'clock and it was only the afternoon.

I just went walking – had a stroll round the pedestrian precinct and checked out the junk shops and I saw that there was a Clint Eastwood film, *Play Misty for Me*, on at the pictures so I wandered in there. And I was sitting in there and it was a half empty Saturday afternoon in the cinema and I look across and see the guitar-player Kev sitting over there, I looked behind me and there's David the drummer, and then I see Russell walking down the aisle. We were all in there, all on our own.

Ian Dury

5
The characters

How do we judge which people we can trust? Which people to value?

Theophrastus (371–287 BC) was a Greek philosopher and botanist who is best known for his unique book, The Characters, a series of portraits of people to avoid. It might be instructive for pupils to devise their own modern equivalents of the following and of other characters included by Theophrastus such as the character, the ingratiating man, the inventor of news, the boaster, etc.

1: THE TOADY

The toady is the sort of person who will say to the man he is walking with, 'Do you notice how people look at you? You're the only man in Athens they study in that way.' Or perhaps, 'You were being complimented yesterday in the Arcade. There was a group of thirty or more sitting talking; and the question cropped up, Who was our best citizen? Starting from that, we all came back finally to your name.' While he is going on like this, he picks a stray thread off the other's cloak; or if a bit of chaff has blown into his hair, he takes it out, and says with a laugh, 'Look at that! Because I haven't seen you for two days, you've got a beard full of grey hairs; though, if anyone's hair keeps its colour in spite of years, yours does.' Then he will tell the company to keep silent while the great man is speaking; he will praise him when he is listening; and when he pauses in his talk he will back him up with 'Hear, hear!' When his patron makes a feeble joke he laughs, stuffing his cloak into his mouth as if he couldn't contain his merriment. He asks people they meet in the street to wait until 'He' has passed. He buys apples and pears, brings them in and gives them to the children when their father is watching, kisses them and says, 'Well, youngsters, you've got a splendid father.'

At a dinner party he is the first to praise the wine, and he may be relied on to exclaim, 'How delicate your food is!' Then he picks up something from the table, and says, 'Now, isn't that choice?' He will ask his friend if he is cold and if he would like to put something more on; and while still asking he puts a wrap round him. What's more, he leans over to whisper in his ear; or, when talking to other guests, keeps glancing at their host.

2: THE SKINFLINT

The stingy man is the sort who, when he is at table with others, will count how many cups each person has drunk; and of the whole company at dinner, he will pour the smallest libation to the gods. If you buy anything for him, however cheaply, he will say, when you send in your account, that it has taken his last penny. If a servant breaks a jug or a dish, he stops the price of it out of his allowance. If his wife has dropped a threepenny-bit, he is the sort of person to start moving the furniture, shifting couches and cupboards, rummaging among rugs. If he has anything to sell, he will only let it go at a price which means a bad bargain for the buyer. He would never let you eat a fig out of his garden, or walk through his land, or pick up one of his windfall olives or dates. Every single day he inspects his boundaries to see if they have been tampered with.

When it is his turn to give the parish dinner, he cuts the meat into tiny slices to serve out. He goes off to market, and comes home again without buying anything. He forbids his wife to lend salt, or lamp-wick, or herbs, or barley-grains, or garlands, or holy-cakes. 'These things all mount up, you know,' he says, 'in a twelvemonth.'

3: A CHIP ON THE SHOULDER

The man with a grievance is the kind of man who, when a friend has sent him his share of a banquet, remarks to the slave who brings it, 'He doesn't invite me to dinner: that way he saves my share of his soup and his nasty wine.' When his sweetheart is caressing and kissing him he says to her, 'I wonder if you genuinely love me as much as you seem to.' He is resentful against Zeus, not for sending rain, but for sending it too late. If he finds a purse in the road, he says, 'But a fortune – no! I've never found that.' When he has bought a slave cheap after much haggling, 'I wonder, now,' says he, 'whether for that money I can have bought anything worth having.' When someone comes to him with the good news, 'You've got a son,' he replies, 'If you add to that, "And away goes half my property," you'll be telling the truth.' When he has won a lawsuit by a unanimous vote, he finds fault with the man who wrote his speech, for omitting a number of strong points. When his friends have contributed to provide him with a loan, and one of them says, 'Now you can feel cheerful,' 'Can I indeed,' he answers, 'when I've got to give every one of you his money back, and on top of that show gratitude, as if I'd been done a favour!'

Theophrastus

6

Great events

The following sequence of readings are contemporary descriptions of great events, written by reporters and news correspondents of The Times. *They are quoted here from the 60,000th edition of* The Times, *dated 11 May 1977, in which they were reprinted.*

1: BLUNDERS OF THE CRIMEA

During the years 1854 and 1855, when the circulation of The Times *was greater than that of all its rivals put together, the country was shocked by the disclosures of its correspondent, W. H. Russell, of blunders and inefficiency in the conduct of the Crimean War and hardships experienced by the troops. His strictures on the lack of surgeons, nurses, clothing and medical equipment led Florence Nightingale and a party of thirty-eight nurses to go to Scutari where, in spite of official obstruction, she revolutionized the medical services using her own resources and money provided from a fund administered by* The Times. *MacDonald, one of the correspondents, who found that the 39th Foot had been ordered from the tropics to the Crimea with no warm clothing, supplied them all with flannel underclothing at his own expense.*

March 29, 1854 – War is declared. A peace, which has lasted the unexampled period of thirty-nine years, which many fondly hoped was to last as many more, is at an end; and the three most powerful states of Europe are once more engaged in a struggle, the duration, the end, and the results of which no man can tell; but, which is too likely to produce disasters and sufferings of which we are mercifully spared the foreknowledge.

Monday, January 15, 1855 – We can entertain no doubt that every one of our readers will heartily join us in reprobating the imputations which have been cast upon the motives of Miss Nightingale and the nurses who have accompanied her to the hospitals of the East. God knows there is but little in the conception or execution of the great expedition itself upon which future generations of Englishmen will be able to look back with complacency or satisfaction. All that authority could do has been ill done, or omitted altogether. The bravest soldiers of England have been sent out to perish of preventible disease and unnecessary exhaustion.

It was to Miss Nightingale that the thought first occurred – and eternal honour to her for the thought – that, whatever the sufferings of our soldiers in the mis-managed hospitals might be, the one sight that would raise their drooping spirits and cheer their failing hearts would be the presence of an Englishwoman among them. Nor has the event contradicted her anticipation. Miss Nightingale invented female nurses at Scutari as one discoverer invented the steam-engine and another the printing press.

Saturday, February 3, 1855 – From Our Special Correspondent. Before Sebastopol, Jan. 19 – There have been severe and sudden alternations of temperature within these last few days . . . Men have been frozen in their tents, and several soldiers on duty in the trenches have been removed to hospital with severe frost bites, and suffering from the effects of the bitter cold winds and frost . . .

I know of regimental hospitals in the front where sick men in wet marquees have only one blanket to lie upon at this very date . . . For myself, I must say one of the most melancholy subjects for reflection in the world is the sight of our present army. It consists of officers, men and regiments almost new to this campaign. The generation of six months ago has passed away . . . What a harvest Death has reaped, and yet how many more are ripe for the sickle of the Great Farmer! On the 16th the thermometer was at 14° in the morning and at 10° on the heights over Balaklava. The snow fell at night and covered the ground to the depth of three feet; but the cold and violent wind drifted it in places to a depth of five or six feet . . . Our men have been seen hobbling about in the trenches and in the camps bare-footed, and yet ankle-deep in snow. They could not get their frozen boots and shoes on their swollen feet.

Tuesday, January 16, 1855 – From Our Own Correspondent, Scutari,

Jan. 4– Since the date of my last letter about 1000 more sick have been brought down here from the Crimea. One transport steamer after another arrives with her sad freight, and anchors in the Bosphorus a short way off the hospitals. It is one of those spectacles which by its protracted painfulness haunts a man's imagination and memory against his will . . .

Of the 4000 now in hospital, three-fourths at least are suffering from causes which a less ambitious share in the siege operations and greater attention to the material wants of an army placed in such circumstances, must have vastly mitigated . . . hospitals here are filled with English soldiers, prostrated by disease, brought on from overwork, want of proper clothing, and want of proper food. The deplorable state of the medical arrangements has no doubt aggravated the amount of sickness.

2: THE JAPANESE WAR

In 1940, Japan, which had been fighting a war in the Far East, joined the side of Germany and Italy in World War Two. The United States of America was still a neutral country.

The following two passages outline the events (including the bombing of Pearl Harbour) that brought America into the war, and describe how the war against Japan ended.

December 8, 1941 – The Japanese, without any formal declaration of war, yesterday attacked American bases in the Pacific. Later the Japanese High Command announced that from dawn Japan was in a state of war with Great Britain and the United States in the western Pacific.

August 6, 1945 – From the cruiser Augusta in mid-Atlantic, President Truman has announced that the United States air force have used, for the first time, against a Japanese target an atomic bomb which has an explosive power equal to 20,000 tons of TNT.

The statement, which was issued through the White House, said that on Sunday an American aircraft dropped one of the new bombs on Hiroshima, an important Japanese army base west of Kobe. The bomb had more power than 20,000 tons of TNT, and more than 2000 times the blast power of the British 'grand slam' (20,000 lb) bomb which until now was the largest bomb ever used in the history of warfare.

The new bomb, said Mr Truman, meant a new and revolutionary increase in destruction to supplement the growing power of the United States against Japan. 'It is an atomic bomb. It is the harnessing of the basic power of the universe.' He added that the new bomb was now in production and that even more powerful forms were being developed.

The use of the new bomb meant victory in a feverish race with German scientists to find some way to harness and release atomic energy . . . Before Pearl Harbour the United States and Britain had pooled their scientific knowledge that could be useful in war, and many priceless aids to victory had come from the arrangement. With American and British scientists working together, the Allies had entered a race of discovery against the Germans. There were two great plants and many lesser works devoted to the production of atomic power. 'We spent $2,000,000,000 on the greatest scientific gamble in history – and won . . . Let there be no mistake; we shall completely destroy Japan's power to make war. It was to spare the Japanese people from utter destruction that the ultimatum of July 25 was issued from Potsdam. Their leaders promptly rejected that ultimatum. If they do not now accept our terms they may expect a rain of ruin from the air the like of which has never been seen on this earth.'

3: MAN STEPS ON THE MOON

The Space Age is generally said to have begun in 1957 when the USSR (Russia) launched Sputnik I, the first artificial earth satellite. This was soon followed by another and then the USA launched Explorer I.

The first manned space flight was in 1961, when the Russians sent Yuri Gagarin into space. In 1969, America achieved the first landing on the moon.

July 21, 1969 – Neil Armstrong became the first man to take a walk on the moon's surface early today . . . It was 3.56 a.m. (British Standard Time) when Armstrong stepped off the ladder from Eagle and on to the moon's surface . . . 'That's one small step for man but one giant leap for mankind,' he said.

The two astronauts (Armstrong and Aldrin) opened the hatch of their lunar module at 3.39 a.m. in preparation for Neil Armstrong's walk . . . Aldrin had to direct Armstrong out of the hatch because he was walking backwards and could not see the ladder. Armstrong moved out to the porch outside Eagle and prepared to switch on the television cameras which showed the world his dramatic descent as he began to inch his way down the ladder . . . Viewers had a clear view as they saw him stepping foot by foot down the ladder which had nine rungs. He reported that the lunar surface was a 'very fine-grained powder'. Clutching the ladder Armstrong put his left foot on the lunar surface and reported it was like powdered charcoal and he could see his footprints on the surface . . . The light was sufficiently bright for everything to be clearly visible.

As the television clock showed the last twenty minutes ticking away second by second and we heard the matter-of-fact voices of the American astronauts, any family with a television set was present at one of the most exciting moments of man's history. July 20, 1969, will be remembered when little children who were brought down half asleep are grandparents. It is the first event of such historic significance to be shared so widely and known so immediately.

The Times

7

Other customs

A series of readings about neighbours with differing customs. (See also Themes 3 and 18.)

1: THREE NEIGHBOURS

Mrs Green and Mrs Brown often stop to chat outside the shops, even when the wind blows chill. We listen-in on this occasion as Mrs Brown speaks of her mother's poor health. The conversation is interrupted by the appearance of Mrs Tariq.

Mrs Green: Hallo Mary – haven't seen you lately. Been staying in the warm? Can't say I blame you.

Mrs Brown: This wind's been blowing for three whole weeks. It's enough to make anyone stay indoors. But I've spent most of my time at Mum's. Had to keep an eye on her.

Mrs Green: Oh, is she bad again?

Mrs Brown: Yes. It's her heart as usual. But this time she really had us worried. We thought we were going to lose her.

Mrs Green: Well, at least you're not too far away. How long does it take you to get there?

Mrs Brown: Only about half-an-hour. But that seemed like eternity when they called us.

Mrs Green: Yes; I always say that when there's real trouble ten miles is as bad as a hundred. No wait! I shouldn't say that. Here's Mrs Tariq coming, and *her* mum's thousands of miles away in Pakistan.

Mrs Brown: Mrs Who?

Mrs Green: Mrs Tariq. The Pakistani lady at number 45.

Mrs Brown: Oh, is *that* her name! I've never plucked up courage to speak to her yet.

Mrs Green: I usually say Hallo; but that's about all. Keep talking and I'll pretend I haven't seen her.

Mrs Brown: Why? Don't you like her?

Mrs Green: It's not that. But I heard in the Post Office that her father's just died in Pakistan, and really I don't know what to say to her.

Mrs Brown: Just talk to her normal I would.

Mrs Green: Yes, but what shall I say about her . . . Oh well, here goes. Hallo Mrs Tariq. Cold wind, isn't it? I bet you'd rather be back in Pakistan on days like this.

Mrs Tariq: Yes indeed. If I were home I could comfort my mother.

Mrs Green: Oh . . . Of course . . . Yes . . . er. We're all sorry to hear about your father.

Mrs Tariq: Thank you. We pray he will go to Jannat and will be free of pain.

Mrs Green: Jannat? Another hospital? But I thought he was . . . I mean . . .

Mrs Tariq: You are right. My father died last week. We pray that he will go to Jannat, like you say Heaven.

Mrs Green: Oh, I see. Yes I'm sure he will. I mean . . . well, God is love, isn't He?

Mrs Tariq: God is also righteous and just, and He expects us to be the same. But we pray that my father will sometime go to Jannat. Now I must shop. Thank you for your sorrow. You are very kind. Goodbye.

Mrs Green: 'Bye. And once again, I'm sorry. Give me your hand . . . 'Bye.

The Revd James Bell

The following Bible passages give some directive on our attitude to people of other faiths: St Matthew chapter 8, verses 5–13 – *Jesus heals the centurion's son;* St John chapter 4, verses 5–10 and 19–26 – *Jesus and the Samaritan woman.*

There are a number of texts in the Quran about people of faiths other than Islam, including this one:

In the Name of Allah, the Compassionate, the Merciful
Say: 'Unbelievers, I do not serve what you worship, nor do you serve
what I worship; I shall never serve what you worship, nor will you ever
serve what I worship. You have your own religion, and I have mine.'

2: THE INDIAN WOMAN IN BRITAIN

This is an excerpt from Joan Lingard's novel, Into Exile, *which is about
Kevin and Sadie, a young married couple from Belfast, living in London.
Sadie has made friends with a neighbour, a young married Indian
woman, Lara.*

Lara came in every Wednesday though she had never asked
Sadie to her house in return. They were on their hands and knees
on the floor cutting a skirt out of a remnant Sadie had bought in
the shop. 'We hardly ever go out so it was a real treat. Do you go
out often with your husband?' Sadie found it difficult to refer to
him as Krishna since Lara did not do it herself.

Lara shook her head. 'No, very seldom.' She lifted the scissors.
'Shall I begin to cut?' she asked.

'Please.' Sadie caught hold of the baby who would have liked
the flashing silver scissors for himself. Lara cut carefully. She
seldom told Sadie anything of her life. She talked sometimes of
her family in India but never of Krishna or her life with him. She
came in every Wednesday for an hour or so and returned home
well before Krishna would come along the street carrying his
newspaper under his arm. Sadie smiled at him and said, 'Hello'
and then he nodded, but nothing more.

'There,' said Lara, folding up the pieces. 'That didn't take long.
You can sew it this evening.'

Sadie nodded. 'Kevin's got his evening class. I'm sick fed up
with him going out so much.'

'You want him to advance in his career, don't you?'

'Oh yes of course.'

'Then you must make sacrifices too.'

'Trouble is I'm not very good at sacrifices.' Sadie made a rueful
face at herself. 'I think you'd be better at that than me, Lara.' Lara
smiled. 'I suppose you were brought up to be docile, you know,
with men,' Sadie went on. 'I used to fight my brother, wouldn't
let him tell me what to do.'

'It's not just a case of being docile,' said Lara. 'Sometimes it is not worth fighting. One has to save one's energy.'

'Well, I dunno. Maybe I'd be better if I'd been brought up with some of that wisdom of the East business too.'

Lara burst out laughing. 'Sadie, you are funny at times.'

'Glad I amuse you,' said Sadie good-naturedly. She filled the kettle to make coffee. 'I like having you coming in here every Wednesday, Lara. You're the only friend I've got.'

Lara hesitated. 'Sadie, I'm sorry I can't ask you to come and visit me. I hope you don't mind.'

'Course not,' said Sadie, though she did. She spooned coffee into the cups.

'It's Krishna –' Lara bit her lip.

'Doesn't he like me?'

'It's not that.'

'Is it because I'm white?'

'Oh no! It is just that he is very private. He does not like strangers.'

'But how can strangers ever become friends if you don't give them a chance in the first place?'

'I know.' Lara sighed. 'But you cannot force people. I am sorry.'

'That's all right. Don't worry about it.' Sadie gave Lara her coffee. 'You can always come here.'

Sadie noticed Lara taking a quick glance at her watch under her sari. Today they were later than usual having their coffee.

'Are you lonely in the evenings when your husband is out?' asked Lara. 'Why don't you go to an evening class yourself?'

'I might,' said Sadie without enthusiasm, 'if I'd someone to go with. What about you, Lara? Would you come with me? Hey, what about woodwork or something like that? Then we could show them. I've always liked banging in nails.'

'I'm afraid I could not. There is the baby.'

'Your husband could baby-sit.'

'I don't think so.' Lara put down her cup. 'I must go now, Sadie. See you next week.'

Next week was a long time. Seven days lay between. Weekends were good for then she and Kevin were together but the other evenings were stretches of time to be filled and she had never seen time in that way before.

'Lara's husband doesn't like strangers,' Sadie told Kevin at tea-time. 'And he's living surrounded by ten million. Not very friendly I call it.'

'Perhaps he's afraid,' suggested Kevin.

'Afraid? I never thought of that. In that case I'll go on smiling at him and saying good morning.'

Joan Lingard

3: 'RECENTLY ARRIVED' RELIGIONS

In a series of programmes made for Radio 4, Professor John Bowker looked at the major religious traditions which have only recently become part of life in Britain.
What happens to those religions when they arrive in this country?

Krishna is an incarnation of the god Vishnu. (Some Hindus may say there are many gods, but for most Hindus the gods are only different aspects of the One Supreme Being.)

Hindu life in an Indian village is one thing; Hindu life in Coventry or Leeds is very different indeed.

Certainly the different styles of these religions have to change, partly because the English weather does not allow for many festivals to be staged out of doors and also because, as one Indian put it, 'We pray loudly'. Complaints from the neighbours mean that you cannot blow conch shells at midnight, to celebrate the birth of Krishna, as Hindus would in India.

Differences of diet also create problems. Many Hindus, Sikhs and Buddhists are supposed to be vegetarians; Muslims and Jews are required never to eat pork or anything connected with pork; but that obviously creates difficulties, as Mr Khan, a lecturer in law, made clear: 'Muslims are not allowed to take pork or any part of pig in any form. Unfortunately, pig is the favourite in this country, and it appears in all forms: that is to say, if I buy bread from the shops, there is lard in it, or if I go to a restaurant nothing is available about which I can be certain that it has been cooked in butter or margarine.'

Even more difficult is the difference between the public calendar in Britain and the many different calendars in each religion. Important religious festivals are not public holidays. If they were, we'd be on holiday every week of the year, which is pretty much how one Hindu described India: 'There is a proverb in India which says that in twelve months you have thirteen festivals. That means that people enjoy festivals more than anything else – that's a part of our life.'

In fact, what happens is that each one of these religions adapts its practices and festivals as much as it can, while respecting the culture and law of the land. They may not like it, but that is simply what they have to do – as a Hindu schoolteacher told me: 'If Christmas Day happens to be on a Wednesday in this country, everything comes to a stop. If a Hindu festival happens to be on a Monday or a Wednesday or a Friday, everything in this country doesn't come to a stop. You would like it to, for your own personal reasons, you would like to celebrate a big family day. But what you do here is, you try and cram in as much as you can before you go to school in the morning, and you cram in as much as you can when you come home in the evening.'

John Bowker

8

Christian saints

NB   Saint: *(1) a person who is officially recognized after death by the Christian church as specially holy and worthy of formal honour; (2) a person with a holy or completely unselfish way of life.*

1: MOTHER JULIAN OF NORWICH

Julian of Norwich was born in 1342, and died, we may gather, well on in the fifteenth century at a considerable age. She was almost certainly educated by the nuns at Carrow, a Benedictine Priory, although she claims to be 'unlettered'. Perhaps by that she simply meant she had little or no knowledge of Latin.

On 8 May 1373 during severe illness, Julian received the series of sixteen 'shewings' of our Lord.

In the spring of 1373, on Sunday the first of May, Julian felt unwell. What could have been a simple indisposition due to change of season soon turned into a frightening illness. She was then about half way through her thirty-first year. The young woman took to her bed, but by Wednesday the fourth of May it was clear that she was already beyond human ministration. Thomas Whiting, the curate of St Julian's, came to administer the last rites. As the priest ended the last exhortation: 'May the Holy Ghost enlighten thee . . . and lead thee to thy heavenly home where God reigneth in perfect Trinity for ever and ever', and Julian's mother and those around the bed answered 'Amen', she was already drifting into unconsciousness.

She endured thus, sometimes in pain, sometimes barely conscious.

It was now Sunday the eighth of May. As dawn crept into her chamber, there came back to Julian's mind a request she had made many years ago: that she should partake of Christ's Passion in her mind and body; and, as the thought came to her, she saw 'the red blood trickle from under the garland' (the crown of thorns). This proved to be the first of sixteen 'Showings' (or Revelations) which would occur between four o'clock in the morning of the eighth of May and nine o'clock on the following morning.

The first fifteen Showings lasted five hours and were received by Julian in a trance-like state. One moment, she had been at death's door and the next, unaware of any pain, she had seen the Saviour's head crowned with thorns and His blood 'all hot, fresh and plenteous and real, so much so that it seemed to me as if it was the very moment when the crown was thrust on this Blessed Head'. She was so surprised that she cried out: 'Bless me, this is the Lord!' At the same time she had a 'ghostly sight' of God's love. God showed her a small round thing in the palm of her hand 'like a hazelnut': the whole Creation which He made and loves and keeps, and she summed up her Revelation: 'God is all that is good, this is what I understand.'

Nicole Marzac-Holland

She became an anchoress or nun, a woman dedicated to religion, living permanently alone in a cell attached to St Julian's Church in Norwich. Julian almost certainly took her name from the Church which would then have been about 400 years old.

For twenty years Julian meditated on the visions she had received, and at length she recorded them and their meaning as The Revelations of Divine Love. *This is the first book known to be written by a woman in English, and is now acknowledged all over the world as one of the great classics of spiritual literature.*

This is one of those meditations, and one which shows how important she thought it is for Christians to trust in God.

He showed me a little thing, the size of a hazelnut, in the palm of my hand, and it was as round as a ball. I looked at it with my mind's eye and I thought, 'What can this be?' And the answer came, 'It is all that is made.' I marvelled that it could last, for I thought it might have crumbled to nothing, it was so small. And the answer came into my mind, 'It lasts and ever shall because God loves it.' And all things have being through the love of God.

In this little thing I saw three truths. The first is that God made it. The second is that God loves it. The third is that God looks after it.

What is he indeed that is maker and lover and keeper? I cannot find words to tell. For until I am one with him I can never have true rest nor peace. I can never know it until I am held so close to him that there is nothing in between.

Her life is commemorated by the Church on 8 May.

2: LORD SHAFTESBURY

Anthony Ashley Cooper, seventh Earl of Shaftesbury (1801–85), is chiefly remembered for his work in reforming working conditions in factories and coal mines. As a young man, he had the title Lord Ashley.

In the year 1815, Lord Ashley was only fourteen years old and still a schoolboy. He was also extremely rich.

One day he saw an event which was to have a great effect on his life. A funeral. A pauper's funeral. The three men carrying a coffin were somewhat drunk. Young Lord Ashley was offended.

'I say, my good men!' he shouted. 'Show some respect. That's a coffin you're carrying.'

'Thish ish George,' answered one of the men.

'Thish *was* George,' said another.

'But this is no way to conduct a funeral,' said the schoolboy, primly. 'Why can't he have a proper funeral?'

'George died without leaving any money. He's a pauper. 'E'll be buried in the pauper's corner.'

The third man then spoke for the first time.

'It's not a grave, governor. Just a shallow hole, for people with no money. They're not buried proper. Only the rich can afford to be buried. People like yourself.'

Lord Ashley was rich. He need never have done any work. He could have spent his whole life just enjoying himself. Except that he could not forget the sight of that man's funeral. As time went by, he made a resolution. 'When I am grown up, I shall use my time to help the poor.'

So he became a Member of Parliament, and set about finding out about the conditions in which the poor had to earn their living.

In those days, round about the year 1830, even very young children had to work in factories and in weaving and spinning mills. They were made to crawl into the moving machines and to oil and grease them; they were beaten if they stopped work for even a few moments; they became weak and deformed and suffered from terrible diseases. Some were forced to work from six in the morning until half past eight at night, or even later. Parents could not object: they needed the money.

Lord Ashley knew that this must be changed. He spoke in Parliament.

'. . . And so I say, we must, I repeat, we must improve the lives of our workers, especially those of our women and children. This is a Christian country, and every citizen is equal in the sight of Almighty God. They must be treated fairly! They must have time to rest, an hour of leisure once a day. We must put an end to this barbaric treatment of our children.'

Other speakers disagreed. As another MP said:

'My Lord Ashley argues convincingly but he is in error. His sentiments do him justice, I agree, but such changes cannot be. If the workers do not labour such hours, factory profits will fall, owners will be forced to close mills and factories and the workers will lose their jobs. Indeed, the workers themselves welcome this opportunity to earn a wage.'

Lord Ashley tried and tried again. It took many debates like that before any improvement was agreed upon – but at last, in 1833, an Act of Parliament was passed. The wording was as follows: 'It is hereby enacted that no child of under nine years may be employed at all, and those aged from nine years to thirteen years may not work for more than forty-eight hours in any one week.'

Gradually more laws were passed. In the end, children were stopped from all work – from working down mines, from working up chimneys and in factories. And many of these improvements were the result of Lord Ashley's untiring efforts to work to help the poor.

He started schools, he persuaded the government to build houses for working people, he worked for improvements in hospitals. Then, when he was fifty, his father died. His father had been the Earl of Shaftesbury, and so Lord Ashley became the new Earl of Shaftesbury – which is the name we remember him by.

And after he died, a statue was put up in the middle of

Piccadilly Circus in London. We call it Eros, but the man who made it called it the Angel of Christian Charity, in honour of the Earl of Shaftesbury.

David Self

3: ARCHBISHOP LUWUM

From 1971 to 1979, Uganda was ruled by a dictator, President Idi Amin. He used violence and torture to suppress anyone who might oppose him.

There was increasing confrontation between Amin and the Christian church in Uganda under its leader, Archbishop Janani Luwum. This confrontation came to a head when Luwum was arrested in February, 1977. This account by another bishop, Bishop Festo Kivengere, tells how Amin got the chance to arrest Luwum. Bishop Kivengere was in his apartment in Kampala one day, when he saw a man being dragged from a building on the opposite side of the street, by a group of men.

The men bound him and threw him into the open truck and drove off. They were not dressed in uniform, so I knew they were the dread Research Unit of the Special Forces. These are the most cruel of all . . .

We found out later that the man they took was called Ben Ongom, of the Langi tribe. They tortured him for five days, making him 'confess' the names of people of his tribe and also of the Acholi tribe – both considered enemies to the present regime – who 'might have been' involved in smuggling guns or plotting subversion. Not satisfied with the people he named, they forced him, by torture, to go on. Finally he named the medical superintendent of Mengo Hospital, who was taken and later released after terrible torture. Then, in desperation, he suggested the name of the archbishop!

Archbishop Luwum's house was searched. Nothing was found. Later, the Archbishop and other bishops went to Amin to complain about this and other incidents. The Archbishop was detained. The other bishops could only wait.

We waited and waited. We saw the intelligence people guarding the door getting embarrassed and angry.

60

Finally we went to them and said, 'What is happening to the archbishop?'

'He is busy with the president.'

'We are waiting for him. We want to go home with him.'

'Well, you can go home now. We'll bring him in another car.'

'No. We want to go with him. We have his car here.'

'Get away! Don't wait here! Get over near that car!' We sat down again. Then an officer came and barked, 'I order you to go. It's an order! Get in that car and go!'

'Where is the archbishop?'

'Oh, he will come. We will bring him. He is still busy.'

'But it is terribly embarrassing and very bad for us to go without him, since we came with him.'

In the end he went away and sent two officers who pointed guns at us. They said, 'Did you hear the order?'

'Yes, we did.'

'Well, get in that car!' So we got into it . . .

Now we know that the archbishop was probably dead at this point. There is a rumour that they were trying to make him sign a confession, which he would not do. We were also told that he was praying aloud for his captors when he died. We have talked with eyewitnesses who claim they saw him shot, and to others who saw the bodies in the morgue with bullet wounds. Evidence suggests that he was shot at about 6.00 p.m. either in the Nile Hotel or in the Nakasero 'torture house'. Prison vehicles were driven over the bodies to make it look like a car accident.

Radio Uganda announced at 6.30 p.m. that the archbishop and the two cabinet ministers had been arrested. By morning they had cooked up a story in order to save face before the world. The government's version in the morning papers was: 'Sorry! Tragic accident with a car!' In the morning, they showed one wrecked car in the paper, and a different one on television in the evening.

A great international funeral had been planned for Sunday, but the government refused entrance to the important foreign visitors who wanted to enter Uganda for it. Nevertheless, on Sunday, February 20, the great cathedral on Namirembe Hill was packed with 4500 people, in spite of threats by Amin's authorities. People could not stay away. It was a powerful service.

Retired Archbishop Erica Sabiti read the angels' message to the women on the day of the Resurrection: 'He is not here. He is risen!' Then he said, 'Our brother's body is not here, but we know that his spirit has gone to be with the Lord Jesus. He has risen. Praise God!' Heaven was near, and people began singing, softly at first 'Glory, glory to the Lamb!' It was picked up and passed on until the hilltop was resounding with victorious singing.

The sound of victory is still being passed on. It rang in the memorial services that were held for Archbishop Luwum in many cities on several continents. He is still speaking the truth in love in the hearts of all suffering Ugandans, and in the minds of those who put him to death.

Bishop Festo Kivengere

9

Work: a good thing?

What do we mean by work? Is work essential or natural? What is it like to lose a job or to have no prospect of getting one? What is the difference between unemployment, freedom from work, and leisure? In the distant future, will there be work?

These are some of the questions and thoughts that may be prompted by this sequence of readings.

1: THE NEED TO WORK

This reading comes from a thoughtful and constructive book called Freedom from Work (which would provide several passages suitable for use in assemblies).

What do we mean by the word 'work'? Is it natural for human beings to work? Do we have to have a job, if we can get one?

People feel they need to work in the same way that they need to eat and drink: this is called the work ethic, or sometimes the Protestant ethic. It is one of the most motivating forces in any industrialized society and means that people want to work for reasons which are over and above the money that they earn. The money, wages or salaries, buy the things that individuals and families need to live, and, hopefully, live well; but work is needed for itself too.

Yet this has not always been the case. The earliest societies worked to live. They hunted, then later cultivated crops and reared animals, but when enough had been done they rested. If, on any particular day, or week, nothing needed to be done, the people simply did no work at all – the notion of a fixed time in which one had to work came much later.

The civilizations that followed the very early days had a

63

stronger attitude to work. The Egyptian, Greek and Roman empires were based on slavery. The slaves, often from countries that had been conquered, did most of the physical work and tended to their owners' needs. The owners themselves, and their families, did not claim that they worked – indeed, to do so would have diminished their status. In short, it was a two-tier society – those who controlled, and those who were subjected and who worked (most often unwillingly) . . .

In a complex industrial country, work is needed to meet the needs and demands of the people of that, and sometimes other, countries. To this extent it is essential. To work for the sake of working is a totally different matter.

In Eastern Europe, full employment is *the* major objective. These countries do not have unemployment problems as we understand them in the West, although there is a cost associated with this policy. The cost is a lack of efficiency, the result of which is fewer consumer goods, such as cars, fridges, TV sets, and slower services. It is certainly one way of running a society which cannot be disregarded out of hand; after all, the work ethic is so very strong, and it at least means everyone has some sort of work.

Regrettably, most people do not enjoy their jobs when they are actually doing them. Some are dirty and dangerous, others noisy, others repetitive and boring and most neither stretch nor fulfil the people doing them. They are only really valued when they are lost. The work ethic has developed a strange attitude to work. Rather like swallowing a nasty tasting medicine, people take it because they think it will do them good – but don't like it. It is actually difficult to see the enjoyment in working on a car assembly line or shovelling chemical waste all day. Those who dignify such work have rarely even visited such areas, let alone worked in them.

The actual act of coping with rush hours, especially for commuters in large cities, attracts as much criticism as work itself.

Why, then, in a rich society, are we all so concerned to spend our lives doing something which we don't enjoy very much, if at all? Why do we put up with boredom, or let ourselves suffer from stress trying to get promotion or beating out adversaries? It must come down to the unquestioning adherence to the work ethic.

If it were possible to provide most of the goods and services using the labour of fewer people, would people be happier? At present the answer must be 'no', even though people's superficial attitudes would suggest the opposite. Yet given the dislike, the strains and the industrial injuries and diseases, less work would be a good thing. The present technologies dictate that mankind still has to work – but will this apply to the new systems just being introduced? Should we follow the Eastern bloc and create jobs willy-nilly, or, if the opportunity arises, cut down on the amount of work that individuals do?

We are on the threshold of a new industrial revolution based on microelectronics. As it will make some other technologies redundant, so it will make a wide range of jobs redundant. We really will be faced with the question – is work essential?

Barrie Sherman

2: WALL STREET CRASH

Nobody fully understands what happened to the United States in October 1929. It was as if the whole nation had been struck by an illness, which became known as the Great Depression.

The centre of the nation's financial world was Wall Street, New York, the exchange where stocks and shares were daily bought and sold. One day, the market would be what was called 'bullish' when the value of shares would rise so fast that fortunes would be made in a flash. On another day, conditions would be 'bearish': in other words, the value of shares would be falling.

(This reading will be particularly effective if it is possible to follow it by playing a recording of 'Buddy, Can You Spare a Dime?')

In the early part of 1929, Wall Street had been a 'bull' market, with shares rising fast for day after day, week after week. People began to have a sneaking fear that this was too good to last. Suddenly, without anybody being able to put a finger on the cause, that sneaking fear turned into outright hysteria, and on October 29, 1929, an extraordinary situation arose. So few people wanted to buy shares that the whole stock market collapsed – or, as the papers put it, 'Wall Street crashed'. Shares went down by millions of dollars overnight, wiping out not only the fortunes of rich families, but the nest-eggs of hundreds and thousands of small savers, too. A nationwide panic set in. People rushed to their banks to draw out what money they had left. The banks simply could not cope with so many unexpected demands, and began to close in their thousands. Eventually, a third of all the banks in the United States closed their doors; and people who had money in those banks simply lost it! The panic spread rapidly to businesses, which cut their losses the obvious way, by lowering wages and dismissing staff. Wages throughout the US dropped by nearly half (40 per cent). Unemployment leapt to a staggering total. Estimates vary, but in the end the figure may well have been as high as seventeen million – which meant that one quarter of all the workers were without jobs.

Hundreds and thousands of people hadn't the money to pay the mortgages on their houses, and were turned out of their homes. They included people from every part of society. Doctors, lawyers, artists, shop owners, farmers – anyone who had a job to lose or a business that could go bankrupt was in danger of finding himself suddenly without a cent in his pocket or a roof over his head. In one town, the homeless included two families who were so well-known locally that they had actually had streets named after them! Not that that is much consolation when you are walking the pavements, penniless.

More than a million Americans were now doing just that. They formed a vast 'vagabond army', as it was called, wandering desolately from town to town searching for any opportunity to earn, beg or steal the means to keep alive. They slept at night under the stars – or headed for the nearest railway station to creep into railway carriages or goods wagons, where they could at least get some shelter if it rained. The South Pacific Railroad turned 683,000 trespassers off their trains in a single year. Then the company took pity on the vagabonds, and began arranging for extra carriages to be available for them to sleep in!

Other destitute people built shanty towns, out of odd bits of wood and pieces of rusty corrugated iron, on the the edges of the big cities. They called these towns 'Hoovervilles', after Herbert Hoover, the president whom they believed had got the country into this mess, and was doing nothing to help them. Hoover became the most hated man in America. An empty pocket turned inside out (a sign that its owner hadn't a cent in the world) became known as a 'Hoover flag'. One enterprising hitch-hiker, it was said, travelled the thousands of miles from New York to California by hanging a notice round his neck threatening: 'Give me a lift or I'll vote for Hoover!'

One unemployed man in Baltimore was photographed with a still more startling notice round his neck:

I AM FOR SALE.
I must have work or starve
Your inquiry appreciated

His simple, bleak message summed up the plight of a quarter of the United States. And the statement 'I must have work or starve' was not much of an exaggeration. In those days to be workless did literally mean to face starvation. Long queues formed wherever the Salvation Army or any other charity organisation handed out soup and food (usually not more than a slice or two of bread). The people in the queues were called the 'breadliners' – and there were soon millions of them.

To understand the misery, bewilderment and bitterness of the time, you only have to listen to the words of the popular hit song of the period – 'Buddy, Can You Spare a Dime?'

W. V. Butler

3: THE FUTURE OF WORK

In a radio programme in 1983, Professor Charles Handy argued that we need to redefine our concept of work – in particular, that we need a new word for 'job'.

Our mistake, I suggest, has been to equate work with job, with employment. We need instead, I believe, to redefine work and so to redistribute it. Not only will jobs get split up and spread out, helped by the new technology, but we could all do much more part-time marginal or pocket-money work and we could all do more gift work for free or for expenses in the home or the community. These forms of work happen already, of course, but they don't 'count' in the same way as jobs do. One reason maybe is that they are not paid for. If they are, then there is a taint of illegality about it, they're not respectable work.

We need rather urgently to make these other forms of work respectable, not only to give our lives meaning, but also because society needs these forms of work. Job work is so expensive today that if everything had to be done by people employed full-time at full wages, a lot more work would be priced out of existence than has already gone. We need, therefore, to change the whole way we think and talk about work. . . .

How's that going to happen? Well, we need some new words and we need to see them used by people of influence. Take, for instance, the concept of ecology and the conservation of our environment. Twenty years ago no one had ever heard of the word ecology or took it seriously. Now every teenager will know what it means. We needed that new word to give an edge to the old word 'environment' and we needed to see it become fashionable, to be taken seriously by people who mattered. The new word we need in the world of work is one to replace 'job'. It has to be possible for the question 'What do you do?' to mean more than 'What's your job?' I'm quite sure we're ready for the word, but I don't yet know what the word is. I've sat with groups trying to redefine work and the best they've come up with is 'meaningful activity'. But that hardly has the ring of the pub about it. You'd have to be very serious or very drunk to ask someone 'Please tell me what is your meaningful activity?' A poor replacement for a three-letter word like job!

Can you think of a word? We need something that allows one to describe a rounded life with more than one form of work or 'meaningful activity' in it.

Charles Handy

10

At worship

One way of beginning to understand what it means to worship is to hear about ways in which different groups, sects and faiths worship.

It may be possible to invite representatives of various faiths to speak about how they worship and perhaps to read or say a favourite prayer, saying why it is important to them.

1: THE QUAKERS

When people are asked what they know about the Quakers, many people say they make porridge. Some think they wear tall black hats and spend their time being gloomy (or miserable). Nothing could be further from the truth.

Their proper name is Friends, or members of the Society of Friends. They have no priests or ministers. They are people who like to think for themselves.Their worship is simple, as this description of a Friends' meeting shows.

The seating consists mostly of wooden benches arranged in an open square facing inwards. In the centre is a table on which are two or three books including a Bible. There are generally some flowers.

Every Sunday morning just before 10.30 people begin to arrive at the Meeting House. Among the first will be the Friend (man or woman) who is acting as 'doorkeeper' for the day. His job is to greet people as they arrive, with a special welcome for any visitor who is coming for the first time. People may sit anywhere they wish, although most of the regulars have their favourite spots.

The actual Meeting for Worship starts when the first Friend arrives and sits down in silence. Others come in and join him, and soon after 10.30 about forty or fifty people, including children, will have taken their places. All have entered the room quietly and there is a lovely sense of stillness, which is a great contrast to the general racket of modern life. Even quite young children seem to enjoy the peace, although they may chatter a bit. This worries their parents, but no one else minds; in fact most people rather like it. After about fifteen minutes the young children leave the meeting and go to other rooms.

The Quaker meeting starts in silence, and sometimes nothing will be said for the whole hour that meeting normally lasts. Usually after a fairly long opening period of quiet, someone, man or woman, boy or girl, will feel that he or she has an experience that will help the other people present. It could be something that has happened during the week, or something they have read. Or they will recall a passage from the Bible, or a poem that has taken on a new meaning. The purpose of speaking, reading or praying out loud in meeting is to express what the speaker feels is happening deep in the silence in which they are all meeting. The object of speaking is to help everyone to be even more aware of their links with one another. Whatever is said should be the sincere experience of the speaker. It will be received in silence, and will help to make the silence itself more profound.

During the hour of the meeting possibly three or four people may speak. Discussion and argument are quite out of place. Friends call spoken contributions 'ministry' and at their best they will blend together to make a whole. Often what someone says will express vividly a vague idea that has been forming in my mind. Sometimes the pattern that emerges is so clear that you would think that the speakers must have got together to plan what they will say. It is difficult to realise that the ministry is spontaneous. This is all the more remarkable as they do not sing hymns or use a prayer book, or have any kind of programme for a service, not even a sermon.

The time for closing the meetings makes itself felt quite naturally by a gentle restlessness among those present. The meeting is formally ended by two Friends (whom we call Elders) shaking hands. Nowadays most people present will also shake hands with the persons sitting next to them.

What Friends have known for over three hundred years is that when people make this kind of experimental journey, sooner or later they reach a quiet place in the still centre of their lives. This actually happens in Meeting for Worship, sometimes quite quickly, sometimes more slowly. Early Friends talked about this as 'centring down'. When you get used to the way of silent worship you can often tell when, to use another old phrase, 'the meeting was truly gathered'. In modern words what has happened is that the individuals in the room have made their journey to the centre of their real selves. When they reach this quiet place two things happen at the same time. Everyone knows, firstly, that he or she is a unique, individual person; and secondly that each person present is unable to be truly himself or herself, without the help of others.

George H. Gorman

2: THE SABBATH

The synagogue plays a less central role in Judaism than the church does in Christianity. Many rituals take place within the family. The Jewish home has played a primary role as the sacred place.

The Sabbath day, or *Shabbat* in Hebrew, begins just before sundown on Friday and lasts till nightfall on Saturday night. During these approximately twenty-five hours Jews are forbidden to do any work and they must celebrate the activity of God as Creator of the world and Lord of history. Three ritual meals are eaten on the Sabbath. On Friday night and Saturday lunchtime a banquet-type meal is served, and a smaller meal is eaten on Saturday afternoon.

Just before the Sabbath begins the woman of the household kindles the Shabbat candles so that the home should be full of light. She uses at least two candlesticks and they are commonly made of silver but sometimes of finely wrought bronze. In the poorer Jewish households these candlesticks are often the most precious possession, and generally they are either family heirlooms or else purchased as a wedding gift for the bride by the groom's parents. A number of Sabbath candlesticks from past generations have survived the pillage of countless pogroms, by being hidden or spirited away by Jewish refugees. They show high levels of craftsmanship, although not all of them were actually made by Jews.

The Sabbath is a day when the household brings out its best ware in honour of the beauty of God's handiwork in His

71

Creation. When the husband returns from synagogue on Friday night he finds the table covered with a white tablecloth. On it are the two specially plaited Shabbat loaves, known as *challah*, which symbolize the two portions of manna given to the Israelites in the wilderness of Fridays. The loaves are usually covered by an embroidered cloth representing the dew which lay over the manna. The husband begins the Sabbath meal with the *kiddush*, or blessing, over wine. The cup used for kiddush is most commonly a silver goblet which may have grape motifs engraved on it. Wine decanters used for holding the kiddush wine may be of silver overlay on glass or of crystal. Sometimes they have a silver plaque hung across the front by a chain on which the word 'le-chaim', or 'to life', is engraved.

At the termination of the Sabbath a special ceremony, *havdalah*, marks the separation between the holy day and the ordinary week ahead.

Alan Unterman

Havdalah takes place in the home. A special candle is extinguished in wine, and a spice box is passed round so the family may savour the sweet scent of the holy day that is ending and to prolong its fragrance into the coming week.

The atmosphere of the Sabbath should be emphasized since it has often been misunderstood. In the glowing words of the prophet Isaiah 58: 13, 'Thou shalt call the Sabbath a delight.' The Sabbath Joy appropriately describes this day of brightness and gladness, commencing on the preceding Friday evening. This is not just absence from work, because the Sabbath is meant to bring man nearer to his heavenly Creator. In its universal sense it becomes a symbol of joyfulness and peace when mankind will be free from worry and oppression. It also suggests a time when the world will recognize the purpose of the Sabbath and lead to a true spirit of co-operation between men and harmony in all spheres of human activities. Throughout the services of this holy day, there is a constant reference to God as king of the world.

Myer Domnitz

3: ISLAM

The Prophet of Islam laid five duties on his followers. One is 'zakat' (see page 254). Another is prayer.

Visitors to Muslim countries cannot fail to be impressed at the way in which people stop whatever they may be doing five times every day to say their prayers. Those who live in the towns can carry on their business until they hear the *muezzin* calling the faithful to worship from the minaret on the mosque. He repeats each statement at least once.

God is most great.
I testify that there is no God but Allah.
I testify that Muhammed is God's prophet.
Come to prayer, come to security.
God is most great.

Travellers throughout the open countryside have to watch the sun as it climbs across the sky so that they can judge the proper time for prayer.

At sunset, last thing at night, at dawn, at noon and in the afternoon, all Muslims kneel down with their faces towards Mecca. They perform the ceremonial prostrations as they repeat the traditional words of worship.

Muhammed put aside one day when the faithful should gather together for communal prayer. Perhaps to show that he was independent both of Judaism and Christianity, he set it on Friday. This is not, however, a Sabbath of the Jewish type, for no restrictions are placed on work. At midday all the men gather at the mosque to say their prayers together. Since Allah dwells everywhere, the mosque is just a meeting place for the faithful and not a place sacred in itself. An *imam* (teacher) stands at the front and the whole congregation follows him as exactly as possible so that all move and chant in perfect unison.

Praise belongs to God, Lord of the Worlds,
The Compassionate, the Merciful,
King of the Day of Judgement,
It is Thee we worship and Thee we ask for help.

Guide us on the straight path,
The path of those whom thou hast favoured,
Not the path of those who incur Thine anger nor of those who
   go astray.

To the Muslim prayer is a duty, and he does not expend his energies worrying about what he gets out of it. It is not a means of pleading with God, but simply the method by which God's creatures give him the honour that is rightly his.

Martin Ballard

11

City lights

A sequence of readings to illustrate the problems that face those who are attracted to a city, believing it will provide work, shelter and food.

1: RAVI

In this first story of 'Ravi', four foreign words are used:

dhoti   *loin-cloth*
charpoy   *a kind of bed*
annas   *pence*
chapatti   *a small, flat round of unleavened bread, little more than flour and water.*

Ravi shivered and dragged closer round him the rags that passed for his dhoti. He knew that within a few moments he would be dizzy again with the heat; but the fever was such a part of his life that he took for granted the alternating shivering and sweating. He shifted his position on the ground and noticed that his legs seemed even thinner. If it were possible, the bones and joints stuck out further than ever. Perhaps the truck that had come round a few days ago would be here today handing out something to eat. Ravi didn't really believe this was likely, but just thinking about it made the constant gnawing in his stomach easier to bear.

He automatically brushed away from his eyes and mouth the flies which hovered for a few seconds and equally automatically settled again. With the gutter as the only and well-used lavatory the flies hung in the air in clouds. Even if his sight had been good, Ravi would scarcely have noticed them, and anyway lack of food, in the end, blurs your vision. Perhaps if he went to the station he'd be able to carry someone's luggage for a few annas and he could get some chapattis . . . Reluctantly he abandoned the idea: the last time he'd tried there had been twenty or thirty men like himself for every bag to be carried and it would be worse now. Besides, he'd lose his place under the wall and have to sleep nearer the gutter.

He'd learned a lot about the value of a good stretch of pavement at night. When he first came in from his village, he'd no idea about such things. Now, two years later, he'd almost forgotten what it was to sleep on a charpoy, to have a roof of sorts. Not that there was any rain to keep off. This would be the fifth year that the rains had failed. When the third crop he'd sown had blown away from his patch of land it had blown away his house and few possessions. Or blown them to the moneylender who had paid for the seed. A well would have saved them all: crop, land, house and family. After dragging and carrying them for miles, they had left the children in the outer streets of the town. His wife had cried at first; but she was already too weak to cry for long. Now there was just himself. Just himself; alone – if you didn't count the hundreds of thousands in the same plight on the streets of the same city.

CAFOD

CAFOD is the Catholic Fund for Overseas Development. See page 281.

More than a thousand families living on the outskirts of Calcutta earn their living from rubbish. The huge, filthy city dump at Dhapa is rich in recyclable materials – half burnt coal, metal, plastic, rubber tyres, rags, glass and waste paper. The ragpickers, mainly women and children, scour the dump each day, and sell their pickings to traders running stalls all round the area. Inevitably they are paid only a fraction of the price the scrap will fetch – the middlemen reaping the major benefit.

The Calcutta Social Project (CSP) a complex community development programme initiated in 1969 and working with some of Calcutta's poorest people, has recently focussed its attention on the problems of the ragpickers.

One of the major considerations was that, although obviously unpleasant and hazardous to health, ragpicking is a comparatively well-paid occupation for these families. So the scheme is focussing on a number of projects to improve conditions – campaigning for legalisation of the occupation; encouraging savings schemes; organising the pickers so that, by working together and developing basic collective marketing, they can eliminate the middlemen and profit directly. Eventually they even hope to set up their own small local recycling units.

Oxfam

2: URBANIZATION

The poor level of agricultural development and the industrial development in town areas has led to an enormous problem in cities all over the world for the last two hundred years. It still exists in Britain, but conditions have been improved because of public action and central organization. Such organization does not exist in some parts of the world. This series of questions and answers (which can be arranged for a number of readers (or as a television quiz show) is designed to illustrate the problems associated with rapid urban growth.

Q. What does urbanization mean?
A. The drift of millions of villagers into the cities.

Q. What proportion of people in the world live in the cities today?
A. Out of every three people, two live in villages, one lives in a city.

Q. What will it be like in twenty-five years?
A. By then, two out of three will live in cities.

Q. Is the world population going up, or down?
A. Up at an enormous rate.

Q. So the cities are going to be several times bigger?
A. Yes.

Q. So the problems of a place like Calcutta are going to get several times bigger?
A. Yes, most likely.

Q. Why do so many millions leave the farms and villages?
A. Because they are starving. Because of drought and famine. Because crops have failed and they cannot afford to buy grain. Because the rich countries suddenly do not want the product they were growing. Because automation and machines have done them out of a job.

Q. Why do they move to the cities?

A. For the same reason as Dick Whittington, they think the streets are 'paved with gold'.

Q. Name a few cities, with tremendous problems of poor and destitute people.

A. Calcutta in India, Lima in Peru, Manilla in the Philippines, Kinshasa in Africa, Cairo in Egypt.

Q. Describe what happens for a newcomer to a city, if all goes well?

A. He starts by begging, sleeping on the pavement. He joins with others and builds a temporary shanty. He moves or improves it to a more permanent shanty. He moves or improves it to a more permanent shack. He begins to get odd jobs, and save for a proper house.

Q. How many sleep on the pavements each night in Calcutta?

A. 600,000 (= the whole population of Liverpool).

Q. What are some of the nightmare conditions in parts of Calcutta?

A. No toilets or sewers. No jobs. Rich people passing by. Disease. Fellow-men dying on the street. No proper food.

Q. Why do they stay?

A. Here, they have some hope. Back in the villages, they had none.

Q. What is a shanty?

A. A do-it-yourself house, made out of boxes and scrap iron, or anything, without police permission.

Q. What kind of jobs do the newcomers hope to start with?

A. Things like carrying loads, for a tip. Street trading. Labouring.

Q. Is there a lot of crime in the shanty towns?

A. Not as much as you would expect. The people there are loyal to one another.

Q. Why cannot the city authorities cope?

A. Usually, they get scared at the size of the problem.

Q. Is there any hope for the future, in the cities?

A. Yes (a) The people are, on average, better off than they were in the villages
   (b) Once a shanty district settles down and clubs

together, it begins to improve its own conditions. This is where the city authorities should help. The squatters eventually run their own schools, dig their own drains.

Q.   Is there any hope for the villages?

A.   Yes. Irrigation schemes to bring water to parched lands, digging of wells, aid from central government, aid from other countries. (These are the kind of schemes that charities like Christian Aid and CAFOD support – seeds rather than bread, helping people to help themselves.)

Q.   Is this a new problem?

A.   No, the problem is as old as cities. The ruins of Ur, the oldest city in the world, show slums on the edges. What is new is the size of the problem today.

CAFOD

3: IAIN'S STORY

Homelessness is not only a problem in a city like Calcutta. It is a problem in Britain as well.

Iain has tried hard to find a job in his native Scotland since leaving school. Through the Youth Opportunities Programme, he found six months' employment making cardboard boxes. But a permanent job did not follow. His unemployment caused tension to build up at home where he lived with his parents, three brothers and a sister. Of the whole family, only his sister was in fulltime employment. His father, deeply depressed at fifty-three, had been out of work for two years.

A crisis developed and Iain was told to get out. He witnessed his father burning his bed on an open space near his home – he feels he can never return. Iain now sleeps on a couch in the small house of a friend where eight others live.

Youth unemployment is a serious cause of homelessness. Young people move to London and other big cities in search of work, but many have little chance of a job and maybe even less opportunity of finding somewhere to live. Unemployment also contributes to pressure at home. It is easy to see how relationships break down under financial problems and grave anxiety about the future.

The recent government report 'Single and Homeless' refers to the vicious circle in which homeless people can get trapped.

'For some a vicious circle of unemployment and accommodation problems traps them in a "homeless circuit". Thus if a person has no accommodation it is difficult to obtain and hold down a regular job. Without such employment it is almost impossible to obtain accommodation other than that in a hostel . . . and so it goes on.'

With only a minority of young people housed under the Homeless Persons Act, most seek rented accommodation on the private market where they are faced with shortage and cost. An agency for the single homeless in London reports: 'A self-contained, one ɔedroom flat could cost anything from £50 per week, and a room in a multi-occupied house, sharing all cooking and bathing facilities, a minimum of £20 to £25 per week. Furthermore, deposits and rent in advance can quite easily amount to £200, or more if accommodation agency fees are included.'

It has been claimed that as many as 30,000 young people are homeless in London alone.

It is becoming increasingly important for voluntary bodies such as Shelter to look out for their needs, to provide accommodation and campaign on their behalf.

SHELTER
(see page 282.)

12
Utopia

In 1516, Thomas More (the hero of Robert Bolt's play, A Man for All Seasons) published a book in Latin. It was called Utopia *and it described an island where life was perfectly organized and the people were happy. The following three excerpts illustrate various aspects of life in Utopia.*

1: WORKING CONDITIONS

First, their working conditions. Well, there's one job they all do, irrespective of sex, and that's farming. It's part of every child's education. They learn the principles of agriculture at school, and they're taken for regular outings into the fields near the town, where they not only watch farmwork being done, but also do some themselves, as a form of exercise.

Besides farming which, as I say, is everybody's job, each person is taught a special trade of his own. He may be trained to process wool or flax, or he may become a stonemason, a blacksmith or a carpenter. Those are the only trades that employ any considerable quantity of labour. They have no tailors or dressmakers, since everyone on the island wears the same sort of clothes – except that they vary slightly according to sex and marital status – and the fashion never changes. These clothes are quite pleasant to look at, they allow free movement of the limbs, they're equally suitable for hot and cold weather – and the great thing is, they're all home-made. So everybody learns one of the other trades I mentioned, and by everybody I mean the women as well as the men – though the weaker sex are given the lighter jobs, like spinning or weaving, while the men do the heavier ones.

Most children are brought up to do the same work as their parents, since they tend to have a natural feeling for it. But if a child fancies some other trade, he's adopted into a family that practises it. Of course, great care is taken, not only by the father, but also by the local authorities, to see that the foster-father is a decent, respectable type. When you've learned one trade properly, you can, if you like, get permission to learn another – and when you're an expert in both, you can practise whichever you prefer, unless the other one is more essential to the public.

In Utopia they have a six-hour working day – three hours in the morning, then lunch – then a two-hour break – then three more hours in the afternoon, followed by supper. They go to bed at 8 p.m. and sleep for eight hours. All the rest of the twenty-four they're free to do what they like – not to waste their time in idleness or self-indulgence, but to make good use of it in some congenial activity. Most people spent these free periods on further education, for there are public lectures first thing every morning. Attendance is quite voluntary, except for those picked out for academic training, but men and women of all classes go crowding in to hear them – I mean, different people go to different lectures, just as the spirit moves them. However, there's nothing to stop you from spending this extra time on your trade, if you want to. Lots of people do, if they haven't the capacity for intellectual work, and are much admired for such public-spirited behaviour.

2: SOCIAL ORGANIZATION

Each household, as I said, comes under the authority of the oldest male. Wives are subordinate to their husbands, children to their parents, and younger people generally to their elders. Every town is divided into four districts of equal size, each with its own shopping centre in the middle of it. There the products of every household are collected in warehouses, and then distributed according to type among various shops. When the head of a household needs anything for himself or his family, he just goes to one of these shops and asks for it. And whatever he asks for, he's allowed to take away without any sort of payment, either in money or in kind. After all, why shouldn't he? There's more than enough of everything to go round, so there's no risk of his asking for more than he needs – for why should anyone want to start hoarding, when he knows he'll never have to go short of anything? No living creature is naturally greedy, except from fear of want – or in the case of human beings, from vanity, the notion that you're better than people if you can display more superfluous property than they can. But there's no scope for that sort of thing in Utopia.

These shopping centres include provision markets, to which they take meat and fish, as well as bread, fruit and vegetables.

Every so often, as you walk down a street, you come to a large building, which has a special name of its own. That's where the Styward (the district Controller) lives, and where his thirty households – fifteen from one direction and fifteen from the other – have their meals. The caterers for such dining-halls go off at a certain time each day to the provision market, where they report the number of people registered with them, and draw the appropriate rations.

But hospital patients get first priority – oh yes, there are four hospitals in the suburbs, just outside the walls. Each of them is about the size of a small town. The idea of this is to prevent overcrowding, and facilitate the isolation of infectious cases. These hospitals are so well run, and so well supplied with all types of medical equipment, the nurses are so sympathetic and conscientious, and there are so many experienced doctors constantly available, that, though nobody's forced to go there, practically everyone would rather be ill in hospital than at home.

At lunch-time and supper-time a bugle is blown, and the whole Sty assembles in the dining-hall – except for anyone who's in hospital or ill at home. However, you're quite at liberty to take food home from the market, once the dining-halls have been supplied, for everyone knows you wouldn't do it unless you had to. I mean, no one likes eating at home, although there's no rule against it. For one thing, it's considered rather bad form. For another, it seems silly to go to all the trouble of preparing an inferior meal, when there's an absolutely delicious one waiting for you at the dining-hall just down the street.

When they're handing out food, they don't work straight along the table from one end to the other. They start by giving the best helpings to the older groups, whose places are clearly marked, and then serve equal portions to the others. However, if there's not enough of some particular delicacy to go round, the older ones share their helpings, as they think fit, with their neighbours. Thus the privilege of age is duly respected – but everyone gets just as much in the end.

Lunch and supper begin with a piece of improving literature

read aloud – but they keep it quite short, so that nobody gets bored. Then the older people start discussing serious problems, but not in a humourless or depressing way. Nor do they monopolize the conversation throughout the meal. On the contrary, they enjoy listening to the young ones, and deliberately draw them out, so that they can gauge each person's character and intelligence, as they betray themselves in a relaxed, informal atmosphere.

3: RELIGION

Finally, let me tell you about their religious ideas. There are several different religions on the island, and indeed in each town. There are sun-worshippers, moon-worshippers, and worshippers of various other planets. There are people who regard some great or good man of the past not merely as a god, but as the supreme god. However, the vast majority take the much more sensible view that there is a single divine power, unknown, eternal, infinite, inexplicable, and quite beyond the grasp of the human mind, diffused throughout this universe of ours, not as a physical substance, but as an active force. This power they call 'The Parent'. They give Him credit for everything that happens to everything, for all beginnings and ends, all growth, development, and change. Nor do they recognize any other form of deity.

On this point, indeed, all the different sects agree – that there is one Supreme Being, Who is responsible for the creation and management of the universe, and they all use the same Utopian word to describe Him: Mythras. [*Mythras (or Mithras) was the name of the Persian god of light. Mithraism had some resemblances to Christianity and was widespread among Roman soldiers.*] What they disagree about is, who Mythras is. Some say one thing, some another – but everyone claims that his Supreme Being is identical with Nature, that tremendous power which is internationally acknowledged to be the sole cause of everything.

Their churches contain no visual representations of God, so that everyone's left free to imagine Him in whatever shape he chooses, according to which religion he thinks the best. Nor is God addressed by any special names there. He is simply called Mythras, a general term used by everybody to designate the Supreme Being, whoever He may be. Similarly, no prayers are said in which each member of the congregation cannot join without prejudice to his own particular creed.

At Ending Feasts they fast all day, and go to church in the evening, to thank God for bringing them safely to the end of the year or month in question. Next day, which is of course a Beginning Feast, they meet at church in the morning to pray for happiness and prosperity during the year or month which has just begun. But before going to church at an Ending Feast, wives kneel down at home before their husbands, and children before their parents, to confess all their sins of omission and commission, and ask to be forgiven. This gets rid of any little grudges that may have clouded the domestic atmosphere, so that everyone can attend divine service with an absolutely clear mind. To do so when one is feeling upset is thought positively blasphemous. For that reason, anyone who's conscious of feeling anger or resentment towards another person stays away from church until he's made it up, and purged himself of these unpleasant emotions, for fear of being promptly and severely punished otherwise.

Thomas More

13
Modern parables

1: THE BEARS AND THE MONKEYS

In a deep forest there lived many bears. They spent the winter sleeping, and the summer playing leap-bear and stealing honey and buns from near-by cottages. One day a fast-talking monkey named Glib showed up and told them that their way of life was bad for bears. 'You are prisoners of pastime,' he said, 'addicted to leap-bear, and slaves of honey and buns.'

The bears were impressed and frightened as Glib went on talking. 'Your forebears have done this to you,' he said. Glib was so glib, glibber than the glibbest monkey they had ever seen before, that the bears believed he must know more than they knew, or than anybody else. But when he left, to tell other species what was the matter with them, the bears reverted to their fun and games and their theft of buns and honey.

Their decadence made them bright of eye, light of heart, and quick of paw, and they had a wonderful time, living as bears had always lived, until one day two of Glib's successors appeared, named Monkey Say and Monkey Do. They were even glibber then Glib, and they brought many presents and smiled all the time.

'We have come to liberate you from freedom,' they said. 'This is the New Liberation, twice as good as the old, since there are two of us.'

So each bear was made to wear a collar, and the collars were linked together with chains, and Monkey Do put a ring in the lead bear's nose, and a chain on the lead bear's ring. 'Now you are free to do what I tell you to do,' said Monkey Do.

'Now you are free to say what I want you to say,' said Monkey Say. 'By sparing you the burden of electing your leaders, we save you from the dangers of choice. No more secret ballots, everything open and above-board.'

For a long time the bears submitted to the New Liberation, and chanted the slogan the monkeys had taught them: 'Why stand on your own two feet when you can stand on ours?'

Then one day they broke the chains of their new freedom and found their way back to the deep forest and began playing leap-bear again and stealing honey and buns from the near-by cottages. And their laughter and gaiety rang through the forest, and birds that had ceased singing began singing again, and all the sounds of the earth were like music.

MORAL: *It is better to have the ring of freedom in your ears than in your nose.*

James Thurber

2: A TRAIN OF THOUGHT

The true story of a train journey in Italy, told by a Roman Catholic priest.

He was only eighteen, an Arab travelling in Europe for the first time. His language was a totally inadequate mixture of Italian, English and French. Yet within two minutes of joining our train he had everyone in the compartment talking and laughing. He was the immediate source and centre of attention and amusement. We had already travelled some 200 miles from Rome before he joined us in Florence, but it took his coming to make us talk to each other. It was then that we discovered what a mixed bunch we were: an Italian secretary, a Brazilian on holiday, a Greek labourer, an English priest, a German business man, and now Karim, a Palestinian Arab.

The conversation ranged everywhere: the Muslim religion, the Arab-Israeli conflict, the English, Germans, and Italians in the last war, the social conditions in Portugal and South America, the political situation in Greece, ourselves and our hopes.

Karim told us of his experiences as a Commando under Joshua Arafat until he had come to realize that to carry a gun would inevitably lead to killing someone who was innocent. Far better to save life. And so his family had gathered the money together so that he could come to Italy to study medicine. Then he could return home and help his own people.

It is over three months since all this happened, but what stands out vividly in my memory is the laughter. The fact that none of us really spoke the others' language only made it all the more hilarious. Out came the food, the wine and the coffee – each contributing his bit. We all drank from the one cup and the only glass. The carriage became a riotous picnic. . . .

Some four hours later, Karim had to leave the train at Milan. There was a flurry of exchanged addresses and a near emotional farewell. As our train left, we crowded round the window, waving to that laughing boy on the platform.

Afterwards we were all anxious to talk about Karim: what a personality he had; what courage in a foreign land; such a pity we would never meet again. Yet somehow he was still with us, and our journey continued full of fun – the happiest I have ever experienced. He had unconsciously broken us out of cocoons of shyness or self-interest and left us aware of each other. One was inclined to remember another journey, to Emmaus, where the travellers had said: 'Did not our hearts burn within us as he talked?'

In all that journey there was no condemnation of others, no moralizing about what 'THEY' ought to do. It was a simple, practical demonstration of people with varying religions and nationalities and politics being totally themselves, enjoying each other's company, and agreeing happily to differ.

MORAL: *We hear too much about the people who cause disruption. Instead, let us thank God that there are also a lot of Karims about, people who make the rest of us better for knowing them.*

Father Robert Manley

3: WHAT HAPPENED TO CHARLES

A warning about the dangers of spreading rumour, pretending it is news.

A farm horse named Charles was led to town one day by his owner, to be shod. He would have been shod and brought back home without incident if it hadn't been for Eva, a duck, who was always hanging about the kitchen door of the farmhouse, eavesdropping, and never got anything quite right. Her farm-mates said to her that she had two mouths but only one ear.

On the day that Charles was led away to the smithy, Eva went quacking about the farm, excitedly telling the other animals that Charles had been taken to town to be shot.

'They're executing an innocent horse!' cried Eva. 'He's a hero! He's a martyr! He died to make us free!'

'He was the greatest horse in the world,' sobbed a sentimental hen.

'He just seemed like old Charley to me,' said a realistic cow. 'Let's not get into a moony mood.'

'He was wonderful!' cried a gullible goose.

'What did he ever do?' asked a goat.

Eva, who was as inventive as she was inaccurate, turned on her lively imagination. 'It was butchers who led him off to be shot!' she shrieked. 'They would have cut our throats while we slept if it hadn't been for Charles.'

'I didn't see any butchers, and I can see a burnt-out firefly on a moonless night,' said a barn owl. 'I didn't hear any butchers and I can hear a mouse walk across moss.'

'We must build a memorial to Charles the Great, who saved our lives,' quacked Eva. And all the birds and beasts in the barnyard except the wise owl, the sceptical goat, and the realistic cow set about building a memorial.

Just then the farmer appeared in the lane, leading Charles whose new shoes glinted in the sunlight.

It was lucky that Charles was not alone, for the memorial builders might have set upon him with clubs and stones for replacing their hero with just plain old Charley. It was lucky, too, that they could not reach the barn owl, who quickly perched upon the weathervane of the barn, for none is so exasperating as he who is right.

The sentimental hen and the gullible goose were the ones who finally called attention to the true culprit – Eva, the one-eared duck with two mouths. The others set upon her and tarred and unfeathered her, for none is more unpopular than the bearer of sad tidings that turn out to be false.

MORAL: *Get it right or let it alone. The conclusion you jump to may be your own.*

James Thurber

14
Pilgrimages

As many young people now get a thrill from actually meeting a famous sportsman or pop star and will go to considerable trouble to see their team in action or idols 'in person', so medieval man made pilgrimages to places associated with saints. Pilgrimage was a traditional and important part of Christianity. It still has an important part in Christianity and in the other world religions.

This series of readings tells the story of different pilgrimages and seeks to communicate and explain some of the joy and peace that pilgrims find by making what are often difficult and testing journeys.

1: PILGRIMAGES SECULAR AND SACRED

First, a football fan describes the excitement of a pilgrimage to an away match.

It's when you're caught up in the crowd on the way to the ground that the excitement really hits you! We're about six, maybe seven deep, I suppose, and must trail back a full fifty, sixty yards.

It's not like anything else, really; you can't even imagine it unless you've been there. You give yourself up completely, suddenly you're part of something you can't control . . . don't want to control, because it's being part of it which is sort of reassuring. You can't stop even if you want to, can't change your direction. Most of the time you can't even get out from inside! Yet the funny thing is, that although in one way you're quite helpless, you feel so very strong . . .

The excitement all round you's like something you can touch; and it's almost excitement for its own sake, because like I said, half the people in the stand can't have a clue what's going on, on the pitch. Perhaps it's just being in a big moving mass of people that makes you feel like this, I don't know, but it's like nothing else.

Peter Fieldson

In medieval times, Rome was the most popular place of Christian pilgrimage.

From all over folk piously trudged there, and when they at last reached the top of the last slope from which they could see the sacred city, redolent of Peter, of Paul, of empire and papacy, of sacred Latin and secular law, of churches and Tiber, of promise of eternity, the eternal city itself – when they at last saw it, they chanted in solumn joy the song:

> O Roma nobilis orbis et domina
> Cunctarum urbium excellentissima
> Salutem dicimus tibi per omnia
> Te benedicimus salve per saecula.

In other words:

> O noble Rome, you mistress of the globe,
> Pre-eminent over all cities
> We say our salutes to you for all your blessings,
> We hail you, bless you, through all time.

It had, in medieval times, no great dome of St Peter's. It was replete with towers and battlements, like a mini-Manhattan. Bell-towers as well as defence-towers abounded. It was not too nice, full of faction, gnats, drains, ruins. But it was the holy city of the faith. Rome was not just a place: it was an idea. Although the middle ages were to end with Rome rebuilt, but the Church in spiritual faction, yet as ever Rome survived to see new triumphs. Why did the pilgrims come? Partly because the earthly voyage was an echo of life, which is itself a pilgrimage. We travel through time to eternity, and through space to the eternal city. They came because Rome summed up all cities seen as founts of wonder and civilisation; the Christian religion itself had first been transmitted from city to city, only it later reached out to peasants and barbarian lands. They came because men in the West saw the bishop of Rome as above all other bishops, and the city therefore worth a sacred visit. And in the manner of men who share in the substance of a thing, by being present with it, the pilgrims came to gain promises of later glory and even earthly welfare.

Ninian Smart

2: LOURDES

In 1858 an illiterate fourteen-year-old peasant girl Bernadette Soubirous had a series of visions of the Blessed Virgin Mary at Lourdes, a small town in south-west France in the foothills of the Pyrenees. Between the months of February and July, 1858, Bernadette experienced eighteen religious ecstasies during which she conversed with the apparition of a celestial lady.

Since 1858 Lourdes has grown steadily as a place of pilgrimage – there are now on average nearly three million pilgrims each year. During one of the Virgin Mary's appearances to Bernadette a miraculous spring appeared whose healing waters then and now provide some of the ingredients of faith healing. Of course there were many sceptics at the time when Bernadette claimed to have seen and talked to the apparitions and there are sceptics today. But now, well over a hundred years later, there are numerous cures, witnessed and apparently inexplicable by the canons of medical science and yet fully admitted by the medical profession as authentic cures.

This is one account of a visit to Lourdes. It is by the Christian broadcaster and writer, Malcolm Muggeridge.

Some years ago I went to Lourdes with Mike Tuchner and a camera crew to make a film for BBC television about the place and the pilgrims. I confess that I had no expectation that the experience, though interesting, would be other than melancholy. Generally speaking, I dislike shrines – especially being told about them – and distrust miracles.

Actually, from the moment I got on the train at Victoria (we travelled to Lourdes with a party of pilgrims so as to be able to film en route), I had an extraordinary feeling of light-heartedness. I don't think I have ever in my life been in so cheerful company as this collection of the sick and the crippled, many of them soon to die, and those who were looking after them. Even the restaurant car waiters when we got to France – men, in my experience, not notable for cheerfulness of disposition, especially when serving breakfast in the early morning to passengers who have just crossed the Channel – responded to the atmosphere. Their smiles and prompt kindly service cannot have been due to the expectation of tips; from this point of view it is difficult to imagine a less promising party than ours.

These people – the fortitude with which they endured their afflictions, the joy with which life none the less filled them, their compassion for those more stricken than themselves, above all their serene confrontation of the prospect of death in the certain knowledge of God's love and mercy – occupied my mind and spirit much more than Lourdes as a place.

Places, as it happens, have never interested me much, as such, and Holy Places, whether Bethlehem or Lourdes, tend to be marred for me by the sellers of tawdry relics, the bric-a-brac of piety, who gather around them. However, in the grotto where St Bernadette is supposed to have had her vision – the very heart of Lourdes – I found a marvellous stillness, not due, let me hasten to say, to absence of people. Never a moment, day or night, when there were not some suppliants coming or going, or kneeling in prayer – as we found when we tried to film the grotto empty. For most of the time, in all seasons, it is teeming with people. No, the stillness is within, not without; wonderfully peaceful and uplifting. Human beings are only bearable when the last defences of their egos are down; when they stand, helpless and humbled, before the awful circumstances of their being. It is only thus that the point of the cross becomes clear, and the point of the cross is the point of life.

Were there any miracles? Any number – almost as many as there were pilgrims. The miracle of faith and the miracle of hope endlessly repeated; of faith that in the totality of our earthly lives we are all – the infirm and the whole, the sick and the well, the crazy and the sane – children of God, participating equally in his loving care; and of hope that, as such, our woes and afflictions are no more than bumps and scratches, scarcely to be noticed, soon to be forgotten.

There was even a tiny miracle for me. A woman asked me to go and see her sister who was very sick. So of course I went along. The sister was obviously at the point of death, and like any other glib child of twentieth century enlightenment, I had nothing to say, until I noticed in the most extraordinary vivid way, as in some girl with whom I had suddenly fallen in love, that her eyes were quite fabulously luminous and beautiful. 'What marvellous eyes!' As I said this, the three of us – the dying woman, her sister and I were somehow caught up into a kind of ecstasy. I can't describe it in any other way. It was as though I saw God's love shining down on us visibly, in an actual radiance. That was my miracle at Lourdes, and whenever I hear the Ave Maria they sing there all the time – otherwise, I expect, a rather banal tune – I remember my miracle with great joy.

Malcolm Muggeridge

3: IN ALL RELIGIONS

In all religions, the most memorable experience which they have in common is the experience which occurs in pilgrimage. For Muslims, pilgrimage to Mecca is an obligation for every man at least once in his life; and it clearly leaves its mark: 'There was a time,' said one Muslim, 'when I stood near the Kaaba (the central shrine containing the Black Stone) and I felt that I wasn't on earth at all. I was on a different plane, completely separated from earth. It's an experience you get there that you can't explain in words. It is so different, so beautiful.'

For Jews, the pilgrimage to Jerusalem used to be an obligation when the Temple was standing, and even now many Jews make the pilgrimage to the Western Wall, which stands on the site of Solomon's Temple. As one Jew said, 'Going to Israel is like going home. The heart of it to me is to go to the Western Wall. When I first went, I think I probably gasped when I saw what I was looking at, and tears poured down my face. I wished that my father could have been there too – because Jerusalem was not a united city in his lifetime. I felt that not only was *I* there but I was there for him and for a lot of other people who are outside our world now.'

For Christians, pilgrimage is not an obligation, but many do make pilgrimage to such places as Lourdes, or, in this country, to Walsingham. Hindus and Buddhists frequently make pilgrimage to holy men or women, or to great teachers – and *that*, for Buddhists, is necessary, because listening to a Buddhist teacher 'is not just listening to a lecture: it's a pilgrimage, because in Buddhism we talk all the time about the transmission of the *dhamma* (that is, the Buddha's teachings), and the transmission for us is not just a talking or a communication but almost a literal, physical passing across – it is a physical feeling of vitality that you get. It is a finding and a being found.'

One of the main consequences of pilgrimage for many people is a sense of urgency to do something more with their lives than they have done so far. That's what one Buddhist felt when he went on pilgrimage to the Samadhi statue of the Buddha in Sri Lanka. 'You are there, and the whole place is filled with peace and love and loving kindness. And I felt, what am I doing as a person? I should be trying harder, I should be doing something to eradicate poverty in the world – I must do something worthwhile. I have quite often stood in front of that statue, and Pandit Nehru always went there when he visited Sri Lanka and felt the same. I think to myself, "Well, this is complete peace." And you are quite oblivious of everything else, the whole world and things like that.'

And Sikhs also have *their* pilgrimage, to the Golden Temple of Amritsar; and for them, too, the prevailing feeling is one of peace. 'I think that the only time that I can remember feeling, as an adult, quite content, and actually feeling that it had something to do with religion, was when I went to the Golden Temple; and I think that was the only occasion on which I felt really good and happy. I felt close to that superhuman power, and it made me feel content – it was peaceful just being there.'

John Bowker

(See also page 234.)

15
Age

———— ·•◦•· ————

We live in an ageing society. In the period 1980–86, it is predicted that the number of people aged sixty-five or over will increase by 24 per cent. The very old will increase significantly in numbers. In 1978, 1 in 104 was eighty-five or older. By 2001, it is likely to be 1 in 65.

Age Concern England is a charity which exists 'to promote the welfare of the aged'. Its policy is outlined by its director, David Hobman:

Age Concern's message for the eighties must be to stop treating old people as objects of pity as though they were a race apart. In doing so, we shall better understand that retirement is not synonymous with old age. The ways in which we respond to the needs of the old today will also influence the quality of our own lives in due course.

We also need to recognise that while poverty, sub-standard housing, inadequate transport schemes or shortcomings in the health and personal social services lead to unnecessary suffering, so do isolation, boredom, rejection and loneliness.

1: PRACTICALITIES

Age Concern believes old people should be allowed to be as independent as possible and welcomes the increased recognition by doctors, social workers and others that rehabilitation into the community is both possible and desirable.

Yet none of us is entirely independent; we rely on others in almost every aspect of our daily lives, and even the most active elderly person is not exceptional in this respect. Indeed, to remain in their own homes the more frail elderly may require a considerable number of different support services – among them are the practical jobs such as gardening, decorating and shopping. When younger, they may either have been able to afford to employ someone to undertake some of these tasks, or, more likely, they carried them out themselves. But gardening and decorating, in particular, can be difficult for the infirm elderly despite the availability of special tools for infirm and disabled gardeners. Many people take great pride in the conditions of their homes and gardens and some even succeed in doing a few of the less strenuous jobs themselves.

Food and shopping

High food prices hit hardest at those with small incomes, and the elderly in particular suffer as they tend to pay more for food than other groups in society. It has been estimated that the average man spends more on tobacco and alcohol than does a supplementary pensioner on food.

The poor may have to spend about 11 per cent more than average families in order to enjoy equivalent goods and services. This stems partly from the fact that poor people generally buy in smaller quantities which work out dearer per pound than larger ones; and partly because they are often limited by lack of transport which makes them dependent upon small neighbourhood shops which are usually more expensive than the big supermarkets. Very few old people can afford the capital cost of a freezer, let alone the luxury of buying their food in bulk to cut costs.

Age Concern believes that the major food stores could do much more in this area by providing goods in small quantities and sizes for elderly people. Nor should this consideration for elderly people only apply to food – why is it not possible for garments with zips down the front to be made readily available for people with arthritic hands? Why is it not possible to ensure that there is ease of access to shelves on which goods are displayed? Again Age Concern urges supermarkets and department stores to arrange for goods to be packaged in such a way that they are easy to handle and open. Some progress has been made in this campaign.

Hairdressing

The recognised importance of a hairdressing service to elderly people has led a number of Age Concern groups to provide a facility for housebound elderly people unable to visit a day centre or a club. In much the same way as someone can become depressed over a deteriorating garden or house, so they can feel dejected when no longer able to take pride in their appearance.

Age Concern Peterborough launched its domiciliary hairdressing service in April 1979, using a professionally trained ladies' hairdresser.

Another 'hairdressing at home' scheme is run by Age Concern Barrow in Cumbria. The group employs three volunteers, one of whom is professionally trained, the others being amateurs with a particular flair for this type of work.

Gardening

Keeping the garden neat and tidy is one of the biggest headaches facing elderly people, and it is especially hard on those who have in the past devoted great care and attention to its upkeep. Rheumatism or arthritis – indeed, any illness – can prevent people from doing as much as before; and a widow may find it hard to tackle the garden after her husband's death. For many years, Age Concern groups have marshalled teams of young volunteers to help with gardening, which can be an excellent way of mixing the generations to the benefit of both young and old.

Decorating

The cost of having one's house painted is beyond the means of most pensioners and 'doing it themselves' would be impossible for all but the young and active elderly. For those with stiff limbs or slightly unsteady balance, tall ladders can be dangerous. Even repairing a frayed carpet or rug which could be of hazard for an old person may be too hard for them the tackle on their own.

To help with decorating, insulation and odd jobs Age Concern volunteers have stepped in. In some areas this is done by groups of young volunteers of school age, working with local branches of Age Concern.

Age Concern

Local branches of Age Concern are listed in telephone directories. See also page 281.

2: TRANSPORT

For an elderly person an efficient, cheap, transport service can mean the difference between being housebound and living a full and rewarding life. Although old people do not, in general, require transport for work, it remains an essential part of their lives; and, particularly in rural areas, they may need some form of public transport in order to visit the doctor, collect their pensions, do their shopping and meet other people.

Travelling by public transport is frequently a difficult and exhausting business for people of any age, and for old people it can be sufficiently traumatic to prevent them from leaving their homes. Bus services are seldom designed to cater for the frail and disabled; routes and schedules are drawn up with other passengers in mind; bus stops often have no seats for waiting passengers, and the boarding platforms are usually set at such a height as to make it very difficult for an infirm person to get on the bus without assistance. As pedestrians, too, the elderly confront a set of situations that can be bewildering and frightening. Road traffic has increased by around 40 per cent in the last ten years with the result that old people are at greater risk of being knocked down than ever before; a pedestrian aged seventy and over, for example, is five times more likely to have an accident than is a young adult pedestrian.

In 1979 Age Concern England launched its campaign to persuade the Government to extend the time allowed to cross roads at the Green Man or Pelican Automatic Crossing System. The campaign received widespread publicity and was given support by the Automobile Association. The Government's response so far has been to initiate trials in order to establish whether alterations could be made to make the Pelican Crossings safer.

Age Concern organisations all over the country continue to campaign for improvements in transport services. For example, Age Concern Huddersfield had been assisting a number of pensioners with transport difficulties. To make it easier for people to collect their pensions, the group persuaded the West Yorkshire Transport Executive to re-route one of their bus services. The group is now trying to divert another bus to help a large number of elderly people who have been rehoused in an area without a service.

In some cases, groups are successful in securing improvements. A complaint from Age Concern Exmouth about unheated buses led to more comfortable travel for pensioners in the Exeter area. The Western National Bus Company issued a statement promising that all faulty heating systems in their buses would receive immediate attention as soon as they were reported.

A key service provided by Age Concern organizations is transporting elderly people to and from day centres, lunch clubs and clinics. In many areas groups have their own minibuses and employ regular drivers, while in others they organise voluntary car services to enable elderly people to visit relatives in hospital and to attend GP surgeries.

Age Concern Lincoln has an ambulance as well as a minibus, and both are used to meet the range of transport needs. The ambulance, which has a tail lift for wheelchairs, is able to provide much needed day outings for the housebound. It visits local places of interest, takes groups for shopping trips as well as for more routine journeys to day centres and clubs.

Voluntary car services are also organised by local Age Concern groups. Many day centres rely on volunteers using their private cars to take old people to and from their premises.

Obviously, the key factor affecting transport is the cost of petrol. The recruitment of voluntary drivers and, where necessary, the reimbursement of expenses is just one of the transport facilities affected by petrol prices.

At both local and national level, Age Concern is active in the transport field, campaigning for improvements in public services, but also involved in supplementing those services for the frail and handicapped.

Age Concern

3: LIVING CONDITIONS

The elderly, and particularly the very old, tend to live in the worst housing conditions. Nearly one in four do not have access to an indoor lavatory and about the same number have no piped water. A third of a million still live in homes without a bath or separate kitchen. Escalating fuel costs are especially dangerous for housebound old people because inadequate heating can lead to a condition known as hypothermia. This means low internal body temperature, and it can result in premature death amongst old people (and also very young babies) who are often unaware of their condition and unable to afford to purchase sufficient fuel; and whose houses are, in some cases, so badly constructed that constant heat loss prevents them even from deriving the full benefit of the heating they do have. For this reason, one of the most helpful contributions to the comfort and health of old people can be made through active programmes of insulation.

Almost 70 per cent of all accidents within the home occur in premises occupied by people of over sixty-five, and less than a quarter of people of this age have a telephone through which they can call for assistance in an emergency. In the case of the over-eighties, a telephone is only readily accessible to one person in ten. Yet these are the people who may be most in need of urgent and immediate contact with the outside world, because over two million pensioners live entirely alone. Effective contact systems are crucial.

Whilst modern technology is leading towards the development of a range of sophisticated systems, which can be connected to the homes of isolated elderly people who are known to be at risk to link them with representatives of the social services, they are often very much of a second best to sustained direct personal contact. Call systems are known to give a sense of security to those who might otherwise be even more apprehensive, but they may not actually use them when a real crisis occurs. This confirms that the most reliable basis for continuous care which is readily available, but not obtrusive, is to have it provided within the locality by those who are ready to maintain regular contact with old people as members of their own family, or their parish, or simply out of neighbourliness.

David Hobman

NB *Some pupils may be able to start up or join Street Warden Schemes designed to provide effective early warning systems for the neighbourhood as a whole – young and old alike. A mother with a sick child may be as housebound as a disabled old person.*

16

Business outstanding

A group of three readings which illustrate just a few of the problems and issues which need to be put right in the world.

1 THE WORLD'S CHILDREN

This is an extract from the third annual 'State of the World's Children' report published by the United Nation's Children's Fund (UNICEF).

If the world's political leaders were to walk together through a village in the developing world they would only recognise about 2 per cent of the child malnutrition all around them. Indeed so invisible is the problem that, in one recent study, almost 60 per cent of mothers whose children were suffering from malnutrition believed that their children were growing normally and developing well.

The Third World's hunger is a hidden hunger. Visible malnutrition is rare. And it is time that the skin and bone image of the starving baby – an image which is too often used to represent the developing countries – was replaced by a greater international understanding of what child malnutrition really means.

Today, an invisible malnutrition touches the lives of approximately one-quarter of the developing world's young children. It quietly steals away their energy; it gently restrains their growth; it gradually lowers their resistance. And in both cause and consequence it is inextricably interlocked with the illnesses and infections which both sharpen, and are sharpened by, malnutrition itself. Perhaps as many as half of all cases of severe child malnutrition, for example, are precipitated not primarily by the lack of food but by intestinal parasites, fever and infection – especially diarrhoeal infection – which depresses the appetite, burns the energy, and drains away the body-weight of the child.

The net result is that every day of this last year more than 40,000 young children have died from malnutrition and infection. And for every one who has died, six now live on in a hunger and ill-health which will be for ever etched upon their lives.

No statistic can express what it is to see even one child die in such a way; to see a mother sitting hour after anxious hour leaning her child's body against her own; to see the child's head turn on limbs which are unnaturally still, stiller than in sleep; to want to stop even that small movement because it is so obvious that there is so little energy left inside the child's life; to see the living pink at the roof of the child's mouth in shocking contrast to the already dead-looking greyness of the skin, the colours of its life and death; to see the uncomprehending panic in eyes which are still the clear and lucid eyes of a child; and then to know, in one endless moment, that life has gone.

To allow 40,000 children to die like this every day is unconscionable in a world which has mastered the means of preventing it.

James P. Grant

2: ABORIGINAL LAND RIGHTS

In 1967 Australian Aboriginals were officially recognised as human beings. Before that, they were classed, along with the kangaroo and the national flower, as flora and fauna of Australia. To black people living in the relative comfort of Britain, this may seem an incredible travesty of human rights but for the Aboriginals it is a prime example of the official racism they have been fighting since the arrival of Europeans to their country.

The Voice
(NB: *The Voice* is a Black London newspaper.)

Of all the injustices done to Aboriginals, dispossession of their traditional land is the loss they feel most keenly. Thus, the question of land rights is seen by many Aboriginals and their supporters as the priority issue still to be resolved satisfactorily. This is particularly true in those States where Aboriginals do not have secure tenure of their reserve land.

The Commonwealth Government's Aboriginal Land Rights

(Northern Territory) Act was proclaimed on Australia Day, 26 January 1977. Its provisions were based on the recommendations of a Royal Commission into Aboriginal Land Rights in the Northern Territory.

The Act provides for Aboriginals in the Northern Territory to gain title to existing reserve land and to make claim to other land—Aboriginal-owned pastoral leases and vacant Crown land – on the basis of traditional ownership.

As with most other land in Australia, minerals on Aboriginal land remain the property of the Crown, but the Act requires the consent of Aboriginals for exploration and mining on Aboriginal land. Pre-existing mining interests are, however, protected from veto.

Australian Government

Australia, like much of the world, is in an economic depression and in the never ending search for minerals such as diamonds, bauxite and uranium, Aboriginal reservaions are constantly being made smaller and moved from region to region.

'The problem', according to one Aboriginal representative, 'is that the multinational corporations in collusion with the government are moving from site to site. This means large groups could be moved many miles away from their burial grounds. One company moved a large group of Aborigines, through the government, off some sacred ground to drill for oil. The government thinks one reservation is the same as another but once the sacred ground has been desecrated, that's it. As it turned out, the search for oil in that instance proved useless.'

Asif Zubaity

Aboriginals saw man as part of nature, sharing a common life-principle with animals, birds and plants. The earth, man and all living things had been created by the great creatures, the heroes of the Dreamtime, which in mythological time had travelled through the land giving it its physical form.

Certain natural phenomena such as features of the landscape are believed by Aboriginals to be marks left by the creation heroes and because they hold the living spirits of the creators, are regarded by them as 'sacred sites'.

The spiritual affiliation between Aboriginals and their land was profound. This special relationship was given emphasis in the belief that for a child to be born, a spirit must first enter the mother's womb to give the child life, the spirit deriving from one of the various sites associated with the Dreamtime heroes. Consequently Aboriginals believe there is a direct and personal link between the spirit being, the child and the place from which the spirit came. That place is the source of the person's life force and he or she is inseparable connected with it. The connection is timeless, beginning before birth and continuing after death.

The arrival of European settlers almost two hundred years ago meant that for Aboriginals life was never to be quite the same again.

Australian Government

3: RIVER BLINDNESS

'River blindness' is a disease which has long troubled large areas of West Africa. This passage tells how the disease is being brought under control.

The old village of Samendini in the Coe Valley in the West African republic of Upper Volta is deserted; a place cursed by a malediction and haunted by evil spirits, according to the old people, which made its inhabitants go blind. Eventually the people fled away from the river to higher ground, leaving the fertile lands of their ancestors to return to the wilderness.

In their new home they are healthier but the crops are smaller. The blindness is not the deadly effect of evil spirits but the work of the blackfly, which breeds in the river and spreads 'river blindness'.

Today the new village of Samendini shelters many victims of the disease. For the old there is unfortunately no cure. A woman of thirty, who has been blind for ten years, explained that her grandfather, her father and her brother had all been blind before they died. A vigorous but blind cultivator came from his field to meet us. Asked how he managed, he said he felt the plants, and laughed gently.

Hundreds of villages throughout the Sahel (the southern edge of the Sahara desert) in the upper valleys of the Volta and the Niger, and including parts of Mali, Upper Volta, Ghana, Ivory Coast, Togo, Benin and Niger, have lived with the scourge of river blindness for generations. In the 1960s it was estimated that some twenty million people in West Africa alone were affected.

Medical science had no cure, no answer. Whole areas of rich land were abandoned because of the danger.

In the early 70s a committee of donor nations agreed to fund a twenty-year campaign by the United Naitons to control onchoceriasis – river blindness – in West Africa. The task was given to the World Health Organisation who set up a special oncho-programme. Its headquarters was in Ougadougou, the capital of Upper Volta. Eight years later the programme has largely proved successful, but the work has to continue until 1990.

River blindness is spread by several species of blackfly. The most dangerous is that which lives in the savannah – the *simuli damnosum*. It lays its eggs in fast running water, waterfalls, rapids, shallows of uplands streams, mainly in the rainy season. The fly feeds on human blood and contaminates the bloodsteam of its human victims.

The plan adopted was to interrupt the life cycle of the blackfly with a massive search and destroy operation using all the resources of modern science and technology. By mapping and monitoring all possible laying sites in the rivers and streams of the region, and capturing samples of the blackfly tempted to come and feed on the legs of special catchers, the source of infection could be traced each week and the likely nesting grounds 'bombed' with a selective insecticide.

It's a huge operation, using spraying helicopters and fixed wing aircraft, a network of supply depots and local laboratory centres, bound together by all-weather road transport and radio control. In human terms it has been well worth it.

No infected children have been reported in West Africa for several years and new drugs have been found to brake the progress of the disease in sufferers infected years ago.

The scale of the oncho-programme is such that it can only be funded at the highest international level. But as the villagers return to their lands to farm and seek to introduce new methods of work or organisation, then Christian Aid, through the World Council of Churches Sahel team, can provide help at the village level to give the returning people a fresh start.

Derrick Knight

17

Music in Worship

It is not so very long ago when the most predictable feature of school worship was the singing of a hymn. An informal survey recently revealed that one is now unlikely to find a hymn being sung in more than 15 per cent of secondary school assemblies.

Even those who have no wish to organize the singing of religious lyrics (especially those of dubious merit) will wish to alert students to the role played by music in religious expression.

It is hoped that the following passages will serve as an introduction to the variety of Christian music and especially Christian hymns.

In his introduction to Hymns for Church and School, *Erik Routley considers the question, 'Why sing hymns?'*

NB *The 'Te Deum' is an ancient hymn, originally in Latin, but sung regularly in English in the Church of England service of Matins. It can be found in the Book of Common Prayer.*

It is difficult nowadays to think of Christian worship without hymns. As long as there has been Christian worship there have been hymns of one kind or another to adorn it. During those two thousand years hymns have been written in an astonishing variety of styles, and the word 'hymn' has not always meant what we now mean by it.

What we now mean by a hymn is a song, usually containing a number of stanzas of identical structure, to be sung by a congregation as an act of Christian worship. But if you try to restrict hymns to this kind of definition, you at once run into exceptions. 'Hymn' is, of course, a Greek word, and its original use was for a song in praise of any deity in whom the ancient Greeks believed. But in Christian use – is a hymn always in verse? No, because the *Te Deum*, a piece of rhythmical prose, is a hymn. Must the verses always be in rhyming lines? 'O come, all ye faithful' had no rhymes. Have hymns always been sung by everybody present at the service? Certainly not: for a thousand years in the Middle Ages hymns were sung only by monks' choirs. Have Christians always used them? No, because until very recently they were never used at a Roman Catholic Mass or at a Quaker Meeting. Are they only used in church? Far from it; what about the Salvation Army and the revivals of the Wesleys?

Yet it remains true that hymns have been used, in some form, in some style, in some part of the Church's worship.

The answer to our opening question is, broadly, this. Hymns are sung, and always have been sung, to help people make the Christian Faith their own. Much of what is done in worship is done by people specially set apart to do it: by the priest, and by the choir. But from the earliest days, Christians have felt that worship is best thought of not as a *lecture* but as a *conversation*.

Hymn-singing is accepted as a proper and helpful addition to this congregational part in the service. And in our own time the use of hymns in this way has become more widespread and more discriminating than it has ever been.

Erik Routley

(See also pages 111 and 195.)

1: ANCIENT AND MODERN

The following two excerpts indicate how one famous and traditional hymn came to be written, and how new trends are developing in Christian churches.

During the Thirty Years' War (1620–1648) the little town of Eilenburg, in Saxony, suffered severely. The Austrians sacked it once and the Swedes twice. The over-crowding caused by the influx of refugees from the countryside produced the plague which ravaged the city four times during the period of war. Only one minister of the town, Martin Rinkart, survived this scourge and it often fell to his lot to take as many as fifty funerals in a single day! Famine was yet another of the miseries of war which left its mark on Eilenburg, while of its 1000 houses nearly 800 were laid in ruins.

But at last came the great day when news arrived that the Peace of Westphalia had been signed and the war had come to an end. The Elector of Saxony at once ordered Thanksgiving Services to be held in every church, and also selected a text from which ministers were to preach, Ecclesiasticus 50:22, 'Now bless ye the God of all, Who everywhere doeth great things, Who exalteth our days from the womb, and dealeth with us according to His mercy. May He grant us joyful hearts, and may peace be in our days for ever.'

A splendid text for the occasion, and one which so struck Martin Rinkart that, as he pondered over it, its words gradually shaped themselves into the form of a hymn, which was doubtless sung at his own Thanksgiving Service, has been translated into other languages, and is now used everywhere. Its notes of gladness are intensified when we remember the horrors of war which its author had experienced, and the close of which it first commemorated. How well Rinkart enshrined the text in the hymn can be seen from the first verse.

W. J. Limmer Sheppard

> Now thank we all our God
> With hearts and hands, and voices,
> Who wondrous things hath done,
> In whom His world rejoices;
> Who from our mother's arms
> Hath blessed us on our way
> With countless gifts of love,
> And still is ours today.

Martin Rinkart
(translated by C. Winkworth)

Pop music has infiltrated the churches. Religious songs of the Third World, with their native beat, have been introduced. Songs like the tradiional African 'Kum ba yah' and the 'Caribbean Lord's Prayer' are sung to a guitar, while the church congregation, usually consisting of young people, joins in.

The Church was quick to react to the introduction of pop music. Volumes of modern hymns including pop or folk tunes have been produced. These have titles like Youth Praise.

Like the old folk songs, modern music includes songs with a

story or a message. Sometimes these are of a religious nature. It is not unusual for a guitar-playing group to sing an item during a normal church service. Even cathedrals and abbeys, the bastions of traditional church music, occasionally hold a Rock Mass. But, generally speaking, at present, pop music has become only a small part of the music in church worship.

Eva Bailey

2: EARLY BLACK RELIGIOUS SONGS

One of the earliest musical contacts between the black and white people in the southern states of the USA was through religious music. The early nineteenth century was a time of great religious activity in America. Black congregations were particularly attracted to the Baptist and Methodist missionaries, because of their very lively and emotional style of preaching and conducting services. In this, they were closer to African religious practices than any other Christian denominations. However, rather than simply copying the European hymns they heard white people sing, the slaves combined the music and the religious traditions with those they had known in Africa. Thus the earliest form of black religious music in America was probably the ring shout. This was a kind of religious dance accompanied by singing in a call-and-response pattern, with the dancers stamping their feet to beat out a rhythm, as they moved round in a circle. This illustrates the very different ideas about religion that exist in Europe and Africa. European churchgoers sit quietly in their seats, but in Africa physical action – dance as well as music – is vital to worship. So also is the call-and-response technique between preacher and congregation. This explains the beginning of the song-sermon among black Americans. Here at religious gatherings, either in churches or in widespread camp meetings in the countryside, the preacher would sing or cry his line and the congregation would shout or sing the response.

What are now known as spirituals grew out of the early ring shouts and song-sermons. To begin with, blacks and whites worshipped together in churches. But the whites increasingly disapproved of this, while blacks were also keen to separate, so that they could worship in their own ways. Therefore, as early as 1816 churches were set up for black congregations only. This meant that, rather than having to sing traditional hymns in a strictly European fashion, they could be adapted and sung with the types of African characteristics we have discussed. Hymns performed in this way are known as spirituals. They had a special significance for the slaves, because they adapted stories from the Bible to their own situation. One of the most popular was that of the Israelites in captivity in Egypt, which is the theme of 'Go Down Moses':

When Israel was in Egypt's Land,
Let my people go!
Oppressed so hard they could not stand,
Let my people go!
Go down, Moses, way down in Egypt's Land,
Tell old Pharaoh, let my people go!

Legend has it that Moses in this spiritual was a reference to Harriet Tubman, a black anti-slavery worker who helped slaves escape to the northern states of America. There, blacks were free men, since most northern states had freed their slaves early in the nineteenth century or before. Such double meaning would have been missed by the whites, who would have interpreted this spiritual as simply a traditional religious hymn, rather than as a protest against slavery.

The black religious singing tradition continues to this day in the form of gospel music, the music of the black churches.

Graham Vulliamy

3: TWO TRADITIONS

This passage requires two actors, one black and one white (the 'vicar') and one narrator.

It may be possible to illustrate the passage with songs and hymns of the various traditions mentioned, between the scenes.

Later, pupils might discuss the issues raised by this scene. For example, has the vicar a point in asking Ben not to 'Praise the Lord' during prayers and the sermon? Is it good that separate black and white churches should grow independently of each other?

Narrator: The Anglican Parish of the Most Holy and Undivided Trinity has a church on Acacia Road, part of a vast new housing estate. There is a busy church life, and newcomers are said to be welcome on Sunday mornings. Young people collect eagerly enough for Christian Aid and support 'starvation lunches'. A few of the middle-aged are enthusiastic about providing Sunday Schools, being involved in local community groups or the like. Some of the elderly wish the new vicar wouldn't fit new tunes to old hymns.

Into this parish comes Ben.

Scene 1 *Enter Ben and Vicar from opposite directions.*

Ben: Hello, vicar. I'm coming with my family next Sunday.

Vicar: Welcome. Where are you from?

Ben: Barbados, via Southampton, Brixton and Birmingham, these past fourteen years. It's been quite a trek, a great adventure. Now a great happiness, for I have a job, and a lovely new house here in Peterborough. Praise the Lord! We're all so happy – my wife and I with a place of our own, here with our children. We feel we're 'home'. God has been good to us. Praise the Lord!

Vicar: Oh! I see. Yes . . . well.

Ben: You're not used to my Gospel ways? My family, we enjoy the Bible, and singing about Jesus. You have 'Songs of Praise' next Sunday . . . we're coming to that!

Vicar: Well . . . it's really only a few hymns and some prayers.

Ben: Praise the Lord: that's good. I enjoy prayers.

They go their own ways.

Narrator: It is now a week later.

Scene 2 *Re-enter Ben and the Vicar*

Ben: That service 'Songs of Praise', vicar – when you have it again, my family would like to sing some of our songs for you.

Vicar: Oh! Yes! Calypsos?

Ben: No – Gospel Songs. Songs of Joy and Peace and Love.

Vicar: Oh! Well, I don't know if my folk would take to that sort of thing . . . we use *100 Hymns for Today*. That's quite modern you know!

Ben: Don't fear . . . I'll teach them.

Vicar: But would we have the music?

Ben: I'll sing . . . and we have our hands . . . (*Clap! clap!*) . . . these Ten Stringed Instruments!

Vicar: Well, we'll see how it goes!

They part.

Narrator: Another week passes.

Vicar: Ben, I really enjoyed your Songs. It was really good of you to share your music with us. I found myself laughing and clapping with you.

Ben: Praise the Lord!

Vicar: The only thing is . . . a few people think we should not 'applaud' in Church. They're thinking of going to the Cathedral. However, a few of us have been talking about it with them, and we seem to have accepted that sometimes it is fun, being together as Christians, and that we are allowed to enjoy being in Church. But, Ben, I really must ask you not to 'Praise the Lord', and 'Amen' during reading and prayers. It makes it difficult for some of the older ones, and it's not only the elderly who find your behaviour during sermons distracting.

It is upsetting when you nod your head and agree with me during sermons. It's frightening for the children.

Ben: How strange! But, I'll try, it's just so natural for us to be happy in our religion.

Vicar: Well – yes. We're happy too in our own way. See you next week?

Ben: Yes. Perhaps.

The Rev. James Bell

18

Inter-racial attitudes

NB *This is a sequence of readings more suitable for use with older students.*

People of one group are often suspicious or even afraid of those who belong to another. When people of different groups have to live close to each other, problems can arise.

1: GYPSIES IN BRITAIN

It is not generally accepted that Britain has become a multi-cultural country. Some people believe that harmony will come through 'pluralism with separatism'. That is, individual groups should be helped to preserve their own languages, customs and beliefs. But while many believe that, for example, settlers in this country should have those rights, they take a different attitude to Travelling People.

It is the nature of Travelling People (or gypsies as they are often called) to travel. Many feel the answer to 'the gypsy problem' is to help them to settle in one place.

This passage comes from a book published in connection with Human Rights Years (1968) which marked the twentieth anniversary of the Universal Declaration of Human Rights.

Their principal problem has been their inability to obtain and retain permanent sites upon which to live either in caravans or more permanent erection although over the years some have acquired land and eventually erected permanent dwellings. Town and country planning makes provision for caravan parks but if these have the accepted standards of roadways, sanitation, etc., gypsy occupations such as car breaking, wood sawing, rag sorting, scrap metal and general dealing have not been accepted as congruous. The result has been that gypsies have sought sites on forest and common land and roadside verges from which in latter years they have been continually moved. We might ask ourselves whether gypsies can be considered to have any special rights not enjoyed by settled communities. Whilst they can and do acquire land, is it unreasonable for society to ask for guarantees of observance of standards of hygiene and social behaviour expected of society generally?

Many of the Human Rights cannot be fully or even partially enjoyed without the benefit of education. The very mode of life of gypsy parents has prevented many of the children from settled schooling and this, coupled with the conditions in which many of the families have been living, has meant that upon reaching employment age the young men and women are not acceptable in a very wide range of employments. The young men have tended to continue in the casual employment of their fathers and the young women to follow the occupations of their mothers, such as flower-selling, rag sorting and washing, and seasonal agricultural and horticultural work such as fruit-picking. Settlement then is a prerequisite to education which is essential if succeeding generations of gypsies are to enjoy a fuller life. One effect of this has a second bearing on employment. Social Security contributions and Income Tax requirements are not adequately understood and the necessary paper work is worrying the gypsy men and women placed in regular employment for the first time. Possible penalties for non-observance in the past of the rules in these respects have an unsettling effect and tend to encourage reversion to casual work.

The attitude of the public to gypsies varies from complete disregard to real fear. In the course of rag and scrap-metal collection and seeking water supplies from houses in the neighbourhood of sites without any services, some apprehension has been engendered in housewives and some public-houses have sought to avoid serving gypsies for fear of the effect of their company upon other customers. The tendency for gypsies to desecrate the countryside with rubbish left from scrap collection and car breaking has hindered their acceptance by neighbours. Foremen in charge of working gangs are not unsympathetic to gypsies who are encouraged to take up regular work, but their fellows in casual work resulting in higher incomes than the lesser skilled regular work the gypsies are able to do, tend to look down on those in orthodox employment. So far as the attitude of the public is concerned we might ask ourselves how far we should tolerate and be sympathetic towards citizens who, through lack of education and amenities, are reluctant to accept the standards of settled communities. It does seem possible that the gypsies would exchange their present conditions for a more settled way of life if they could receive more goodwill from society.

The above article went on to describe a settlement programme in detail and concluded:

It seems conclusive that ultimate placements not in groups of gypsy families but interspersed throughout the community is the answer to the problem but it is essential that the following must have been achieved during their stay in the rehabilitation centres:

1. Regular employment by the head of the household – to ensure good standards of accommodation, feeding, clothing and recreation.
2. Acceptable domestic standards in the home.
3. Acceptable personal standards of dress, cleanliness and behaviour.
4. Regularity of school attendance and good neighbourliness.

F. J. Bryan Long

2: COCKNEY ATTITUDES

This reading is from a book called 'The Muvver Tongue', which is about Cockneys (traditionally described as people born 'within the sound of Bow Bells' in London's East End), and about their dialect and attitudes. Its two authors are both Cockneys. Their views are widely held – but are not those of everyone.

Cockneydom is an uneasily multi-racial society. Those who regard themselves as 'native' East Enders are mostly descendants of families which came in from Essex, Suffolk and Hertfordshire in the nineteenth century for work in the docks, factories and markets and on the railways. Some have an older East London lineage, and others represent the half-a-million Irish who poured into the riverside areas in the 1840s. In addition, there have always been other-coloured immigrants. Before the last war there was a well-established little Chinese colony in Limehouse, and a small number of black people. Lascar seamen were plentiful round the docks; and Sikhs who carried suitcases full of cheap haberdashery, bought in Shoreditch warehouses, to sell on door-steps. The most conspicuous additions, however, have been the wave of Russian and Polish Jews between 1880 and 1900, and the influx of Pakistanis and Bengalis in the last twenty years.

A small minority of Cockneys are openly racist and have it in for Jews and coloureds. A large number grumble about them but would not accept trying to harm them or drive them out 'now they're here'. The grumbling is mostly connected with grievances over Social Security, housing and so on. As mixing takes place, it gives way to the sentiment 'there's good and bad among all people'; this acknowledges progress in relationships while leaving room to criticize when the speaker feels like it. The fear of getting a lot of Asian immigrants in 'our' street is not racial hostility so much as unease when neighbours with whom one converses easily on the basis of a common background are replaced by families whose style makes a barrier. After a generation this softens a good deal. The second-generation black man has assimilated a lot of East End culture, and his teenage daughter talks pure Cockney.

By enlightened middle-class standards in which the wrong word is outrageous, practically all Cockneys are racist in their talk. They refer to black people as 'darkies' or 'niggers'; all people from the Indian continent, and the Asians who have come from Kenya and Uganda, are 'Pakkys'. Jews are 'Jewboys', 'Yids' or 'four-by-twos' – an older word was 'sheeny'. A Jewish man working among gentiles is likely to be called 'Ikey', just as a Scot is 'Jock' and an Irishman 'Paddy'. Italians are 'Tallyarners', a free-and-easy rendering of 'Italianos'.

In fact it is doubtful if these are racist words. If they are, it ought to be offensive to call somebody 'Ginger' or 'Lofty'. Though there is a mild cruelty in some of them, as there is in many nicknames and epithets – calling a spectacled person 'Foureyes', for instance – they are simply descriptive tags which, in general, do not carry malice.

The nicknames and jokes are part of the flow of East End folklore and help to make the terms on which different nationalities and races live cheek-by-jowl with, on the whole, not much trouble. To call a cash register 'Yiddisher piano' conveys the legend about the Jews, but an amused tolerance as well. Something of the sort appears in comments about 'Pakky colours' (usually bright pinks and blues) for painting houses; they imply recognition and back-handed acceptance of another culture. In a more gracious environment, better consummations might be wished. In East London, harsh-sounding banter expresses relationships which may be the best obtainable when the whole population is aware of life as a collection of struggles.

Robert Barltrop and Jim Wolveridge

3: THE JEWS OF NORWICH

In the Middle Ages, Norwich was the third largest city in England. It had a large Jewish community, living alongside the Christian community in apparent harmony.

But one event, the murder of a boy called William, led to the growth of hatred, the massacre of many Jews and the eventual expulsion of all Jews from England in 1290.

'The Jews were expelled not because they were ostentatious, nor because they were secret proselytisers [seeking converts] nor because they were failing . . . as money-lenders, but because they were victims of that dark streak within the human personality which leads us to believe that we can turn our misfortunes away from ourselves by inflicting sufferings on others.'

This is the story of William of Norwich.

A boy's dead body was found in Thorpe Wood outside Norwich on March 24, 1144. William was eleven or twelve years old, the son of a well to do farmer and the grandson of a priest. His aunt was also married to a priest. He was apprenticed to a skinner and naturally, in this trade, he had frequent dealings with Jews, saw them in their houses and was said to be close friends with a number. His uncle, however, Godwin Sturt, a priest, warned him against them.

Nevertheless, a man who may have been a Jew or a Christian, who said he was the Archdeacon of Norwich's cook, offered the boy a place in the Archdeacon's kitchen and took him away. On Easter eve, his body was found in Thorpe Wood, dressed in his jacket and shoes, with his head shaved and punctured with countless stabs. Thomas of Monmouth's story in that in the

Passover week the boy was kindly treated by the Jews but after synagogue service on the Wednesday, he was bound as if on a cross, his hand and feet pierced with nails and boiling water poured over the corpse. On Good Friday, the body was taken on horseback to Thorpe Wood. Five years later, a Norwich citizen confessed on his deathbed that he had seen the two Jews bearing the body entering Thorpe Wood. The body itself was buried where it lay in the woods but afterwards, exhumed and re-interred. Godwin Sturt, the priest told the story to his wife, who then told him that she had had a vision on the previous Saturday week warning her against the Jews. The boy's mother then accused the Jews. The priest then demanded justice against the Jews, who were summoned to appear the next day before a synod. The Sheriff rescued the Jews from the Bishop and his followers and escorted them to the Castle. The Bishop, however, organized the cult of St William who was afterwards buried in the Cathedral, despite strong opposition from Elias, Prior of the Benedictines from 1146 to 1150. The local clergy, who knew the Jews best, strongly denied the so-called 'evidence', and the Jews continued to live in Norwich for the moment undisturbed. However, in 1146, a Norwich Jew was murdered and his murderer was defended by Bishop William Turbe.

Looking back on the story, the facts may well have been a sexual crime against a child of the kind so common today. There is no evidence to identify the criminal, whether Christian or Jew. Perhaps the whole story was got up owing to the need for a saint to stimulate the offerings of pilgrims. William's remains were identified as someone who had died for the faith, hence the suggestion that his death was the result of some kind of ritual murder. Prior Elias at the Cathedral, and those who supported him, insisted that it was not the sufferings of the boy but the cause of the suffering which made the martyr. He denied that William was a ritual victim, killed for religious reasons.

But the evil story did its work. Similar accusations were made at Gloucester in 1168, at Bury St Edmunds in 1181 and in Bristol in 1183. Still, however, the peace held and it was only when the Third Crusade began that anti-Jewish feeling broke out into violence, as Steven Runciman put it, 'Crusading fervour always provided an excuse for killing God's enemies.' So in 1189, houses were burned at the centre of London and thirty Jews lost their lives. A series of massacres took place at York in 1190 and at

King's Lynn, and a substantial number also died at Norwich. There were accusations of abduction and circumcision and on this occasion, the Prior of Norwich was amongst the accusers. It is as if the poison which had at first been rejected by the Cathedral clergy and the other lower clergy gradually seeped into the Christian community and they were more prepared to punish and to cause suffering. A number of Jews were hanged by the Crown. In 1290 all Jews were expelled from England and did not officially return until the time of Cromwell. However, the evil story continued to circulate and may have been one of the sources of the Nazi propaganda leading to Belsen.

The Very Reverend Alan Webster

19

Successful living

1: BE YOURSELF

At least three things are involved in fully being ourselves, in achieving all we are capable of achieving.

First, imagination. Great living starts with a picture, held in some person's imagination, of what he would like some day to do or be. Florence Nightingale dreamed of being a nurse, Edison pictured himself as an inventor; all such characters escaped the mere shove of circumstance by imagining a future so vividly that they headed for it.

Think of the poet John Keats: orphaned in early boyhood, pressed by poverty, hurt by the cruelty of his literary critics, disappointed in love, stricken by tuberculosis, and finally shoved off the scene by death at twenty-six. But with all his ill fortune, Keat's life was not driven by chance. From that day when, as a youth, he picked up a copy of Spenser's *Faerie Queene* and knew beyond doubt that he too was born to be a poet, Keat's life was drawn by a masterful purpose which gave him a lasting place among the world's renowned. 'I think', he said once, 'that I shall be among the English poets after my death'. He got that picture in his imagination, and to him it was a constant encouragement.

Hold a picture of yourself long and steadily enough in your mind's eye and you will be drawn towards it. Picture yourself vividly as defeated and that alone will make victory impossible. Picture yourself vividly as winning and that alone will contribute immeasurably to success. Do not picture yourself as anything and you will drift like a derelict.

Second, common sense. There is no use in a round pegs imagining itself fitted in a square hole. As a matter of fact, many people flounder about pitifully before they discover the true direction of their lives. Whistler, the artist, started out to be a general and was dropped from West Point Military Academy because he could not pass in chemistry. Sir Walter Scott wanted to be a poet and turned to novel writing only when Byron outshone him in his chosen field. Study yourself and use your head in picturing your goal. But whether with wisdom or without, pick a goal; don't drift.

Third, courage. Real personalities always have the kind of faith that produces courage. When his generation was against him, Richard Wagner had faith in his music, and it overcame the world. After centuries had borne unimpeachable testimony to the devastating virulence of yellow fever, a little group of American medical men in Cuba had faith that it could be conquered, and it was. Charles Darwin worked for twenty years in a little English garden succeeding and failing, trying and keeping on because he had faith that he had found a clue, and he conquered. Faith is not credulity. It is creative power. It is vision plus valour.

Imagination, common sense and courage – even a moderate exercise of these will produce remarkable results. If a man is primarily after wealth, the world can whip him; if he is primarily after pleasure, the world can beat him; but if a man is primarily growing a personality, then he can capitalize anything that life does to him.

Harry Emerson Fosdick

2: WHEN YOU'RE IN THE WRONG

When one is at fault, it is frequently disarming to admit it quickly. Ferdinand Warren, a commercial artist, used this technique to win the good will of a petulant art director. 'Recently I delivered to him a rush job,' Mr Warren told me, 'and he phoned me to call at his office immediately. When I arrived, I found just what I had anticipated – he was hostile, gloating over his chance to criticize. He demanded with heat why I had done so and so. Trying a new strategy, I simply said, "I am at fault and there is absolutely no excuse for my blunder. I have been doing drawings for you long enough to know better. I'm ashamed of myself."

'Immediately he started to defend me. "Yes, you're right, but after all, this isn't a serious mistake –"

'I interrupted him. "Any mistake may be costly. I should have been more careful. I'm going to do this drawing again."

' "No! No!" he protested. "I wouldn't think of putting you to all that trouble." He praised my work, assured me that he wanted only a minor change, a mere detail – not worth worrying about. My eagerness to criticize myself took all the fight out of him. Before we parted, he gave me a cheque and another commission.'

Dale Carnegie

3: THE GOLDEN RULE

We are invited by the great and wise to be kind – to treat our neighbours as we would have them treat us. We ourselves, of course, are included in this embracing love – an important point. Healthy persons wish to develop their own potentialities, to be themselves. But this need not be at the expense of others.

Our neighbours, however, include everybody, the whole human race. That is the difficulty. Kindness to those we are fond of, and who are fond of us, comes naturally enough to normal people. Most of us realize that life is not easy. We expect our friends to be kind to us and we see the point in being kind to them. Generally kindness in our own little circle or 'in-group' comes fairly naturally to healthy people. But kindness to everyone is a different matter. The brotherhood of man – one huge 'in-group' – is a concept that has to be learned. Kindness towards those in the 'out-group', those who feel and think perhaps very differently from us, those who do not accept our code, those who have hurt or wronged us, is in practice an ideal which frequently goes against the grain. Yet that is what we are invited to show.

An important step towards such embracing concern and kindness is the development of the desire to understand our fellows rather than to pass judgement. It is here that the little child may lead us. In our dealings with children we think of what they need rather than what they deserve. We realize that they need our help. In the same way we must try to understand our fellows – not because they are little children or necessarily in any way inferior to ourselves, but because we all need the co-operation of our fellows.

One of the lessons of history is that the best in us brings out the best in the worst of others, while the worst in us brings out the worst in the best of others. This is the psychological insight expressed by 'turning the other cheek'.

The great enemies of kindness and magnanimity are vindictiveness, jealousy, pride, and prejudice. Vindictive persons are insufficiently mature to take the knocks of everyday life. They think too much about their injured pride and the possibilities to 'getting their own back'. They are small and mean.

To think well and speak well of others is an important habit of mind to acquire. And it pays dividends. Identify yourself with the good points of others. This elevates you as well as them. All this is really nothing but a special case of generally paying attention to the good things of life. Such an attitude does not overlook or neglect the less acceptable facts. It is not delusion. It is the general habit of looking up to the stars rather than peering down at the mud.

V. C. Chamberlain

20

The human:
A unique animal

Denying that we have a special position in the natural world might seem modest, but it might also be used as an excuse for avoiding our responsibilities. The fact is that no species has ever had such control over the earth as we now have. That lays a huge responsibility upon us. It is not only our own future that lies in our hands, but that of all other living creatures with whom we share the earth.

That is the concluding paragraph of David Attenborough's book, 'Discovering Life on Earth'. The following three passages illustrate some of the stages in the development of civilization that led to that 'special position'.

1: BASIC COMMUNICATION SKILLS

Human beings have more separate muscles in their face than any other animal. So they can move the various parts of the face – lips, cheeks, forehead, eyebrows – in a great number of ways. There is little doubt that the face was the centre of early people's gestural communication.

One of the most important pieces of information the human face passes on is identity. We take it for granted that all our faces are very different from one another, yet this is very unusual among animals. If individuals are to cooperate in a team, then they must be able to tell one from another. Many social animals, such as hyenas and wolves, do this by smell. Human beings' sense of smell, however, was much less sensitive than their sight, so their identities were made clear by the shape of the face.

Since the features of the face can be moved, they can reveal a great deal of information about moods and intentions. We have little difficulty in understanding expressions of enthusiasm,

125

delight, anger and amusement. But quite apart from such feelings, we also send messages with our faces – of agreement and
disagreement, of welcome and invitation.

Are the gestures we use today ones that we have learned from
our parents and share with the rest of the community because we
have the same social background? Or are they an inheritance
from our prehistoric past? Some gestures, such as ways of count-
ing or insulting, vary from society to society and are clearly
learned. But others appear to be more universal. Did early
people, for example, nod agreement and shake their heads in
disapproval as we do? Clues to the answers can come from the
gestures used by people from another society who have had no
contact whatever with our own.

David Attenborough goes on to describe an encounter in New Guinea.

New Guinea is one of the last places in the world where such
people might be found. Ten years ago I was there with an expedition looking for people of the Biami tribe who had never seen
Europeans before. One morning, we awoke to find seven of them
standing in the bush nearby. As we scrambled out of our tents,
they stood their ground. It was an act of great trust and we tried to
show that we were friendly. We spoke to them, but the Biami
understood nothing. We had to rely entirely on such gestures as
we had in common, and it turned out that there were many of
them. We smiled – and the Biami smiled back. The gesture may
seem an odd one as a sign of friendliness, for it draws attention to
the teeth which are the only natural weapon that human beings
have. The important part, however, is not the teeth but the
movement of the lips. In other primates, this is a gesture of
peace-making. Among humans the gesture has changed by
upturning the ends of the mouth and is used to show welcome
and pleasure. We can be sure that this expression has not been
learned entirely from our parents, because even babies that are
born deaf and blind will smile when they are picked up to be fed.

David Attenborough

2: LANGUAGE, TECHNOLOGY AND FAMILIES

Of all the special features of humans, spoken language is probably the most important. Although other animals can signal simple messages to each other, human language goes much further than this. With hundreds and hundreds of words to choose from we can send much more complicated messages.

This allows humans to discuss important matters and plan ahead. We have evidence that our ancestors lived in bands and shared their food. Some members of the band probably collected fruits, nuts and roots, while others hunted animals. At the end of the day, everyone brought their food back to a base camp where it was shared out. We can guess that they needed to talk to each other to decide when they would meet up again. It would also enable them to tell each other if they had seen a tree full of fruit or a herd of animals somewhere nearby. When a group of them hunted a fairly large animal, language must have been useful in working out their hunting tactics beforehand.

One important human characteristic, that marks us out from other animals, is the way we make and use tools. A few animals use very simple tools: sea otters use stones to break open shells, for example, and chimpanzees use twigs to extract termites from the ground. But these 'tools' are basically natural objects that the animals have found a use for. Usually they use the object just as it is, and even if they adapt it for their use the changes made are very small: the chimpanzee, for example, takes a twig, removes the leaves, and breaks it into a suitable size and shape, but that is all. When a human being turns a natural object into a tool, far greater changes are made to it, and the finished product often looks nothing like the raw material. No animal makes tools in the imaginative way that humans do.

The simplest tools which early people used were made by knocking chips off a stone to produce sharp flakes. As our ancestors became more skilful they learned to make more specialized tools such as harpoons, fish hooks and knives. With these they could be better hunters and even start making clothes and building houses and boats. Today we have developed technology to the point where we can make highly complex tools like computers, lasers, space satellites and electron microscopes.

Unlike most other animals, humans live in family groups and take a long time to grow up to the point where they can look after themselves. Human babies, that are a few weeks or even months old, are helpless. Most week-old animals can walk and run but human babies don't learn to do this until they are more than one year old. Young animals can generally obtain food for themselves a few months after birth but human children, if left to their own devices in the wild, would be incapable of doing this until six or seven years of age. Because human babies take so long to become independent they must be looked after for several years, and humans live in family groups in order to care for their children.

A long childhood is an important part of being human, because we are essentially *cultural* animals. While we are growing up we are busy learning all the complicated ideas and skills we will need for our lives as adults in a human world, as well as the customs and manners which govern human behaviour . . .

But with all our technology, we now have the power to destroy our planet and all life on it. An understanding of our past, and an appreciation of our common heritage, will help us to preserve and develop the world for a better future.

Richard E. Leakey

3: CIVILIZATION

About 8000 years ago, the human population began to increase. The trigger may have been a wild grass that grew on the sandy hills and fertile river banks of the Middle East. It bears lots of nourishing seeds that are easily plucked and separated from their husks. Doubtless people had gathered it and eaten it whenever they came across it. But a change came when they realized that if they planted some of the seeds that they gathered, they would no longer have to search for the plant the following summer. They could stop wandering and become farmers. They could build themselves permanent huts and live in villages. So they founded the first towns.

Uruk, in Iraq, was built on what was then the marshy delta between the Tigris and Euphrates Rivers. Now it is a desert. The town was a complex one. The people planted fields of grain around it and kept herds of goats and sheep. They made pottery. This settled life enabled them to make an important advance in communication. People who travel all the time cannot have many possessions but people who live in houses can do so. In the remains of one of the buildings at Uruk the earliest known piece of writing has been found. It is a small clay tablet, covered with marks. No one yet knows exactly what it means. The marks are simple diagrams but ones that must have been recognized by the people for whom they were meant.

When people baked that tablet they changed the course of evolution. Now individuals could pass on information to others without being there. People in other parts of the world and in future generations could now learn from them. Other people elsewhere, in the valley of the Nile, the jungles of central America and the plains of China, made the same discoveries. Pictures of objects became simplified and took on new meanings. Some came to represent simply sounds. At the eastern end of the Mediterranean, people developed them into a system in which every sound they spoke had a shape that could be cut in stone, scored on clay or drawn on paper. So writing was developed. The revolution based on the sharing of experience and the spread of knowledge had begun. Later, the development of printing spread the knowledge even further. Today, our libraries can be seen as huge communal brains, memorizing far more than any one human brain could hold, and it is this stored knowledge that enables us to find ways of controlling our environment. Our knowledge of agriculture and machines, of medicine and engineering, of mathematics and space travel, all depend on stored experience. Cut off from our libraries and all they represent and marooned on a desert island, any one of us would be quickly reduced to the life of a hunter-gatherer.

David Attenborough

THOUGHTS FOR A DAY

Each of the following thirty passages can serve as the basis of a single assembly. Though all the passages are intended to develop moral awareness and to widen emotional responses, there is a greater emphasis on the social and practical in the first fifteen passages and on the imaginative and spiritual in the later ones.

1: PLAGUE

Daniel Defoe's Journal of the Plague Year *is an account of the Great Plague (1665), based on various sources and official documents. It was published in 1723.*

The narrator is a citizen of London and he describes the fears of his fellow citizens and the effects of the plague on their lives. In this excerpt he meets a boatman who keeps away from his family because they have the plague and he must try to remain healthy in order to provide for them.

Much about the same time I walked out into the fields towards Bow; for I had a great mind to see how things were managed in the river and among the ships; and as I had some concern in shipping, I had a notion that it had been one of the best ways of securing one's self from the infection to have retired into a ship; and musing how to satisfy my curiosity in that point, I turned away over the fields from Bow to Bromley, and down to Blackwall to the stairs, which are there for landing or taking water.

Here I saw a poor man walking on the bank, or sea-wall, as they call it, by himself. I walked a while also about, seeing the houses all shut up. At last I fell into some talk, at a distance, with this poor man; first I asked him how people did thereabouts.

'Alas, sir!' says he, 'almost desolate; all dead or sick. Here are very few families in this part, or in that village' (pointing at Poplar), 'where half of them are not dead already, and the rest sick.' . . . 'Why,' says I, 'what do you here all alone?' 'Why,' says he, 'I am a poor, desolate man; it has pleased God I am not yet visited (by the plague), though my family is, and one of my children dead.' 'How do you mean, then,' said I, 'that you are not visited?' 'Why,' says he, 'that's my house' (pointing to a very little, low-boarded house), 'and there my poor wife and two children live,' said he, 'if they may be said to live, for my wife and one of the children are visited, but I do not come at them.' And with that word I saw the tears run very plentifully down his face; and so they did down mine too, I assure you.

'But,' said I, 'why do you not come at them? How can you abandon your own flesh and blood?' 'Oh, sir,' he says, 'the Lord forbid! I do not abandon them; I work for them as much as I am able; and, blessed be the Lord, I keep them from want;' and with that I observed he lifted up his eyes to heaven, with a countenance that presently told me I had happened on a man that was no hypocrite, but a serious, religious, good man. 'Well,' says I, 'honest man, that is a great mercy as things go now with the poor. But how do you live, then, and how are you kept from the dreadful calamity that is now upon us all?' 'Why, sir,' says he, 'I am a waterman, and there's my boat,' says he, 'and the boat serves me for a house. I work in it in the day, and I sleep in it in the night; and what I get I lay down upon that stone,' says he, showing me a broad stone on the other side of the street, a good way from his house; 'and then,' says he, 'I halloo, and call to them till I make them hear; and they come and fetch it.'

At length, after some further talk, the poor woman opened the door and called, 'Robert, Robert.' He answered, and bid her stay a few moments and he would come; so he ran down the stairs to his boat and fetched up a sack, in which was the provisions he had brought; and when he returned he hallooed again. Then he went to the great stone which he showed me and emptied the sack, and laid all out, everything by themselves, and then retired; and his wife came with a little boy to fetch them away, and he called and said such a captain had sent such a thing, and such a captain such a thing, and at the end adds, 'God has sent it all; give thanks to Him.' When the poor woman had taken up all, she was so weak she could not carry it at once in, thought the weight was not much neither; so she left the biscuit, which was in a little bag, and left a little boy to watch it till she came again.

'Well, but,' says I to him, 'did you leave her the four shillings too, which you said was your week's pay?'

'Yes, yes,' says he, 'you shall hear her own it.' So he calls again, 'Rachel, Rachel,' which, it seems, was her name, 'did you take up the money?' 'Yes,' said she. 'How much was it?' said he. 'Four shillings and a groat,' said she. 'Well, well', says he, 'the Lord keep you all;' and so he turned to go away.

As I could not refrain contributing tears to this man's story, so neither could I refrain my charity for his assistance. So I called him, 'Hark thee, friend,' said I, 'come hither, for I believe thou art in health, that I may venture thee;' and so I pulled out my hand, which was in my pocket before. 'Here,' says I, 'go and call thy Rachel once more, and give her a little more comfort from me. God will never forsake a family that trust in Him as thou dost.' So I gave him four other shillings, and bid him go lay them on the stone and call his wife.

I have not words to express the poor man's thankfulness, neither could he express it himself but by the tears running down his face. He called his wife, and told her God had moved the heart of a stranger, upon hearing their condition, to give them all that money, and a great deal more such as that he said to her. The woman, too, made signs of the like thankfulness, as well to Heaven as to me, and joyfully picked it up; and I parted with no money all that year that I thought better bestowed.

Daniel Defoe

2: WORKING FOR OTHERS

Just as the boatman in the previous passage made sacrifices for his family, so Anne Sullivan devoted her life to helping her pupil Helen Keller.

The following story is a reminder of the need to be ready to help friends even if it means putting oneself at a disadvantage, and might also serve as a 'discussion starter': 'When and to what extent should one put the needs of others before one's own?'

In the spring of 1887, a twenty-year-old arrived in Tuscumbia, Alabama, to attempt the tutoring of a deaf-blind creature. The tutor's name was Anne Sullivan and the student's name was Helen Keller. They were to develop one of the most admired friendships of the century.

At seven, Helen Keller was a wild vixen who uttered unintelligible animal sounds. When in a rage, she would snatch dishes from the table and throw them and herself on the floor. More than one person had told Mrs Keller that her child was an idiot.

For weeks Anne spelled words into Helen's small hand, but

she could not break through to her consciousness. Then, on April 5, something wonderful happened. Here are Helen Keller's recollections of that day, written more than sixty years later:

It happened at the well-house, where I was holding a mug under the spout. Annie pumped water into it, and when the water gushed out into my hand she kept spelling w-a-t-e-r into my other hand with her fingers. Suddenly I understood. Caught up in the first joy I had known since my illness, I reached out eagerly to Annie's ever-ready hand, begging for new words to identify whatever objects I touched. Spark after spark of meaning flew from hand to hand and, miraculously, affection was born. From the well-house there walked two enraptured beings calling each other 'Helen' and 'Teacher'.

Annie Sullivan gave most of her life to Helen Keller. When her famous pupil decided to go to college, she sat beside her in every class at Radcliffe, spelling out the lectures into Helen's hand and overusing her own defective eyes to spell out books that were not in Braille.

Anne Sullivan recognized that Helen was a prodigy and had unlimited possibilities for thinking and feeling. There was no question as to which of the two had the higher IQ. By the time she was ten, Helen was writing to famous persons in Europe in French. She quickly mastered five languages and displayed gifts which her teacher never pretended to have.

But did that change Anne Sullivan's devotion? Not so far as we know. She was satisfied to be Helen's companion and encourager, allowing her to be applauded by kings and presidents and to be her own unique personage. In short, she gave her friend room to grow.

Alan Loy McGinnis

(See also passage 22 on pages 169–71.)

3: THE WORLD OF ENERGY

A reading for an occasion when an energy 'crisis' or debate is in the news.

Energy comes to us in many forms: as electricity to power our factories and warm our homes, as gas to cook our food, as petrol to drive our vehicles, and most vital of all as the heat and light we get from the Sun. In fact, the Sun is the Earth's ultimate source of energy. It not only radiates a plentiful supply of warmth, but has also helped to create coal, oil and the Earth's radioactivity, which are also vital sources of energy. Even the food we eat contains a dose of energy that originated in the Sun.

So what do we mean when we call all these things energy? A clue can be found in the origin of the word in the Greek language: it means action. And that is a very good description of energy in all its forms. Whenever energy is used, some sort of action takes place, so we can only begin to understand the nature of energy if we also look at what we mean by action.

We often think of action as some kind of bodily exertion. However, we also build powerful machines that are many times stronger than the human body. These can only function if they have a supply of fuel, just as we can only carry on working if we have a regular intake of food. Human beings and the machines they operate are therefore continually using up Earth's energy reserves and it is important to realize just how limited these are. Our present rate of consumption cannot carry on indefinitely, and energy is far too valuable to waste.

So are we really living in an age when our energy supplies are rapidly running out? Has the world become so dependent on dwindling reserves of oil that we can never again look forward to the abundance of energy we have enjoyed in the past? Is the outlook so bleak that only those who are very rich will be able to afford adequate amounts of increasingly expensive fuel and power?

These are the kinds of questions we are confronted with almost every day as newspapers and television remind us of the 'energy crisis'. What this really means is that there is a danger of a crisis arising in the future if we go on using energy as recklessly as we have in the past and we find nothing to replace oil on which we now depend for nearly half our energy needs.

Whatever breakthroughs occur in the search for alternative forms of energy, it is unlikely that there will ever be a single source of energy giving us all the power we need. The world's present over-dependence on oil may have taught us a valuable lesson in this respect. The threat of an energy crisis has arisen because we have come to rely so much on oil that we have tended to forget that oil would become more expensive as supplies became scarce. The only way to avoid such costly mistakes in the future is to have a greater variety of energy sources, or perhaps better still to learn to use much less energy in our daily lives, so that readily available supplies will go a lot further.

Frank Frazer

4: HUMAN NEEDS

A recent report suggested that the signs of being poor in Britain were (a) not being able to afford a holiday, (b) not being able to afford a weekly joint of meat and (c) not having a television set.

Bede Griffiths is a Christian monk. He went to India and followed a Hindu way of life while remaining a Christian. This passage, from his book Return to the Centre, *is a reminder of how those of us in the West tend to class luxuries as necessities.*

India has a way of reducing human needs to a minimum. One full meal a day of rice and vegetables – at best with some curds and ghee (clarified butter) – is considered sufficient. Tea or coffee with some rice preparation and some pickle is enough for breakfast and supper. Nor are tables and chairs, spoons and forks and knives and plates considered necessary. One sits on the floor on a mat and eats with one's hands – or rather with the right hand, as the left hand is kept for cleansing one's self. For plate there is a banana leaf. There is thus no need of any furniture in an Indian home. The richer people who have adopted Western ways may make use of tables and chairs and beds and other conveniences, but the poor man – and that is the vast majority – is still content to sit and sleep on the floor. Nor are elaborate bathrooms and lavatories considered necessary. In the villages the majority of people will take their bath at a pump or a well or in a neighbouring tank or stream, and most people still go out into the fields or by the roadside or by a stream to relieve themselves. There is a beautiful simplicity in all this, which makes one realize something of the original simplicity of human nature. Even clothes are hardly necessary. Most men today, it is true, wear a shirt and a 'dhoti' – a piece of cloth wound round the waist and falling to the feet – and women wear a sari and a blouse to cover the breast, but this is comparatively recent. . . .

Does this not bring us very near to the first disciples of Christ, who were told to take 'no gold, nor silver, nor copper in your belts, no bag for your journey, nor two tunics, nor sandals, nor a staff', and to the Son of man himself, who had nowhere to lay his head? What a challenge this presents to a world which takes pleasure in continually increasing human needs and so makes itself more and more dependent on the material world.

Bede Griffiths

5: HUMAN ENERGY

A passage from the writings of Jiddu Krishnamurti

Born in south India, Krishnamurti was brought to England by a woman called Annie Besant who believed he was a new messiah. At the age of thirty-two he disbanded the organisation that had proclaimed him its leader and said he did not want any followers or disciples. Since then he has travelled all over the world, preaching that peace and harmony in society can come about only through a change in the heart of each individual.

Many human beings do not have a great deal of energy, and what little energy they have is soon smothered and destroyed by the controls, threats and taboos of their particular society with its so-called education; so they become imitative, lifeless citizens of that society.

When you are very young, as you all are, you are full of energy, are you not? You want to play, to rush about, to talk; you can't sit still, you are full of life. Then what happens? As you grow up your teachers begin to curtail that energy by shaping it, directing it into various moulds; and when at last you become men and women the little energy you have left is soon smothered by society, which says that you must be proper citizens, you must behave in a certain way. Through so-called education and the compulsion of society this abounding energy you have when you are young is gradually destroyed.

What is this energy which we all have? This energy is thinking, feeling; it is interest, enthusiasm, greed, passion, lust, ambition, hate. Painting pictures, inventing machines, building bridges, making roads, cultivating the fields, playing games, writing poems, singing, dancing, going to the temple, worshipping – these are all expressions of energy; and energy also creates illusion, mischief, misery. The very finest and most destructive

139

qualities are equally the expressions of human energy. But, you see, the process of controlling or disciplining this energy, letting it out in one direction and restricting it in another, becomes merely a social convenience; the mind is shaped according to the pattern of a particular culture, and thereby its energy is gradually dissipated.

So, our problem is, can this energy, which in one degree or another we all possess, be increased, given greater vitality – and if so, to do what? What is energy for? Is it the purpose of energy to make war? Is it to invent jet planes and innumerable other machines, to pursue some guru, to pass examinations, to have children, to worry endlessly over this problem and that? Or can energy be used in a different way so that all our activities have significance in relation to something which transcends them all? Surely, if the human mind, which is capable of such astonishing energy, is not seeking reality or God, then every expression of its energy becomes a means of destruction and misery. To seek reality requires immense energy; and, if man is not doing that, he dissipates his energy in ways which create mischief, and therefore society has to control him. Now, is it possible to liberate energy in seeking God or truth and, in the process of discovering what is true, to be a citizen who understands the fundamental issues of life and whom society cannot destroy? Are you following this, or is it a little bit too complex?

You see, man is energy, and if man does not seek truth, this energy becomes destructive; therefore society controls and shapes the individual, which smothers this energy. That is what has happened to the majority of grown-up people all over the world. And perhaps you have noticed another interesting and very simple fact: that the moment you really want to do something, you have the energy to do it. What happens when you are keen to play a game? You immediately have energy, have you not? And that very energy becomes the means of controlling itself, so you don't need outside discipline. In the search for reality, energy creates its own discipline. The man who is seeking reality spontaneously becomes the right kind of citizen, which is not according to the pattern of any particular society or government.

So, students as well as teachers must work together to bring about the release of this tremendous energy to find reality, God or truth.

Krishnamurti

6: TERRORISM IN TODAY'S WORLD

This passage (the first part of which might be arranged for several 'reporters' or 'newsreaders') could be used on one of the many occasions when terrorist activity sadly makes the headlines. A topical report may be included where shown.

It was a Friday night in Birmingham, England, 21 November 1974. The pubs were filling up. Two, in particular, were crowded – the Mulberry Bush and the Tavern of the Town, both in the centre of the city. Suddenly, just after eight o'clock, explosions ripped their way through the buildings. In the horror and confusion, twenty-one people lay dead, 162 were injured. It was an IRA bomb attack.

In March 1968 an American company of soldiers, under Lieutenant William Calley, entered a Vietnamese village called My Lai. They had been brutalized and demoralized by war. Their orders were to 'clean up' the village, though what this should involve was not clear. On Calley's orders, they began to shoot the villagers. Over 500 civilians died.

In May 1972 members of a Japanese terrorist group, who had formed links with the Popular Front for the Liberation of Palestine, managed to get into Lod Airport in Israel. They opened fire with machine guns at waiting passengers. Twenty-six were killed and eighty wounded. Most were Puerto Rican pilgrims who had been visiting the Holy Land.

11.30 a.m., 30 April 1980. The Iranian Embassy, London. Six gunmen burst into the Embassy seizing twenty-six hostages. The gunmen demanded the release of ninety-one prisoners held in Iran. For over five days the world watched, as police tried to negotiate with the gunmen. At last, the gunmen lost patience. They shot one of the hostages. Minutes after his body had been passed out of the building, the Embassy was stormed by the SAS, a highly trained commando troop. All the remaining hostages except one were released alive. Five of the six gunmen were killed.

Here a similar report of recent terrorist activity could be included.

Such are the dramas of terrorism, dramas which are flashed on to our television screens, even (as in the case of the Iranian

Embassy) as they happen. They are dramas which are headlined in newspapers throughout the world.

It is not just the violence which shocks the world, but *the fact that this violence is used so indiscriminately*. The terrorists seem to mock the values of those communities who have learned to live in peace. They threaten not only the lives but the ways of life of us all.

Some people have argued that terrorism has a simple cause. It is a weapon of the poor against the rich, of the oppressed against the oppressor. It only occurs when there is a grievance that cannot be voiced in any other way. Looking back at the sorts of situation in which terrorism had been used against governments, we can see that such a simple explanation is not enough. And, also, there are so many cases of oppression and poverty where terrorism has not been used. Are we ever likely to pinpoint what actually causes the use of terrorism?

Terrorism has been used by guerrilla groups as part of their struggle against colonial governments. The IRA would argue that they too are fighting a colonial government, the British government, which is continuing to occupy part of Ireland.

Terrorism has been used against a state which occupies territory claimed by the terrorist groups. This is the case of the Palestinians. They believe that Israel occupies their traditional homeland and they are fighting to destroy her.

Terrorism has been used by separatist movements, who wish to form an independent nation by breaking away from the state of which they are now part. . . .

The gunmen who occupied the Iranian Embassy in London were also separatists. They wanted greater independence for the province of Khuzistan. . . .

Terrorism has been used by revolutionary groups, both big and small, in an attempt to overthrow their governments, be they authoritarian or democratic.

As yet there is no way by which the international community can effectively bring pressure to bear on a terrorist government. There are obvious reasons why this is difficult. When is a government defined as terrorist? What exactly do you do about it? Economic sanctions may only bring increased hardship to the people as a whole. A military invasion may only lead to more bloodshed. These problems have frustrated many who wish to fight government terrorism by means of international sanctions.

But each case of terrorism not dealt with firmly will simply encourage imitations in other parts of the world and so a new spiral of terrorism begins. At present, action by the world community has managed to contain some forms of terrorism such as hijacking, and this united and determined stand must continue.

The use of terrorism is one of the greatest threats to democracy. It is not only that terrorism involves the use of violence to achieve political ends by groups who are self-appointed. It is also that their use of terrorism encourages governments to use counterterrorism, in which case many democratic freedoms disappear. It is certainly possible to argue that the greater threat to democracy is not the act of terrorism against the government, but the methods a government can use in return. A democratic government seeking to fight terrorism is faced with possibly its most challenging task. The need for political wisdom, rigorous control of the forces of law and order, and a refusal to give in to terrorism, demands the greatest political expertise.

Charles Freeman

7: THE 'JUST' WAR

For centuries, Christians and other believers in peace have debated whether it is ever right to go to war. Is there such a thing as a 'just' war?

The thirteenth century Christian philosopher, Thomas Aquinas, said there were three conditions for a 'just' war:

1   *It must be on the authority of the sovereign;*
2   *The cause must be just; and*
3   *Those fighting should have 'a rightful intention'.*

A later Christian teacher added that, for a war to be just, it must be fought by 'proper means'.

No one who has studied the development of warfare in the twentieth century can fail to be aware of the far-reaching side-effects of even the most limited conflict. The course of any war is unpredictable. Violence used for whatever end cuts deep. It destroys and embitters, arouses the desire for revenge. Very seldom does any use of violence neatly achieve the objective for which it was used.

One response to this knowledge is pacifism, the refusal to use

143

violence in any situation, even in self-defiance. Pacifism has an impressive following, especially among members of the main religious traditions, but it has always remained a minority belief. For most, there continues to be the concept of 'the just war', the belief that, in certain circumstances, force, used in a limited way, can be justified.

Statesmen, church leaders and philosophers have debated the nature of the just war for centuries. In what circumstances is violence justified? How much violence is justified in achieving your objective? What rules of war should be observed to minimize the effects of conflict?

The concept of the 'just' war has always rested on the ideal that, if war is used, its effects must be limited as far as possible. The developments of modern technology have shown just how vulnerable this ideal has become in the modern world.

In recent months, much of the discussion on the 'morality' of modern warfare has centred on the possession of nuclear weaponry. It has been argued that any reliance on nuclear weapons, even if they are held only as a threat, is inherently immoral. A nation possessing such weapons must thus abandon them irrespective of whether its enemies do so.

Opponents of this view would argue as follows. The fundamental 'moral' duty of a nation is to protect its citizens. In a nuclear age, the most 'moral' policy is that which offers least risk of nuclear attack. If (and, of course, only if) you believe that the possession of nuclear weapons to be used in retaliation if attacked will significantly reduce the risk of being attacked in the first place, then it can be seen as moral to possess them. This argument would not, of course, explain why retaliatory nuclear weapons need to be aimed at civilian targets nor why more than a very few such weapons need to be possessed, when the destructive power of each is so great.

Charles Freeman

8: LOOKING AFTER THE OLD

Once upon a time there was a little old man. His eyes blinked and his hands trembled; when he ate he clattered the silverware distressingly, missed his mouth with the spoon as often as not, and dribbled a bit of his food on the tablecloth. Now he lived with his married son, having nowhere else to live, and his son's wife was a modern young woman who knew that in-laws should not be tolerated in a woman's home.

'I can't have this,' she said. 'It interferes with a woman's right to happiness.'

So she and her husband took the little old man gently but firmly by the arm and led him to the corner of the kitchen. There they set him on a stool and gave him his food, what there was of it, in an earthenware bowl. From then on he always ate in the corner, blinking at the table with wistful eyes.

One day his hands trembled rather more than usual, and the earthenware bowl fell and broke.

'If you are a pig,' said the daughter-in-law, 'you must eat out of a trough.' So they made him a little wooden trough, and he got his meals in that.

These people had a four-year-old son of whom they were very fond. One suppertime the young man noticed the boy playing intently with some bits of wood and asked what he was doing.

'I'm making a trough,' he said, smiling up for approval, 'to feed you and Mamma out of when I get big.'

The man and his wife looked at each other for a while and didn't say anything. Then they cried a little. Then they went to the corner and took the little old man by the arm and led him back to the table. They sat him in a comfortable chair and gave him his food on a plate, and from then on nobody ever scolded when he clattered or spilled or broke things.

Joy Davidman
(based on the Brothers Grimm)

9: FACING THE FACTS OF DEATH

Tony Whiteley discovered, in the spring of 1974, that he had lung cancer, and only months, perhaps only weeks, to live. He was thirty-four. He had just had a successful exhibition of his paintings, and his wife, Vivien, was expecting the birth of their second child. He agreed to make a film for television Remember All the Good Things, *as a record for his family, and in the hope that it would help others in his situation.*

Nobody is prepared for death at thirty-four, and my immediate reaction was it's such a shame to die so young when everything was going so well. We had such a happy marriage, and one child, another on the way, and all my plans for becoming an exhibiting artist, all these were going to come to nothing. I felt more sorry for my wife, Vivien, because my release was going to come soon; I might go through some suffering. I didn't know what, I still don't know what sort of suffering, but Vivien is going to be bringing up two children on her own. We had to start thinking my future was going to be very short and getting my affairs sorted out.

I'm keeping a diary for the children and Vivien afterwards. I started writing about the last weeks, or whatever it is going to be, so that the children would know their dad, what their dad thought.

One of the hard things we immediately started doing, we told our close relatives as soon as we could, and I have written in the diary that some people broke down and cried, and others, preferable to me, took it much more calmly, saying, 'Well, what are you going to do?'

I have had people of all shades of religion praying for me – letting me know that they are praying for me. I think it really hurts when people find out that a young man like myself is dying. It really moves them. I'm an atheist. I have been since the age of eighteen, and my religion of atheism has carried me through this because I have been able to plan, to behave normally. I am not wondering where I am going after death, or worrying about that at all, I am just worrying about Vivien and the children and leaving everything all right here.

I smoked for ten years, which is not very long. I'm unusual, too, in that I've got lung cancer at this early age. It doesn't normally strike at this age and I suppose it could be caused by smoking. I might be particularly receptive. I didn't smoke that heavily. It may be the main cause and I wish I'd never done it, and yet people will be thinking, 'It's different, I'll be all right.' But they won't, they won't.

The doctors decided to try a new course of treatment which, although it would not cure the cancer, would give Tony a few months longer – possibly two years at the outside – to live.

The future may not be the full two years, but at least we have got some time. Thanks to this treatment, it's a stay of execution, or a new lease of life, but it's only a stay, or a lease, it's not a cure yet, but while I'm alive there is the possibility that a cure may come. It's a bit hard, just having to sit back and watch it all. At first, we were so busy with all the arrangements to be made that I didn't do any painting, but now I've started again. And the funny thing is, you would expect my paintings to change. The myth of artists is that when they get bad news they start using tubes of black instead of tubes of yellow, but I'm still using the yellow. The art is not changed, it is still joyful where it was joyful and still critical of the world where it was critical.

I know I'm going to die sometime, probably in the near future, but I don't know exactly when, so we're having to put it out of our minds for the most part. We know it's there, it's planned for, and every time I get ill, we think, hello, is this it? I'm under sentence, but we don't know when it's going to be carried out.

Tony Whiteley

Tony Whiteley died on 28 July 1974.

10: POLITICAL ACTION

This parable is a reminder that sometimes charity is not enough: it is necessary to become involved in the politics of a problem.

There was once a factory that employed thousands of people. Its production line was a miracle of modern engineering, turning out thousands of machines every day. The factory had a high accident rate. The complicated machinery of the production line took little account of human error, forgetfulness or ignorance. Day after day, men came out of the factory with squashed fingers, cuts, bruises. Sometimes a man would lose an arm or a leg. Ocasionally, someone was electrocuted or crushed to death.

Enlightened people began to see that something needed to be done. First on the scene were the churches. An enterprising minister organized a small first aid tent outside the factory gate. Soon, with the backing of the Council of Churches, it grew into a properly-built clinic, able to give first aid to quite serious cases, and to treat minor injuries. The town council becàme interested, together with local bodies like the Chamber of Trade and the Rotary Club. The clinic grew into a small hospital, with modern equipment, an operating theatre, and a full-time staff of doctors

147

and nurses. Several lives were saved. Finally, the factory management, seeing the good that was being done, and wishing to prove itself enlightened, gave the hospital a small annual grant, and an ambulance to speed serious cases from workshop to hospital ward.

But, year by year, as production increased, the accident rate continued to rise. More and more people were hurt or maimed. And, in spite of everything the hospital could do, more and more people died from the injuries they had received. Only then did some people begin to ask if it was enough to treat people's injuries, while leaving untouched the machinery that caused them.

Brian Wren

11: WAR ON WANT: ERITREA

The following was written in 1983. However the conflict is resolved (if it is indeed resolved), it is a reminder of how a people can suffer when they become pawns in a super-power chess game. In this case the game is (or was) for control of access to the oil rich Gulf.

For more than twenty years the Eritrean people have faced the devastation of war.

More than 60,000 civilians have been killed. Two million people have been made homeless. Thousands of people have been left seriously injured as a result of the Ethiopian regime's (the Derg's) air attacks on villages, agricultural settlements and nomadic encampments.

Eritrea is located next to the Red Sea in the Horn of Africa. Its access to the Suez trade route gives the area strategic importance for outside powers, particularly for the economic interests of an otherwise landlocked Ethiopia.

It was colonised by the Italians in 1889 until the British occupation in 1941. In 1952 Eritrea was given self-government in a federation with Ethiopia, as a result of the United Nations resolution. At the time, most Eritreans wanted total independence.

In 1962, Ethiopia unilaterally and illegally went against the UN resolution and annexed Eritrea as a province. The Ethiopian regime crippled the economy of the area, destroyed the power of local political parties, imprisoned political leaders and suppressed the freedom of the press and of individuals to voice their opinions.

In the early 1960s the armed struggle of the Eritreans against this oppression began. Until the Ethiopian revolution in 1974, the United States provided arms and support to the Ethiopian forces. Following the revolution, however, the USSR has provided the military hardware and technical advisers to support the increased efforts to occupy and control Eritrea.

Super-power intervention in the region continues with competition for spheres of influence in this strategic area of Africa. The latest move has come from the United States with the build-up of its Rapid Deployment Force to patrol the Indian Ocean and the Arabian Gulf.

It is this rivalry which is prolonging the suffering of the Eritrean people and delaying a just solution representing the interests and basic rights of the local population.

The hundreds of thousands of casualties brought about by this conflict have placed a severe strain on the medical support teams working in Eritrea. Recently, the Ethiopians have been using more sophisticated weapons, such as defoliants and anti-personnel devices, which have made the problems faced by Eritrean medical teams more acute. The use of napalm, which burns the flesh over a period of weeks, and cluster bombs, which spray minute needles that 'swim' through the flesh and organs and can result in a slow death, have increased the cases of lost limbs, paralysis or partial paralysis, blindness and disfigurement.

Attempts are now being made to rebuild the horribly distorted and mangled faces of the war victims through bone grafting and plastic surgery. The condition of the paraplegics has changed dramatically – from being hopelessly bed-ridden with sores and infections to healthy, confident individuals participating in the activities of the centre with renewed hope for the future.

When they have improved sufficiently and have gained basic control over their disability, the paraplegics join training courses at the Solomuna Refugee Camp in Sudan. Here, skills training is given in carpentry, watch repair, metal work and radio repairs. Production workshops have been established. Classes are held in English, mathematics, geography, sciences, Arabic and local languages. Sports facilities are provided, and though popular, are limited by lack of equipment. This recreation has had a positive effect on the general health and well-being of the disabled.

149

War on Want is supporting the Eritrean rehabilitation programme for the disabled by making grants towards the cost of equipment for the training centres.

War on Want is a registered charity founded in 1951 in response to a letter from the publisher, Victor Gollancz, to the Guardian. He asked those who wanted to act against poverty – to produce 'tractors not bombs' – to reply with their name and address on a postcard with the word 'Yes'. In two weeks 5000 replied and War on Want was founded. The name was suggested by a founding member, Harold Wilson. Since then over £10 million has been raised for development projects.

(See page 282.)

12: ALCOHOL ABUSE

It is usually not a crime for a young person to drink alcohol at home or at somebody else's home, but this does not mean that it is possible for a young person to go out and buy alcohol. It is also illegal for a person under a certain age (usually eighteen) to go into a bar and have a drink . . .

It is against the law to drive a car or a motor cycle after drinking more than the legal amount. If you do, you're going to be a danger to yourself and to others. Alcohol slows your reactions and may change the way you see things. Imagine trying to drive using only one hand and closing one eye – it would hardly be easy! Even a small amount of alcohol may make you unsafe on the road. The skills needed to drive are impaired by any alcohol in the blood-stream. By the time your blood alcohol is at the legal limit of 80 mg per cent everyone is clearly impaired.

Driving after drinking is a crime that may lead to a loss of your driving licence and, in some cases, a prison sentence. If you cause an accident as a result of your drunken driving, then this will make it even more serious. Then there is also the question of how you would feel if your bad driving had caused somebody to lose his life or to be seriously injured. This may be the worst part – as this story shows.

Mike had just passed his driving test and he took his father's car out one Saturday night. Driving was still something quite new to him, and he got a lot of fun out of it. He was not a bad driver, and his father trusted him to bring the car home in one piece.

Mike drove round to pick up his friends. Altogether there were four people in the car – Mike, his girlfriend Anne, his friend Jim and Jim's girlfriend Jane. They drove round for a while and then they went on to a house where they knew there was going to be a party. When they arrived the party had already started. The music was loud and everybody seemed to be having a good time.

There was quite a lot of beer at the party. Mike knew that he would have to be careful if he was to drive back, but he thought that he would just have one or two beers, and that would be quite all right.

After the second beer (which seemed to go quite quickly) Mike found himself in a really good mood. He started a third beer and then a fourth. With all the fun of the party, he forgot about driving.

Jane had to be back at twelve and Jim asked Mike if they could go. Mike now remembered about the car. He wondered if he might be too drunk to drive, but because of the good mood he was in, he decided to go ahead anyway. If he didn't drive back, then he would get into trouble with his father for not bringing the car back. 'I've got no choice,' he said to himself. 'I'll just be extra careful.'

Mike began to drive. Jim and Jane were in the back seat and were laughing over something that somebody had done at the party. Anne was fiddling with the switch on the radio trying to find a good station.

Mike blinked. He felt good inside, but he found it a bit difficult to deal with the traffic. There were cars coming from the other side of the road and their lights seemed very bright. Anne suddenly said something to him.

'Slow down, you're going too fast.'

Mike looked at the speedometer. Anne was right – he was going too fast. Putting his foot on the brake pedal, he began to press it down. There were lights in front of him, red lights, the back of a truck. Mike pushed hard on the brakes, but there was not enough room to stop. With a thud and a crumpling, Mike felt the car go into the truck. He felt himself going forward and he heard screaming. Then there was nothing.

Mike and Anne were very lucky. In spite of the fact that they had piled right into the back of the truck, they suffered only concussion and a few scratches and bruises. Jim was all right as well. He wasn't even knocked unconscious by the impact. Jane wasn't so lucky. When the car hit the truck, she was catapulted forward into the front seat and actually ended up against the car's instrument panel. Her face was badly cut and she lost some teeth. She had to have stitches across her cheek and under her chin. When the stitches came out, she was very badly scarred.

Of course, it could have been much worse. Nobody was killed or crippled in that accident, but Jane would have to go through life with ugly scars across her face. Mike still sees her from time to time, and each time he sees her he is reminded of the fact that it was his stupidity that had caused the accident.

If Mike had not driven after drinking, then it wouldn't have happened.

Of course there was one other consequence. The police were called to the accident and Mike was breathalysed and taken to the police station. A blood sample was taken and this was over the legal limit. In Court he was fined and lost his driving licence. So now he has to walk everywhere and when he gets his licence back he will find it very hard to get car insurance, and if he does get it, then it will cost him much more.

Fiona Foster and Alexander McCall Smith

13: GLUE-SNIFFING

It is not suggested that this passage will be relevant in every school and the assembly leader must consider whether it will prove a deterrent or an incentive. (Some readers may decide to omit the phrases in square brackets.)

It has been selected because it does tackle a serious problem in a way that is sobering without being hysterical.

Did you know?
* On average between 45 and 50 young people, mostly teenage boys, die each year as a result of sniffing glue or other solvents.
* It is believed that up to 10 per cent of pupils, aged between twelve and sixteen, are involved in solvent abuse in some British schools.
* Sniffing glue began in the USA in the 1960s, and has since spread among youngsters in many industrialized nations.

Ask Phil why he sniffs glue and he'll reply that it's cheaper than alcohol and not illegal like LSD or heroin. Phil, seventeen, has been a 'gluey' for three years. He's out of work and spends his unemployment benefit on cans of glue. Not even three months in a detention centre – for mugging a younger teenager after a two-hour sniffing session – has stopped the habit.

It started when Phil was still at school. 'We'd go into parks, sheds, derelict houses – anywhere quiet – and sniff glue. Sometimes only for an hour or two, sometimes till late at night. Glue is easy and cheap to get hold of.'

For a few months Phil had a job on a demolition site, and during that time he stopped sniffing. 'But then I lost the job and went back to the glue,' he says. 'It helps the boredom – even when I'm on the dole I can afford to buy enough to escape into another world. Without a job I've no money to go out at weekends and there's nothing to look forward to. When people say I'm ruining my life by sniffing, I think so what?'

But Phil continued: 'Although I'm hooked, I still wouldn't want other kids to end up like me. I've been to hospital several times and I'm always falling down and injuring myself after I've been sniffing. One of the lads round here got himself killed, after he'd been sniffing. He had no idea what he was doing, he was so high. He jumped out in front of a lorry and it went right over him. If I don't go like that I reckon that one day I'll just bury my head in the glue and not come round again.'

It is not correct to think that sniffing glue is the only form of solvent abuse. Certain types of glue are used, but sniffing often involves a wide variety of household and industrial products [including paint strippers, lighter fuel and hair lacquer]. Many of these products are even more dangerous than glue. One spray into the mouth or nostrils from an aerosol could be fatal.

Side effects from sniffing glues and nail varnish remover include dizziness, fainting and vomiting. Sniffing [petrol and rubber solutions] can cause headaches, nausea and possible liver damage. Long-term inhaling of cleaning fluids can damage the kidneys, liver, lungs and intestines.

Solvent sniffing can also produce states of intoxication and euphoria, causing sniffers to injure themselves by falling, or walking into traffic.

Fortunately, most youngsters only sniff for a short length of time, and stop after a few months. A few, usually the solitary sniffers, may continue for much longer. These people may have an underlying emotional problem, and sniffing provides a simple means of 'escaping' from pressures.

Vanora Leigh

14: PROBLEM PAGE

All or a selection of the following letters to an imaginary agony column could be used as a reading (perhaps arranged for several voices) to alert an assembly to the problems faced by many young people, and maybe to encourage individuals that they are not 'alone'. If several pupil readers are being selected, it could be wise to avoid 'type-casting'.

Where prayer is part of assembly, the letters could illustrate 'prayers for those in need'.

Discussion and drafting of constructive answers would be a useful classroom follow-up activity.

Dear Problem Page,

My parents will not let me out of the house unless I'm sensibly dressed. I have to wear long skirts, nice jumpers, etc. I'm not allowed to wear anything remotely fashionable. I get laughed at by my class at school. I know my mother thinks she's saying it all for the best, and I know it would really worry her to see me in what she calls punk clothes. Should I do what I think? Or should I 'honour and obey' my parents.

> Yours sincerely,
> Worried

Dear Problem Page,

My father is out of work and my mother works all day at a tiring job. My father feels I should work very hard at school to get good grades, but I don't really think I'm going to do very well and I think I'm doing quite enough work as it is. He says John next door spends all night doing homework but even if I do that I still get poor marks. So what should I do?

> Yours,
> Fed-up

Dear Problem Page,

I am adopted. My new parents are very good to me, but sometimes I disagree with what they say or want more freedom than what they give me. Sometimes we even row. Afterwards I feel very guilty because I am sure I have hurt them. I am sure I would not row with them if they were my real parents. What do you think?

Yours sincerely,
Confused

Dear Problem Page,

People discriminate against me because of where I live. I agree it's not a very nice area, but the people are great and I like it. But when people ask me where I live or I have to tell someone my address, they give me a look as though to say, 'Oh, so you'll be a right trouble maker, won't you?' And I bet all the advice you can give me is 'Move house'. Well?

Yours,
Disgusted

Dear Problem Page,

My boy friend says I'm a coward because I say no. Am I?

Yours sincerely,
Cautious

Dear Problem Page,

How do you say 'No' to a dare when you'll be called a coward or a pouf all round the school, if you don't join in?

Yours,
Annoyed

Dear Problem Page,

I'm got at because, as school, I work hard. When everyone else is being disruptive, I get on with some reading. Because of this, the disruptive people pick on me and a couple of times they've ripped up my homework. But I want to do well at O-level. Why do they discriminate against me? Is there anything I can do?

> Yours sincerely,
> (and this is what they call me),
> Creepy

David Self

15: SKIN CARE FOR BOYS

This reading is offered slightly tongue-in-cheek. It has however proved highly effective on a number of occasions, offering (as it does) help to the boy who would never dare to ask for help and creating a general interest in clean and healthy skin – among both boys and girls.

There is a tale of a Charles of the Ritz salesgirl, who was invited on to a North Sea oilrig to give a talk on skincare, and sold to the very toughest rigger of the lot a £40 jar of nourishing cream. Luckily we do not need to spend so much in order to have healthy skin.

While boys are keen to experiment with make-up and hair ideas, they often shy away from thinking about their skin. You slap a bit of soap and water on your face in the morning, towel it dry, and the skin care routine is complete. You don't think about your skin unless very dry skin or acne turn it into an embarrassing problem.

The truth is that your skin collects dirt, oil, dead skin cells, sweat and bacteria just like a girl's. If you don't cleanse your skin properly you'll start to notice whiteheads, which will turn into blackheads, and before you know where you are you've got a crop of rather nasty-looking spots!

Taking sensible care of your skin won't always mean a trip to the local chemist to stock up a pile of beauty products. It may just mean that when you do use soap and water, you take a little more care that you are using them to your skin's advantage. The one product that you might think about using is a moisturizer, but more about that later.

The best way to clean your face is a way that removes the dirt, oil and dead skin cells without irritating your skin. In most instances soap will meet these requirements, but make sure it's the right kind of soap. Some soaps are better than others. It's best to avoid deodorant or highly perfumed soaps on your face. They are often too harsh and irritating. Try to buy a 'simple' soap – one that has very few ingredients and doesn't contain perfumes or colouring.

The best way to use such a soap is:

1. Wet face thoroughly, by splashing water on it with your hands. It's far more hygienic to use your hands than a face-cloth.
2. Rub the soap in your hands to create a lather. Use your fingers to spread the soap on to your face. If you suffer from blackheads or spots, a complexion brush is also a good idea. . . .
3. After rubbing the soap gently all over your face, rinse thoroughly. Don't stop until every trace of soap has been removed from your face. Any soap that remains will only be furthering the blackhead cause.
4. Splashing aftershave on your face at this point can only have a drying effect. If you've noticed that your skin tends to dry out after washing, then use a moisturizer suited to your skin type (i.e. dry, normal, or oily). It might surprise you to learn that even oily skin benefits from the use of a moisturizer.

If your skin tends to be *very oily*, then twice a week you could follow your evening wash with a facial scrub. These 'scrubs' contain harsh particles suspended in a cream and they can help keep those pores unclogged. Astringent used after your wash will remove oil and soap left behind. You can also use the astringent on its own during the day to help control the build-up of oil. Though you can use the astringent fairly frequently, don't use the scrub more than twice a week, as it is quite harsh on the skin. Use a moisurizer to complete your routine.

If your skin is on the dry side, look at the type of soap you're using. A simple soap will be kinder on your face. If you already use a simple soap, you might need to use a liquid cleanser instead. A moisturizer is obviously a good idea, too!

The most common and worrying problem that boys face is spots. These blemishes come in various forms, some worse than others. Whiteheads and blackheads aren't particularly nice, but they aren't often so obvious as to be a positive embarrassment. Spots and acne are.

An excess of oil or sebum is produced while you're a teenager and this clogs up your pores and encourages blackheads to develop. Sometimes, controlling the number of blackheads will help to control your spots. Try to get rid of your blackheads before they turn into pimples.

How to get rid of a blackhead:

1. Warm the area around the blackhead by soaking a clean facecloth or piece of cotton wool in very warm water and holding it against your face.
2. Squeeze out the blackhead either with fingers covered by paper tissues, or with a special 'blackhead extractor' bought from a chemist. Be very gentle. If the blackhead is obstinate, leave it for a couple of days and try again.
3. Dab the area with a little antiseptic.

By keeping the number of blackheads down, you can usually keep spots or acne under control. However, if you have very bad acne, don't hesitate to visit your doctor. He'll be able to prescribe an effective treatment which will not only suit your skin, but also be a little cheaper than buying it over the counter at a chemist's.

Maggie Philbin

16: JUST IMAGINE

A reading designed to develop an appreciation of what it is to possess and use one's imagination.

A plumber can't mend a burst pipe without a tool-kit. If he is to get on with the job of being a plumber he must be given tools, otherwise he's just going to stand there unable to do much to help himself or others. Man has been given the tools for being human; he doesn't have to stand around waiting like the powerless plumber, for equipment. In his tool-kit is the imagination. It is his most powerful weapon for attack, defence, survival – but above all for invention and creativity. All he has to do is to exercise his imagination and so become fully human.

The poet Wordsworth called the imagination 'that inward eye which is the bliss of solitude'. With this inward eye man can see beyond himself, beyond his immediate environment and circumstances. He can see a picture in his mind and then make the picture into something more real, more concrete outside himself – a painting, a sculpture, a machine, a building, a bowl, a design, a poem, a play, a story, a loaf of bread. The inner vision can be transformed into a work, a creation. Man then becomes a creator and this process of being creative is what makes man distinctively human. . . .

It is possible for a man to go through life with so little imagination that he is virtually a machine. He doesn't see beyond the immediate, the material. He doesn't initiate or begin anything. He copies what is already there, he makes only what is already made, he says only what has already been said. He is a machine responding to a programme. He has no power of selection since without the use of the imagination he can see no alternative to his thoughts, words or actions. No one is really without the gift of imagination; it is part of being human. But having the gift is not necessarily the same as using it – like the parable of the talents in the New Testament, in which a man, given money buries it in the ground and fails to use it. He wasn't just being lazy or foolish. He was being less than human. He was not realizing his full humanity and for this he was completely responsible. Failures to use the gifts which have been given to us are far more serious sins than the comparatively insignificant lapses in conduct that are so often given the name 'sin'. It could well be the work of the Devil that we are kept thinking about unimportant and irrelevant 'sins' while a falling away from our real humanity through not using some talent that has been freely given to us, goes unnoticed.

The marks of imagination are that a person lives creatively – creative in the way that he can see alternatives in life; he is sensitive to the needs and feelings of others because he can imagine what it is like to be in someone else's shoes; he can be sympathetic, he can suffer with, rejoice with, another; he is alert because all the things and people around him excite and activate his imagination – there is no limit to the possibilities which surround him. Beauty in shape or form or person kindles the imagination into further creativity.

Ralph Rolls

The parable of the talents: Matthew 25: 14–19.

17: MAKING A DOOR

There is much satisfaction to be gained from a job well done, especially if the job involves making something, like a door. This passage is a reminder of that pleasure. Even though this door is a very simple one, it is right for its purpose.

Father sawed logs the right length for the door. He sawed shorter lengths for cross-pieces. Then with the axe he split the logs into slabs, and smoothed them nicely. He laid the long slabs together on the ground and placed the shorter slabs across them. Then with the auger he bored holes through the cross-pieces into the long slabs. Into every hole he drove a wooden peg that fitted tightly. That made the door. It was a good oak door, solid and strong.

For the hinges he cut three long straps. One hinge was to be near the top of the door, one near the bottom, and one in the middle. When he had fastened the three hinges to the door, he set the door in the doorway. It fitted. Then he pegged strips of wood to the old slabs on either side of the doorway, to keep the door from swinging outward.

Next he made a latch on the door, because, of course, there must be some way to keep a door shut. This was the way he made the latch: first he hewed a short, thick piece of oak. From one side of this, in the middle, he cut a wide deep notch. He pegged this stick to the inside of the door, up and down and near the edge. He put the notched side against the door, so that the notch made a little slot.

Then he hewed and whittled a longer, smaller stick. This stick was small enough to slip easily through the slot. He slid one end of it through the slot, and he pegged the other end in the door.

But he did not peg it tightly. The peg was solid and firm in the door, but the hole in the stick was larger than the peg. The only thing that held the stick on the door was the slot.

This stick was the latch. It turned easily on the peg, and its loose end moved up and down in the slot. And the loose end of it was long enough to go through the slot and across the crack between the door and the wall, and to lie against the wall when the door was shut.

But there must be a way to lift the latch from the outside. So he made the latch-string. He cut it from a long strip of good leather.

He tied one end to the latch, between the peg and the slot. Above the latch he bored a small hole through the door, and he pushed the end of the latch string through the hole.

The door was finished. It was strong and solid, made of thick oak with oak slabs across it, all pegged together with good stout pegs. The latch-string was out; if you wanted to come in, you pulled the latch-string. But if you were inside and wanted to keep anyone out, then you pulled the latch-string in through its hole and nobody could get in. There was no doorknob on that door, and there was no keyhole and no key. But it was a good door.

Laura Ingalls Wilder

18: SCREWTAPE

The Screwtape Letters by C. S. Lewis is a famous collection of letters, supposedly written by a senior devil in hell, called Screwtape. He writes to his nephew, Wormwood. Wormwood is a young and inexperienced devil who is trying to tempt a human along the road to Hell.

The human, who is described by Screwtape as Wormwood's patient, has just become a Christian. Wormwood is in trouble. In the letter, the 'Enemy' is of course God.

What C. S. Lewis is saying in the letter is that many Christians are disappointed by their local church. This disappointment can be a great help to Wormwood.

My Dear Wormwood,

I note with grave displeasure that your patient has become a Christian. Do not indulge the hope that you will escape the usual penalties; indeed, in your better moments, I trust you would hardly even wish to do so. In the meantime we must make the best of the situation. There is no need to despair; hundreds of these adult converts have been reclaimed after a brief sojourn in the Enemy's camp and are now with us. All the habits of the patient, both mental and bodily, are still in our favour.

One of our great allies at present is the Church itself. Do not misunderstand me. I do not mean the Church as we see her spread out through all time and space and rooted in eternity, terrible as an army with banners. That, I confess is a spectacle which makes our boldest tempters uneasy. But fortunately it is quite invisible to these humans. All your patient sees is the half-finished, sham Gothic erection on the new building estate. When he goes inside, he sees the local grocer with rather an oily expression on his face bustling up to offer him one shiny little book containing a liturgy which neither of them understands, and one shabby little book containing corrupt texts of a number of religious lyrics, mostly bad, and in very small print. When he gets to his pew and looks round him he sees just that selection of his neighbours whom he has hitherto avoided. You want to lean pretty heavily on those neighbours. Make his mind flit to and fro between an expression like 'the body of Christ' and the actual faces in the next pew. It matters very little, of course, what kind of people that next pew really contains. You may know one of them to be a great warrior on the Enemy's side. No matter. Your patient, thanks to Our Father below, is a fool. Provided that any of those neighbours sing out of tune, or have boots that squeak, or double chins, or odd clothes, the patient will quite easily believe that their religion must therefore be somehow ridiculous. At his present stage, you see, he has an idea of 'Christians' in his mind which he supposes to be spiritual but which, in fact, is largely pictorial. His mind is full of togas and sandals and armour and bare legs and the mere fact that the other people in church wear modern clothes is a real – though of course an unconscious – difficulty to him. Never let it come to the surface; never let him ask what he expected them to look like. Keep everything hazy in his mind now, and you will have all eternity wherein to amuse yourself by producing in him the peculiar kind of clarity which Hell affords.

Work hard, then, on the disappointment or anticlimax which is certainly coming to the patient during his first few weeks as a church-man. The Enemy allows this disappointment to occur on the threshold of every human endeavour. And there lies our opportunity. But also remember, there lies our danger. If once they get through this initial dryness successfully, they become much less dependent on emotion and therefore much harder to tempt.

Keep him in his present state of mind as long as you can.

Your affectionate uncle
SCREWTAPE

C. S. Lewis

19: THE DUCKLING

A prose poem by the Russian writer, Alexander Solzhenitsyn, in which he meditates on the miracle of life.

A little yellow duckling, flopping comically on its white belly in the wet grass and scarcely able to stand on its thin, feeble legs, runs in front of me and quacks: 'Where's my mummy? Where's my family?'

He has no mummy, because he has been fostered by a hen: ducks eggs were put in her nest, she sat on them and hatched them with her own. To shelter them from the bad weather their home – an upturned basket without a bottom – has been moved into a shed and covered with sacking. They are all in there, but this one is lost.

Come on then, little thing, let me take you in my hand.

What keeps it alive? It weighs nothing; its little black eyes are like beads, its feet are like sparrows' feet, the slightest squeeze and it would be no more. Yet it is warm with life. Its little beak is pale pink and slightly splayed, like a manicured finger-nail. Its feet are already webbed, there is yellow among its feathers, and its downy wings are starting to protrude. Its personality already sets it apart from its foster-brothers.

And we men will soon be flying to Venus; if we all pooled our efforts we could plough up the whole world in twenty minutes.

Yet with all our atomic might we shall never – never! – be able to make this feeble speck of a yellow duckling in a test-tube; even if we were given the feathers and bones we could never put such a creature together.

Alexander Solzhenitsyn

20: PORPOISE SONG

It's very easy to be over-sentimental about animals and to make them out to be more clever or more intelligent than they really are, but we can still learn from their ways.

This passage is part of a novel called 'Porpoise Song' by Michael Clegg. It takes place in the North Sea – literally in it. It tells a lot about kindness and caring, and about what a true community is.

Under the wine dark water, above which the stars blazed in summer brilliance, three porpoises held station. The youngest was about to give birth and the others were there to lend their support if it was needed. She was young, but this was her fifth calf in the eight years that made up her life so far. Her attendants were aged twelve and eighteen respectively and the younger of them was only weeks away from calving herself.

They communicated wordlessly, and not very often. The expectant cow arched her back from time to time as though to ease tired muscles. From time to time they rose a few feet and breathed at the surface but each time sank again to about ten feet below the gentle waves.

The pup's tail appeared first and expanded like a pair of ancillary flippers. The attendants noted this and relaxed. So far so good. Slowly but smoothly the calf began to emerge and the mother turned as far as she could to see it. The umbilical cord floated out like a strand of wool and as the calf fell free she made a sharp turn which snapped it off short.

Her impetus carried her down and round below the calf and rising, she batted it upwards towards the surface with her flipper. The two old cows rose with it. Then the calf's head cleared the surface and it drew its first breath, though whether it was the upward slap or the summer wind on its skin which inspired it cannot be known. It breathed and was alive.

The four of them lay at the surface together and the little bull calf's blow hole winked as it sucked in the soft, moist air. Twenty minutes later the afterbirth was shed, and drifted down to the sea-bed. There had been no sharks or violent interruptions of any sort and, with their duty done, the two elders departed to spread the news among the school.

The slap of wavelets rocked the thirty-inch calf and tended to drift him away from his mother's side. She used her flippers to correct the tug of the current and moved her bulk so that she broke the force of the ebbing tide. She listened with half an ear to the gossip of the school as they mustered five hundred yards away. . . .

Two of the cow's earlier young, both females, were with the pod (school or shoal). One of them had been sired by the mature bull, now seven years old, who was the father of the present calf.

The young cows swam over to look at the new arrival and the elder of the two, who had lost her first calf a fortnight earlier in a summer gale, muzzled him closely. His mother had to retrieve him eventually.

A young male, excited by the onset of maturity, jostled the cow from below and barrel-rolled round her. The calf, startled by this disturbance, took refuge below his mother's belly and then, almost as if allaying his fear, took suck for the first time. The big bull watched with mild interest while the calf fed and then turned away and they all followed him. The rest of the pod picked up the message and eleven porpoises in all moved out to sea.

Michael Clegg

21: CONVALESCENT HOME

In this short story, a voluntary helper describes her work in a charity shop, and raises questions about why some people work for charities and what they hope to gain from such work.

I didn't take much notice of her at first. Well, I mean she was just one more bargain-hunter . . . till you got a second look and then you could see she was just put together with spit. One good puff of wind and she'd be ready for planting in Adam and Eve's Garden! Still, I'd better begin at the beginning.

You see there was this junk shop. For charity. People gave the stuff and we worked for nothing so what was made was pure profit. And at least we got a good laugh for our pains. You get these women, dressed up to the nines, wandering in with a parcel as though they were Her Majesty handing out the Maundy money. And after all their swank, when you look inside it's rubbish. You know, threadbare and all that. And then there's the one's that've come in for a bargain but they'd sooner die than admit it. They're buying for their 'chah-lady' or a 'pooah femmily who live neah meah'. This town's swarming with swanky women who live next door to 'pooah femmilies'.

Of course there's some who're past caring what anyone thinks. They live in a concentration camp of credit and the tallyman in the watch-tower'll make damn sure they never get out of it. What this lot've got is tuppence and their bus fare home . . . and yet nine times out of ten they'll say 'Keep the change . . . it's in a good cause' . . . and just for a minute you know what it's all about. But for every one of them there's a dozen of the other kind . . . out for themselves and clever with it. They'll beat you down on the price and then tell you they've given you the money when they haven't. My God, I wish I had their nerve, that's all. Anyway, to get back to what I was saying . . . .

This woman came in every day, raking round. I watched her but I kept my distance. Well, it pays you to in those places. I mean some of them are walking! Believe me, there was days when I killed so many fleas and nits I considered applying for a fresh meat licence. Anyway, this day she came over to me. 'Are you closing tomorrow?' she said and I said we were . . . and then it all came out. She'd been ill. Well, you didn't need a Bachelor of Medicine to tell you that bit was true. She was off to a Convalescent Home soon so she needed what she'd done without for long enough . . . a few decent underclothes.

I know all about Convalescent Homes. They're run by rules and if you're a naughty girl the nurse threatens to fetch Dr Who to you. In the end you're that fed up you say you're better and they send you home . . . which was probably what got you down in the first place! What that poor soul really needed was a pair of arch supports and a pound of purple hearts but they're not part of the Welfare State so she was being 'sent up' for a fortnight. I knew what she was worried about . . . there was sure to be one or two who'd managed to wangle themselves a fortnight off from hubby and the household chores and they'd be dressed to kill. You know, transparent nighties and a string of pearls. And there she'd be in her flannel nightgowns from the Guild of Help . . . who'd got them from Lady Muck . . . who'd been in the habit of wearing them between the wars. Crimean and Boer!!

Well I should have understood but home-time was stopping up my earholes so I told her we'd be sure to get fresh stuff in tomorrow and shunted her off. To be perfectly truthful I forgot all about her . . . so it was a bit of a shock when she turned up the next day and I realized she was relying on me to kit her out. Not because I've got a kind face but because there was just no one else. You try telling a social worker you want a nylon nightie and see how far you get. She had a daughter who'd been in with her once or twice but she wasn't the type you'd turn to in a crisis. She had a couple of dozen rollers on permanent sentry-go underneath her headsquare . . . and a faraway look in here eyes like she was dreaming of having it off with Batman. When it came to providing her mother with a few status symbols she'd be a dead loss. So that left little me!

I didn't let on I'd forgotten. I made out I was still waiting for fresh stuff and I've never prayed so hard in my life for someone to walk through the door with a decent bundle. But you might know they wouldn't . . . not when it really mattered. So there I was when the shop shut . . . taking her name and address and promising I'd be at her place the next day with the goodies. There was one moment when I wavered . . . when I realized I only had one decent nightie. Oh, the rest of them had been very glam when I was on my honeymoon but I'm about due for the seven year itch and they were looking a bit jaded. So it had to be the one and only . . . and once I'd climbed that hurdle the rest was easy. I felt ten feet tall, I can tell you, and growing all the time. I could imagine the look on her face when she opened the door and saw I'd kept my word. She'd be surprised and grateful and I'd have a hard time refusing when she tried to pay me. I wouldn't take it, of course. 'No, my dear,' I'd say . . . 'you keep it till you're better and then give something to help someone less fortunate than we are.' Less fortunate than her you couldn't get but that 'we' would boost her ego no end.

When I saw the house I felt even better. You had to hold the door up when you knocked on it in case it fell in. I'm not kidding! Windows cracked and broken . . . and the muck! Poor bee, I thought, and I got ready for my big scene. And then came the anti-climax. The door opened but it wasn't her standing there. It was this little kid, two foot tall with an old man's face. 'Is that the parcel,' he says, cool as you please. 'Me mam's out but she said to leave it and I was to say thank you' . . . and before I could pull myself together he was back inside the door and my best undies in a paper bag under his arm. Well, a slap in the kisser's never pleasant but when your mouth's full of the milk of human kindness it's enough to make you choke. I was furious! How dare she be so sure I'd turn up. And no mention of money! What about that for cheek!

I was half way home before I asked myself what the hell I was bellyaching about. I meant her to have the things, didn't I? Well, she'd got them. OK, she hadn't paid but I hadn't intended her to, so what odds? And why should she wait in specially to grovel to me . . . because that was it, of course. I'd expected her to know forty different ways of saying thank you and if she could roll over and play dead and do a few more tricks to show grateful . . . well, all the better. Her sort are still not supposed to have pride. There's only a very thin line, now, between the haves and have-nots . . . and we don't take the peasants beef-tea and junkey . . . but nothing's really changed. We join things and sit on committees and wait to be made JPs for our pains. Maybe a few do it for the right motives but I'm not one of them. I'm just a Grade A Bitch who'd like to have her boots licked. I saw it all clearly then and what I saw I didn't like. But I'll be back next year, working hard for a good cause and quivering with pleasure when somone tells me I'm a Lady Bountiful.

Denise Robertson

22: IVAR'S STORY

This Icelandic story is over 700 years old. It shows one way in which loneliness or loss can be cured. It shows how important it is that we listen to the people around us when they need someone to talk to.

A man called Ivar was staying at the court of King Eystein. Ivar was an Icelander, well-born and intelligent and a good poet. The king thought very highly of him, as is borne out by the following episode.

Ivar had a brother called Thorfinn, who also went to Norway to visit the court of King Eystein. But Thorfinn soon grew discontented with court life and decided to return to Iceland.

Before the brothers parted, Ivar asked Thorfinn to take a message to a woman called Oddny, Jon's daughter, telling her to wait for him and not to marry anyone else, for he loved her more than any other woman.

Thorfinn put out to sea, and had a good passage. He decided to propose to Oddny and married her himself. When Ivar arrived in Iceland some time later and heard about this, he felt his brother had played a cruel trick on him. Ivar was very unhappy and went back to Norway, where he stood as high in favour with the king as ever before.

As time went on, however, Ivan's anguish only grew worse.

The king noticed this and summoned Ivar to his presence, to ask him why he was so distressed.

'What troubles me, my Lord, is something I may not disclose,' said Ivar.

'Then we'll guess it,' said the king. 'Is there someone here whose presence offends you?'

'No, my lord, it's not that,' said Ivar.

'Do you feel we show you less honour than you'd wish?' asked the king.

'No, my lord, it's not that,' said Ivar.

'Is there anything you've seen in this country that you covet?' asked the king.

Ivar said no.

'The guessing grows harder,' said the king. 'Are there any estates you wish for?'

Ivar said no.

'Is there a woman in your own country you're pining for?' asked the king.

'Yes,' said Ivar.

'Then put your sorrow aside,' said the king. 'When spring comes, you'll go to Iceland, and we'll give you money and letters under our royal seal to her guardians. We don't know of anybody who wouldn't wish to act in accordance with our friendly words or with our royal threats, and marry this woman to you.'

'It's impossible, my lord,' said Ivar.

'No,' said the king, 'it's not impossible, we'll go further still, and even if she's already married we'll obtain her for you if that's what you desire.'

'It's a harder problem than that, my lord,' said Ivar. 'The woman's already married to my brother.'

'We must think of something else then,' said the king. 'I know what. After Christmas we'll be making our royal tour, and you shall come with us. You'll meet many gracious women, and as long as they're not of royal blood, we'll obtain any one of them for you.'

Ivan said, 'My lord, my difficulty's even more acute than that. Whenever I see a beautiful woman I'm reminded of the one I love, and my grief's redoubled.'

The king said, 'Then we shall give you the authority and estates we've already offered, and you can devote yourself to them.'

'I have no heart,' said Ivar.

'Then we shall give you money,' said the king, 'and you can travel wherever you wish.'

Ivar said he didn't want that either.

'Our problems grow worse,' said the king, 'for now we've tried everything we know. There's only one suggestion left, of very little value compared with our previous offers, but it's hard to guess what will be for the best. Come to me every day before the tables are cleared when I'm not engaged in matters of state, and I shall talk with you. We'll talk about this woman to your heart's content for as long as you wish, and I'll devote my time to it. Sometimes a man's grief is soothed when he can talk about his sorrows. And I also promise you that you'll never leave my presence without some gift.'

'Yes, my lord, that's what I'd like to do,' said Ivar, 'and thank you for your consideration.'

And now, whenever the king was not engaged in matters of state, he would talk with Ivar about this woman. The plan succeeded, for Ivar's grief was cured sooner than he'd hoped; his happiness came back, and all his old cheerfulness returned to him.

And he remained with King Eystein.

Translated by Herman Pálsson

23: NOTHING VENTURE

'The Pilgrims and the Peas' was written two hundred years ago by a man called John Wolcot. It's about two men who had sinned wickedly, and as a penance were ordered to walk fifty miles to a holy shrine at a place called Loreto – a sort of pilgrimage to cancel out their sins. To make it more painful, the priest ordered them to put dried peas into their shoes. The word 'peccavi' in the third verse means 'I have sinned'.

A brace of Sinners, for no good,
Were ordered to the Virgin Mary's shrine,
Who at Loreto dwelt . . .

170

Fifty long miles had those sad Rogues to travel,
With something in their shoes much worse than gravel:
In short, their toes so gentle to amuse,
the Priest had ordered peas into their shoes;
The Knaves set off on the same day,
Peas in their shoes, to go and pray;
But very different was their speed, I wot:
One of the Sinners galloped on,
Swift as a Bullet from a gun;
The other limped as if he had been shot.

One saw the Virgin soon; *peccavi* cried;
Had his Soul whitewashed all so clever;
Then home again he nimbly hied,
Made fit with Saints above to live for ever.

In coming back, however, let me say,
He met his Brother-rogue about half-way,
Hobbling with . . . bended knees,
Damning the souls and bodies of the peas;
His eyes in tears, his cheeks and brows in sweat,
Deep sympathizing with his groaning feet.

'How now,' the light-toed, white-washed Pilgrim broke
'You lazy lubber?'
'Odds curse it,' cried the other, ''tis no joke
My feet, once hard as any Rock,
Are now as soft as Blubber.

'Excuse me, Virgin Mary, that I swear;
As for Loreto, I shall not get there;
No, to the Devil my sinful soul must go,
For damme if I ha'nt lost every toe.

'But, Brother-sinner, pray explain
How 'tis that you are not in pain;
What Power hath worked a wonder for your toes;
Whilst I just like a Snail am crawling,
Now swearing, now on Saints devoutly bawling,
While not a rascal comes to ease my woes?

'How is't that you can like a Greyhound go,
Merry as if that nought had happened, burn ye?'
'Why,' cried the other grinning, 'you must know,
That just before I ventured on my journey,
To walk a little more at ease,
I took the liberty to boil my Peas.

John Wolcot

*Many people think that it is somehow wrong or immoral to use your
wits. Compare Luke 16: 1–8.*

*A Christian prayer which might be shared in conjunction with the above
passage:*

O Lord God, prevent us from hurting or harming anyone, but at
the same time, make us wise and shrewd. Teach us to use our
wits in thy service and in the proper management of our daily
lives.

Amen.

24: GURU JESUS

*Robert Van de Weyer left school believing in nothing and with no real
purpose in life. In the next eight years he made two trips to India and kept
a diary. This diary has been published with the title 'Guru Jesus' ('guru'
meaning teacher).*
This is the entry for Christmas Day, 1970.

I have decided to try an experiment: to make Jesus my Guru for a
test period of six months. During this time I shall act as a full
disciple, studying his teachings closely and following them as far
as I can, regardless of whether I fully understand or agree with
them. Then on June 25th next year I shall stand back and review
what has happened to me.

On 9 February, 1971, just six weeks later, he wrote the following
entry:

As I try to follow Jesus's instructions my agnosticism is beginning
to waver. When I am angry or depressed or in any other unloving

172

mood, I make myself say little prayers asking for help to over-come the mood. I do this because Jesus instructs me to, and for the purposes of the prayer I conjure up in my mind an image of a loving father who is able to help me. To my surprise, however, I am generally finding the prayer works, and my bad mood quickly disappears. To give a typical example, the other night I became very irritated with Sarah (my girl friend) over a series of trivial domestic mishaps (many of which were my fault, of course) and usually in the past a black cloud would have hung over us for the rest of the evening. But on this occasion I went out for a short walk and prayed to my imaginary loving father, and by the time I returned the irritation had gone completely.

I realize that there could easily be some natural psychological explanation for these experiences. But what leads me to think that this is not the case is that I also have the strong impression of an outside force working within me. It seems to demand my submission, and having submitted to it I feel I have no control over it. Two or three times I have had the fleeting sensation of standing outside myself and watching my own mind and emotions being manipulated. I am also now aware of the force each evening as I say the Lord's Prayer when I reach the phrase 'thy will be done'. As I turn the phrase over in my mind I sense the presence of a will greater than my own, pressing upon me. Sometimes this presence becomes so strong that I can almost feel it draw close to me in the darkness, as if the warm night air was suddenly heavy and humid.

Robert Van de Weyer

25: PERPLEXITY

This is another Sufi tale or parable. (See page 25.) This story tells us how we can learn to recognize truth through experience.

There was once a man who lived quietly in a certain place, not far from a mountain. He was well-behaved and refined, but the ordinary people did not see anything very remarkable about him. But he had an attractive manner and there was something about his kindness and understanding which made many people visit him and ask his advice.

Whenever anyone came to see him, he gave them advice. One, for instance, he told to open a shop, another to learn how to build rafts, a third he recommended to learn about the growing of plants and how gardens were maintained.

One day a number of people who had set out to try to find Truth paused in their journey and were talking to one another.

The first one said, 'I was able to bring the whole group safely across the treacherous torrent which we have just crossed because a certain man once recommended me to learn raft-building.'

The second man said, 'When, on this journey, we were all captured by brigands, I secured our release by showing the chief of the robbers how to cultivate his garden. I was able to do this because of the instructions given me by a certain man, who suggested to me that I learn about flowers and gardens.'

A third man said, 'We have escaped the terrors of wild animals during this journey because of the instructions given me by a certain man. He it was who, when I asked him what I should do in my life, said, "Learn how to overcome wild animals."'

And the same was true of all the other people in the caravan. When they compared notes, each discovered that he had been told one simple thing about how to progress in life, though few of them had realized how important to their survival it might become.

The guide who was with them on the journey said, 'Just remember that if you had not taken the advice of that man, none of you would be here; for there are many people who went to him for counsel, and who laughed at him or forgot his lessons, because they did not recognize that there could be any inner meaning in what he advised.'

When the travellers arrived at the end of their journey, they saw that their guide was the very same man who had lived at the bottom of the mountain, who had given them advice. They had hardly recovered from their amazement when he took them into the presence of Truth – and then they saw that Truth was nothing less than that very same man.

Then the travellers were perplexed, and their spokesman asked, 'Why, if you are the Truth, as we now all see, did you not tell us at the very beginning, so that we would have been spared this journey and all these discomforts?'

But, no sooner had these words been spoken, then they realized – because they had seen Truth – that they would never have been able to perceive Truth unless they had been through the three stages: the stage of advice and taking it, the stage of travel and applying their knowledge, and the stage of recognizing Truth itself.

They had been able to arrive at their destination only because something in their inner selves had been able to recognize, in the ordinary advice of the man at the foot of the mountain, some inner ringing of truth, some fragment of reality. In this way can man come to the recognition of the Absolute Truth.

Idries Shah

26: THE CONTEST IN GENEROSITY

Zadig is the amiable hero of a story by the French writer, Voltaire. In the course of the story, Zadig travels to various countries and is involved in a series of unlikely adventures.

The time drew near for the celebration of a great festival which took place every five years. It was the custom in Babylon at the end of the fifth year to make a solemn proclamation declaring which citizen had performed the most generous deed. . . .

When this memorable day arrived, the King ascended the throne, surrounded by the nobles and the delegates of all nations who had assembled to witness a contest where glory was to be achieved not by swiftness of horses, or by strength of body, but by virtue alone. The chief satrap (viceroy or local governor) loudly proclaimed those deeds deserving the prize.

He first introduced a judge who had passed sentence against a plantiff by an error for which he was in no way responsible. To make amends, he had then given all his property, though it was of the same value as that which the plaintiff had lost.

He next produced a young man who had married his mistress to a friend. He was devoted to the lady, but his friend was dying of love for her. And he had paid her dowry too.

Next he presented a soldier who had shown an even greater example of generosity in the Hyrcanian war. The enemy had attempted to seize his mistress, and he was defending her, when news reached him that not far away some other Hyrcanians had seized his mother. He left his mistress in tears, and rushed to his mother's assistance; but when he was able to return to his loved one, he found her dying. He was about to kill himself, but his mother declared that she had no one else to look after her, and he found the courage to go on living.

The judges were inclined towards the soldier, but the King intervened and said:

'His was certainly a noble action, and so were those of the others. But they do not give me any surprises; whereas yesterday a deed of Zadig's did surprise me. A few days ago I dismissed Coreb, my chief minister and favourite. I bitterly complained about his behaviour, and all my courtiers assured me that I had treated him too mildly: indeed they vied with each other in maligning him. I asked Zadig what he thought of Coreb, and he had the courage to speak well of him. I can recall examples in history of men who have paid for a mistake with their whole estate, who have given their mistresses away, who have preferred their mothers to the objects of their affections; but I have never read of a courtier supporting a disgraced minister who had put his Sovereign in a rage. I award twenty thousand pieces of gold to those whose generous deeds have just been recited, but I award the cup to Zadig.'

Voltaire

27: COURAGE

Jerry Renault, the hero of a powerful novel called The Chocolate War, *is a teenage student at an American high school called Trinity. He is the victim of a gang of bullies and towards the end of the story has almost no friends at all. One of the reasons for this is that he has been sticking to a course of action which he believes right, but which makes him unpopular with everyone else.*

Jerry shows great courage. He is prepared to stick to what he believes is right, even if everyone else thinks he is stupid. Jerry is prepared to disturb the universe. He is prepared to stand by his belief, even if that makes him a person alone.

Jerry opened his locker. He had thumbtacked a poster to the back wall of the locker on the first day of school. The poster showed a wide expanse of beach, a sweep of sky with a lone star glittering far away. A man walked on the beach, a small solitary figure in all that immensity. At the bottom of the poster, these words appeared – *Do I dare disturb the universe?* by Eliot, who wrote the Waste Land thing they were studying in English. Jerry wasn't sure of the poster's meaning. But it had moved him mysteriously.

It was traditional at Trinity for everyone to decorate the interior of his locker with a poster. Jerry chose this one.

He had no time now to ponder the poster any longer. The final bell rang and he had thirty seconds to get to class.

During the days that follow, Jerry is bullied and picked on in a variety of ways at school and at home, where he receives a number of anonymous, threatening phone calls.

The morning after that first night phone call, Jerry opened his locker and shook his head in disbelief. His poster had been smeared with ink or some kind of blue paint. The message had been virtually obliterated. *Do I dare disturb the universe?* was now a grotesque jumble of unconnected letters. It was such a senseless, childish act of vandalism that Jerry was more awed than angered. Who'd do such a crazy thing? Looking down, he saw that his new gym sneakers had been slashed, the canvas now limp shreds, rag-like. He'd made the mistake of leaving them here overnight.

Ruining the poster was one thing, a gross act, the work of the animal – and all schools had animals, even Trinity. But there was nothing prankish about ruining the sneakers. That was deliberate, somebody sending him a message.

The telephone calls.

That attack on the football field.

Now this.

He closed the locker quickly so no one would see the damage. For some reason, he felt ashamed.

After the next lesson, he returned to his locker.

Jerry opened his locker.

The mess was still there. He hadn't torn down the poster or removed the sneakers, letting them remain there as symbols. Symbols of what? He wasn't certain. Looking wistfully at the poster, he pondered the damaged words: *Do I dare disturb the universe?*

The usual corridor pandemonium surrounded him, slammed locker doors, wild yells and whistles, pounding feet as the guys hurried to the after-school activities, football, boxing, debating.

Do I dare disturb the universe?

Yes, I do, I do. I think.

Jerry suddenly understood the poster – the solitary man on the beach standing upright and alone and unafraid, poised at the moment of making himself heard and known in the world, the universe.

Robert Cormier

28: SACRIFICE

For Christians, this story provides a kind of parallel to the story of the sacrifice Jesus made on the cross. There are of course several important differences between the two events which might be explored in class.

There's a story told among Chinese about a young Chinese scholar and statesman named Gaw Hong, who was sent by the Emperor of China to govern the island of Formosa. The island was inhabited then by savage tribes who worshipped fierce gods and offered human sacrifices on their altars. For many years Gaw Hong ruled over these people; and he became very fond of them. He was a just and kindly ruler whom people loved and trusted, as a friend.

And all that time Gaw Hong was troubled about this custom of human sacrifice. Time and time again he called the tribes together and tried to persuade them to give up this cruel practice; but, much as they loved and respected him, they would not do it, because they feared the anger of their gods. But after many years Gaw Hong's love and friendship prevailed and they said they would do as he asked. And then that very year they had a bad harvest and, threatened with famine, they thought that the angry gods were punishing them for not offering a human sacrifice. So the chief went to Gaw Hong and said, 'We must sacrifice again, for the gods are displeased;' and Gaw Hong said: 'But you have promised not to sacrifice again. It is an evil thing to slay your fellow men on the altar of sacrifice, and if you do evil, you do harm to your own selves. Would I be a true father to let you do evil to yourselves?' But he pleaded in vain. The chief begged and implored that just this once they might be allowed to offer human blood on the altar. At last Gaw Hong said: 'Listen. If I allow you to offer just one more human life on your altars, will you swear to me that this will be the very last time?' 'Yes,' said the chief, 'I swear to it.'

'Then,' said Gaw Hong sadly, 'I will arrange for the victim to be awaiting you tonight in the forest after sundown. You will find him bound to the sacred pine.' The chief thanked him and went.

That same night, after sundown, the chief, the witch doctors and a band of warriors went into the forest, where they saw the victim bound hand and foot and lashed to the sacred pine tree, clothed in the red robe of sacrifice and with the red cloth of sacrifice tied round his face. At a word from the chief the warriors drew their bows and within a few moments the body of the victim was riddled with arrows. At once the drums were beaten and the people were summoned to let them know that the victim was ready for the sacrifice. When the people were all assembled, the chief stepped forward and pulled the red cloth of sacrifice from the victim's face. Immediately the air was filled with cries of dismay and sorrow. 'What have we done?' cried the chief, 'What have we done?' cried the people. 'We have slain our father and our friend. We have slain Gaw Hong.'

And then, turning to the weeping people, the chief spoke to them. 'See what Gaw Hong has done,' he said. 'He believed it was wicked to sacrifice a human life, and if he had given us a victim he would have shared our wickedness. So he gave us himself. He has given his own life to save us from this evil.'

John G. Williams

29: THE CAGE

What is the mark of an intelligent or rational being?
This passage is part of a story by Bertram Chandler called The Cage *and it's about four members of a space expedition from Earth who are stranded on an unknown planet. The strange beings of that planet put the humans in cages.*

On either side of them were other cages. In one of them was Mary Hart – alone. She could gesture to them, wave to them, and that was all. The cage on the other side held a beast built on the same general lines as a lobster, but with a strong resemblance to a kind of squid. Across the broad roadway they could see other cages, but not what they housed.

Hawkins, Boyle and Fennet sat on the damp floor and stared

through the thick glass and the bars at the beings outside, who stared at them.

'If only they were humanoid,' sighed the doctor. 'If only they were the same shape as we are, we might make a start towards convincing them that we too, are intelligent beings.'

'They aren't the same shape,' said Hawkins. 'And we, were the situations reversed, would take some convincing that three six-legged beer barrels were men and brothers.'

Later in the story the inhabitants of the planet put Mary in the same cage as the men. Later still, in the middle of the night, suddenly she is frightened.

Mary screamed.

Hawkins jerked into complete wakefulness. He could see the pale form of Mary – on this world it was never completely dark at night – and, on the other side of the cage, the forms of Fennet and Boyle. He got hastily to his feet, stumbled to the girl's side.

'What is it?' he asked.

'I . . . I don't know. . . . Something small, with sharp claws. . . . It ran over me. . . .'

'Oh,' said Hawkins, 'that was only Joe.'

'Joe?' she demanded.

'I don't know exactly what he – or she – is,' said the man.

'I think he's definitely he,' said the doctor.

'What is Joe?' she asked again.

'He must be the local equivalent to a mouse,' said the doctor. 'Although he looks nothing like one. He comes up through the floor somewhere to look for scraps of food. We're trying to tame him –'

'You encourage the brute?' she screamed. 'I demand that you do something about him – at once! Poison him, or trap him.'

And this they do. They trap Joe and put him in a small cage they have built out of their bedding materials.

Joe was not killed. The three men were rather attached to him. With the coming of daylight they transferred him to a cage that Hawkins had fashioned. Even the girl relented when she saw the harmless ball of multi-coloured fur bouncing indignantly up and down in its prison. She insisted on feeding the little animal, exclaimed gleefully when the thin tentacles reached out took the fragment of fungus from her fingers. For three days they made much of their pet.

On the fourth day beings whom they took to be keepers entered the cage with their nets, immobilized the occupants and carried off Joe and Hawkins.

'I'm afraid it's hopeless,' Boyle said. 'He's gone the same way . . .'

'They'll have him stuffed and mounted in some museum,' said Fennet glumly.

'No.' said the girl. 'They couldn't!'

'They could,' said the doctor.

Abruptly the hatch at the back of the cage opened.

Before the three humans could retreat, a voice called, 'It's all right, come on out!'

Hawkins walked into the cage.

'Come on out.' he said again. 'Our hosts have apologized very sincerely, and they have more suitable accommodation prepared for us. Then, as soon as they have a ship ready, we're to go to pick up the other survivors.'

'Not so fast,' said Boyle. 'Put us in the picture, will you? What made them realize that we were rational beings?'

Hawkins face darkened.

'Only rational beings,' he said, 'put other beings in cages.'

Bertram Chandler

30: THE THREE RINGS

Nathan der Weise *(Nathan the Wise) is a dramatic poem by the German writer, Gotthold Lessing. It first appeared in 1779.*

Nathan is a Jew, living in Jerusalem. Other characters in the play include a Christian knight templar and a Muslim sultan.

At one point in the story, the sultan asks Nathan which, out of Judaism, Christianity and Islam, is the true religion:

Saladin: *Since you are wise, tell me as to a friend,*
What faith, what law, have satisfied you best.
Nathan: *Sultan, I am a Jew —*
Saladin: *A Muslim I. The Christian stands between us. Of these three Religions only one can be the true one.*
Come, then, impart to me your insight!

181

Nathan the Wise decides to answer warily, by means of a parable, the story of the three rings.

There lived a man in a far Eastern clime
In hoar antiquity, who from the hand
Of his most dear beloved received a ring
Of priceless estimate. An opal 'twas
Which split a hundred lovely radiances
And had a magic power, that whoso wore it,
Trusting therein, found grace with God and man.
What wonder therefore that this man o' the East
Let it not from his finger, and took pains
To keep it to his household for all time.
Thus he bequeathed the jewel to the son
Of all his sons he loved best, and provided
That he in turn bequeath it to the son
Who was to him the dearest; evermore
The best-beloved, without respect of birth,
By right o' the ring alone should be the head,
The house's prince.
Well, this ring,
From son to son descending came at last
Unto a father of three sons, who all
To him, all three, were dutiful alike,
And whom, all three, in natural consequence,
He loved alike. Only from time to time
Now this; now that one; now the third; as each
Might be alone with him, the other twain
Not sharing his o'erflowing heart, appeared
Worthiest the ring; and then, piously weak,
He promised it to each. And so things went
Long as they could. But dying hour drawn near
Brought the good father to perplexity.
It pained him, the two sons, trusting his word,
Should thus be wounded. What was he to do?
Quickly he sends for an artificer,
To make him on the model of his ring
Two others, bidding spare nor cost nor pains
To make them in all points identical;
And this the artist did. When they are brought
Even the father scarcely can distinguish

His pattern-ring. So, full of joy, he calls
His sons, and each one to him separately;
And gives to each son separately his blessing,
Gives each his ring; and dies.
For what still follows, any man may guess.
Scarce was the father dead, but each one comes
And shows his ring, and each one claims to be
True prince o' the house. Vainly they search, strive, argue,
The true ring was not proved or provable –
Almost as hard to prove as to us now
What the true creed is.

Gotthold Lessing

SEASONAL READINGS

To everything there is a season, and a time to every purpose under Heaven. A time to be born, a time to die . . . A time to weep, a time to laugh, a time to mourn, a time to dance . . .

Ecclesiastes 3: 1–4

Autumn Term

1: MICHAELMAS

Michaelmas Day, the Christian Festival of St Michael and All Angels, falls on 29 September. See Revelation, *chapter 12, verses 7–9. St Michael was regarded as a protector of Christians against the devil, especially at the time of their death.*

In Britain, for practical and business reasons, the year is divided by law into four quarter-days and four terms. Michaelmas appears in both lists.

Quarter-days are the days when rent, paid 'quarterly' or four times a year, becomes due, and when tenancies on properties begin and end. In England and Ireland these quarter-days are: Lady Day, 25 March; Midsummer Day, 24 June; Michaelmas, 29 September; Christmas Day, 25 December.

The four terms, which now only apply to Law Sittings, but which formerly applied also to universities, are Hilary, Easter, Trinity, and Michaelmas. For convenience' sake universities cut their terms down to three per year of about nine weeks each, and schools follow suit. Oxford University's terms are called Hilary, Trinity and Michaelmas; at Cambridge they are Lent, Easter and Michaelmas. The Michaelmas term is the start of the academic year in universities and schools.

Michaelmas is a major landmark in the farmer's year. Not only is it the great season for the sale of livestock but most farm tenancies run from one Michaelmas to the next. With the harvest gathered in and animals disposed of, it is the obvious time for making a move, starting afresh – or giving up altogether!

Michaelmas fairs provided the ideal meeting place for buying and selling animals, for hiring labour, and for finding work. Fairs were, and still are, held at other times of year, but the great agricultural fairs were mostly held in September and October. Flocks of sheep and herds of cattle changed hands; horses found new owners, and geese, grown fat from gleaning the stubble after the harvest, were driven in their thousands along the roads to 'Goose Fairs'. A 'stubble goose' was an annual treat at Michaelmas. . . .

In towns and villages en route to some famous shrine, the date of the fair was sometimes altered to catch the custom of thousands of pilgrims making for the shrine. Fairs for miles round Canterbury were known as 'Becket Fairs'.

As time went on, more and more people came to disapprove of the mixing up of 'piety, feasting, greed and folly'. Gingerbread stalls selling gingerbread 'saints' were denounced as 'a basket of popery, a nest of images, and a whole legend of gingerwork'. The Reformation finally stamped out any religious element, and fairs were then able to concentrate on their practical purpose. But, as the old songs tell us, there was also plenty of 'fun at the fair'.

Nowadays, these two sides of the fair have separated. We have important Trade Fairs where people from all over the world gather to buy and sell, or just to look at, the latest products. Each Trade Fair is concerned with one particular commodity – cars, antiques, or books, for example.

But the fairs we enjoy most are the 'fun-fairs', with their merry-go-rounds and shooting galleries, their Big Wheels and Dodg'em cars. Although they are much smaller, tamer affairs than those of the past, our ancestors might perhaps recognise the gaudy, worthless prizes, and even the fairground 'barker' himself.

Some Famous Fairs

For I want to go to Widecombe Fair,
With Bill Brewer,
  Jan Stewer,
  Peter Gurney,
  Peter Davey,
  Dan'l Widden,
  'Arry 'Awk,
Old Uncle Tom Cobley, an' all . . .

Widecombe Fair in Devonshire is held in September. It was started for the sale of Dartmoor Ponies. Tom Cobley was a real person who died in 1794 at the age of ninety-six.

St Bartholomew's Fair is featured in a book of that name written by Ben Jonson in 1614. This famous, or infamous, London fair, was held at Smithfield on St Bartholomew's Day, 14 August. By Charles II's reign it was lasting for up to two weeks. People came from all over England to trade, to stare at 'monsters' and watch puppet-shows, to swindle or be swindled, and probably to have their pockets picked.

It was at *Weyhill Fair* in Hampshire that the wife-selling incident in Thomas Hardy's *The Mayor of Casterbridge* is supposed to have taken place.

Hatfield Fair gave a new word to the English language. It was held on the feast day of the town's patron saint, St Etheldreda, or 'Awdry' as she was affectionately known. The cheap and nasty goods sold there eventually produced the adjective 'tawdry'.

Peter Watkins and Erica Hughes

2: JEWISH NEW YEAR FESTIVALS

The Jewish year begins with the month of Tishri (September–October) and a series of important festivals.

New Year

The Jewish New Year, known as *Rosh ha-Shanah*, occurs in September or October. It is a solemn occasion, for although it celebrates the creation of the world the main emphasis is on judgement. There is a tradition that on this day God opens the 'book of life', in which the names of all people and the deeds they have performed are recorded. During the next ten days (known as the Ten Days of Penitence) God assesses whether or not the bad deeds should be punished with death, and so prayers and repentance are very important.

However, an enjoyable and happy ceremony is held in homes on the eve of the festival. Just before the evening meal pieces of apple are dipped into honey, and eaten by each member of the family. This reminds everyone to hope that the new year will be a sweet and prosperous one.

The Day of Atonement

This is known in Hebrew as *Yom Kippur*, and it is the most solemn day in the Jewish calendar. It happens ten days after *Rosh ha-Shanah*, and it is then that God makes a final judgement, and forgives those who have truly repented. Jews fast for twenty-five hours, and spent most of that time in the synagogue, praying for forgiveness.

Sukkot

A few days later the Feast of Tabernacles, or *Sukkot*, is observed. This is a very happy festival, and most families build a *succah* (booth) in their garden. The *succah* is like a hut with no roof, and it is decoraged with foliage and fruit. Many families eat their meals in it, and even sleep in it if the weather is fine. In addition, in many synagogues, people build a *succah* for the whole congregation to enjoy. These are all a symbol of trust in God, who protected the Jewish people during their forty years' wandering in the wilderness.

During synagogue services people wave palm branches, myrtle and willow leaves, and a citrus fruit called the *etrog* in all directions, to show that God can be found in all directions and in all lands.

The last day of the festival is really a new holiday, called *Simhat Torah*: the Rejoicing of the *Torah*. It marks the end of the yearly cycle of readings from the *Torah** (the five books of Moses, the Law of Moses). All the *Torah* scrolls are removed from the Ark, and processions are made with them around the synagogue. Then the people with the scrolls dance around in celebration. Children often join in too, carrying flags. The last chapters of the Book of Deuteronomy are read out, and followed with the first chapters of the Book of Genesis – showing that God's word never ends, but continues to speak again and again to every generation.

Douglas Charing

3: DIVALI

Two accounts of the Hindu 'Festival of Lights':

Divali falls in the Hindu month of Karttika (October–November).

---

* These books form the first five books of the Old Testament.

Its name comes from the Sanskrit word *dipavali*, which means a row of lights. Divali marks the return of the god Rama to his kingdom to become the rightful king. People light rows of small oil lamps or candles along windows and balconies to welcome Rama home.

Lakshmi, the goddess of wealth, is also worshipped on Divali. In most parts of India, Divali marks the new year. Businesses open new account books at this time. A ceremony called the Lakshmi puja is performed to bring good fortune in the coming year. An oil lamp is left burning in most homes all night to welcome the goddess.

Divali is also a time when people wear new clothes, visit friends and exchange sweets.

Patricia Bahree

Family vows are renewed. Husbands and wives remember their duties to each other; likewise children to their parents, and vice versa. Houses are cleaned, clay oil lamps lit to welcome Lakshmi, and gifts are exchanged. Divali means 'cluster of lights'. Everywhere is lit up with lights. Firecrackers scare away evil spirits. Thus light or good overcomes darkness or evil. There is a lot of music and dancing. Festival floats carry scenes from the lives of the gods. Papier-mâché tigers and cows are on sale. Sweets made of thickened milk and sugar or coconut and sugar are distributed. Businessmen celebrate by opening new account books with prayers to Lakshmi for success in the coming year.

J. R. S. Whiting

4: GUY FAWKES DAY

Throughout the reign of Elizabeth I, Roman Catholics in Britain suffered much persecution. James I promised that while he was king, things would be better.

The Roman Catholics had cherished strong hopes, not only of freedom from persecution, but of seeing their religion once more established by law; and James certainly did not allow them to be molested during the first year of his reign. But, soon after, persecution began again, and with greater bitterness and severity than ever, and six thousand Catholics were brought before the courts

191

in one single year for refusing to attend Church of England worship. They now saw what the promises of James were worth. Driven to despair, and with no hope of help from abroad, a small band of them came to the desperate resolution of destroying, at one terrible blow, both Parliament and King. Robert Catesby – a Northamptonshire gentleman – was the chief ringleader.

After disposing of the King, the Lords, and the Commons, Catesby and his followers planned to make for the country, raise the Roman Catholic nobility and gentry, and proclaim one of the king's younger children. A vacant cellar under the Houses of Parliament was hired. Thirty-six barrels of gunpowder were piled against the wall and covered with faggots of firewood; and Guy or Guido Fawkes, a Yorkshire gentleman, who had served in the Spanish army, was induced to carry out the dark and desperate design. Everything was ready; the king was to open Parliament on the 5th of November; and on that night the mine was to be fired. Fawkes was ready in the cellar with his lantern and a slow match.

J. M. D. Meiklejohn

Some of the conspirators, however, who were in any case too numerous to preserve their secrets, were understandably reluctant that the Catholic peers in the House of Lords should be blown to pieces in this Catholic endeavour and dispatched a warning. A peer who received an anonymous letter at once informed the Government and a search party unearthed the gunpowder beneath a pile of coals and wood in the presence of Guido Fawkes who intended to apply the torch. At least that was the official story. The discovery of the plot meant a renewal and increase of penalties against English Roman Catholics, and the introduction of a day of thanksgiving which was officially celebrated for 250 years.

Maurice Ashley

But why the alternative name for Guy Fawkes' Day – Bonfire Night?

When we set light to our bonfires that evening early in November, we are doing something that our ancestors have done over countless generations. There has been a bonfire festival at this time of year since pagan times – first at the Celtic Feast of

Samain, and then at the Hallowe'en festivities which replaced it.

The Puritans were not happy about the intermingling of heathen rites and Christian worship. When a thankful Parliament ordered a public holiday on 5 November to mark the failure of the Gunpowder Plot, it was seized upon as a replacement for Hallowe'en as a festival day. Effigies of Guy Fawkes were burnt on bonfires, church bells were rung and cannons fired. There was also a special service which was not deleted from the English prayer book until 1859.

November 5 became a day when hatred was stirred up against all Roman Catholics, especially the Pope as head of their Church.

Sometimes his effigy was also burned, and a second verse tacked on to the Guy Fawkes rhyme:

A rope, a rope, to hang the Pope,
A piece of cheese to toast him;
A barrel of beer to drink his health,
And a right good fire to roast him.

Peter Watkins and Erica Hughes

5: REMEMBRANCE SUNDAY

Remembrance Sunday exists not to glorify war but to remember those who have lost their lives in war, those who still suffer its effects and those who have been bereaved. (A passage about the work of the Royal British Legion can be found on page 157 of Anthology for Assembly, *the companion volume to this handbook.)*

In the first of these two poems by Wilfred Owen (the first World War poet killed only a week before the armistice in 1918), a Cockney soldier with the BEF (British Expeditionary Force) writes a letter home. The second poem describes the deaths of three soldiers.

The Letter

With BEF. June 10. Dear Wife,
(O blast this pencil. 'Ere, Bill, lend's a knife.)
I'm in the pink at present, dear.
I think the war will end this year.
We don't see much of them square-'eaded 'Uns.
We're out of harm's way, not bad fed.
I'm longing for a taste of your old buns.

(Say, Jimmie, spare's a bite of bread.)
There don't seem much to say just now.
(Yer what? Then don't, yer ruddy cow!
And give us back me cigarette!)
I'll soon be 'ome. You mustn't fret.
My feet's improvin', as I told you of.
We're out in rest now. Never fear.
(VRACH! By crumbs, but that was near.)
Mother might spare you half a sov.
Kiss Nell and Bert. When me and you –
(Eh? What the 'ell! Stand to? Stand to!
Jim, give's a hand with pack on, lad.
Guh! Christ! I'm hit. Take 'old. Aye, bad.
No, damn your iodine. Jim? 'Ere!
Write my old girl, Jim, there's a dear.)

Wilfred Owen

The Last Laugh

'O Jesus Christ! I'm hit,' he said; and died.
Whether he vainly cursed, or prayed indeed,
The Bullets chirped – In vain! vain! vain!
Machine-guns chuckled, – Tut-tut! Tut-tut!
And the Big Guns guffawed.

Another sighed, – 'O Mother, mother! Dad!'
Then smiled, at nothing, childlike, being dead.
    And the lofty Shrapnel-cloud
    Leisurely gestured, – Fool!
    And the falling splinters tittered.

'My Love!' one moaned. Love-languid seemed his mood,
Till, slowly lowered, his whole face kissed the mud.
    And the Bayonets' long teeth grinned;
    Rabbles of Shells hooted and groaned;
    And the Gas hissed.

Wilfred Owen

6: ST CECILIA
(22 November)

St Cecilia is the patron saint of music and 22 November may therefore be a suitable date for an assembly that is largely musical.

Cecilia was a Roman Christian, martyred in AD 176. Her story is told by Chaucer in the second nun's tale in The Canterbury Tales.

She was Roman, we read, born nobly, and born a Christian. She was given in marriage to a young pagan whose name was Valerian, but she had privately taken a vow of virginity. On her wedding night she revealed this to him as tenderly as she could, not forgetting to add that she was often visited by an angel, who would certainly strike him dead if he molested her. Valerian received this news unfavourably, yet loved her enough to seek baptism. Returning, he found his wife in conversation with the angel, who thereupon crowned them with flowers – with lilies and roses, picked in no earthly garden. It must have been Winter; for when Valerian's brother entered the room he remarked on the overwhelming fragrance that filled it; but to him the floral crowns were invisible. He too was baptised; and in course of time the brothers were martyred. Then Cecilia was put to the question, and condemned to be roasted to death in a dry bath. All night and all the following day she reclined there, miraculously cool, and at last an executioner was sent to cut off her head. The operation horribly miscarried, and it was three days before the girl bled to death, still gay at heart, and encouraging her companions.

That is the story that Chaucer tells, in the Second Nun's Tale. It may be asked in what manner the saint was connected with music, and the answer, such as it is, will only be found in one couplet:

And whil the organs maden melodie
To God allone in herte thus sang she.

On that couplet, or rather on the equivalent words in the Golden Legend, Cecilia's musical reputation must stand. At any rate it was thought to be well established in the Middle Ages, when the guilds of musicians adopted her as their patron saint. She was even supposed to have invented the instrument named in her legend, as Dryden describes in his 'Song for St Cecilia's Day'.

Laurence Whistler

195

Song for Saint Cecilia's Day

The trumpet's loud clangour
   Excites us to arms
With shrill notes of anger
   And mortal alarms.
The double double double beat
   Of the thund'ring drum
   Cries hark the foes come!
Charge, charge, 'tis too late to retreat.

The soft complaining flute
In dying notes discovers
The woes of hopeless lovers,
Whose dirge is whisper'd by the warbling lute.

Sharp violins proclaim
Their jealous pangs and desperation,
Fury, frantic indignation,
Depth of pains and height of passion,
   For the fair, disdainful dame.

But oh! what art can teach
   What human voice can reach
The sacred organ's praise?
Notes inspiring holy love,
Notes that wing their heav'nly ways
   To mend the choirs above.

John Dryden

7: ST NICHOLAS
(6 December)

Since Santa Claus is believed by many to have replaced Christ as the central person in the observance of Christmas, it will be well to describe the background from which our modern Santa Claus has emerged.

Although present-day Santa Claus is taken to be a myth, there was a real Saint Nicholas, an early Christian bishop who presided over Myra, a city in Asia Minor. Because of his remarkable childhood and his selection while still a youth as a high church official, he has become known as the Boy Bishop. Because of his love for and relationship to children and because of his generosity, many chapels have been dedicated to his memory. Russia took him as its patron saint, as also did Greece. More churches have been named after him than after any of the apostles – 300 in Belgium, 60 in Rome, and 400 in England.

Dutch seamen are supposed to have first carried to Europe the reports of the bishop's generosity, as a result of which children in Holland received special presents on 6 December. The traditional appearance of Saint Nicholas in Europe is that of a bearded saint riding on a white horse and carrying a basket of gifts for the good children and a bunch of birch rods for the naughty ones.

In Holland, Saint Nicholas Day, 6 December, has remained the great day for children. It seems that the honoured saint is at home here more than in any other country.

On the last Saturday in November the words, 'Look there is the steamer bringing us Saint Nich!' are acted out:

Look, there is the steamer from faraway lands,
It brings us Saint Nicholas; he's waving his hands,
His horse is a-prancing on deck up and down,
The banners are waving in village and town.

Black Peter is laughing and tells every one,
'The good kids get sweets, the bad ones get none!'
Oh please, dear Saint Nicholas, if Pete and you would
Just visit our house, for we all have been good.

Accordingly, Saint Nicholas, wearing a bishop's robe and mitre, white gloves, and an enormous bishop's ring on his left hand, seated on his white horse and accompanied by Black Peter (the name given to the devil for this occasion), arrives by steamer in Amsterdam's harbour and in other harbour cities, cheered by thousands of children and adults, and majestically descends the gangplank.

Amid deafening cheers and with all the church bells ringing, the parade is set in motion. First come a motorcade of the police force and a brass band. Then comes Saint Nick on horseback, wrapped in his scarlet mantle, with Black Peter at his side. The mayor and other city dignitaries follow, decorated floats, a caval-cade of students and more brass bands. The procession stops in the main square in Amsterdam, in front of the Royal Palace, to be welcomed by the Queen.

While the translation of the name (originally from the Latin, *Sanctus Nicolaus*; the German, *Sank Nikolaus*; the Dutch, *Sinter Klaus*) into Santa Claus is readily understandable, it is somewhat more difficult to see how a staid saint of long ago should become the chubby, jolly character who too largely rules the Christmas season. . . .

When the Dutch settled in New Amsterdam, now New York, they brought along their tradition of Saint Nicholas, even naming their first church, though Protestant, after him – the St Nicholas Collegiate Church (recently dissolved to make way for real-estate development). His image had also been placed on the vessel that brought the Dutch settlers, the *Goede Vrouw*. Quite naturally he was represented by a broad-brimmed hat and a long Dutch pipe, and his long churchly robe was replaced by short breeches.

In 1809, a writer called Washington Irving pictured Santa Claus as a jolly, chubby fellow riding through the air in a sleigh drawn by reindeer. On 22 February, 1835, a literary society was organized by Washington Irving which met that year on 6 December, to honour the famous bishop.

From this group, a short, chubby Hollander seems to have become the personification, as to form and spirit, of Santa Claus, which was indelibly enshrined by a Dr Clement C. Moore in his poem 'A Visit from St Nicholas'. On December 22, 1822, Dr Moore, a professor in the General Theological Seminary in New York, read the poem to his children. A visitor in the home was so pleased with the lines that he copied them and had the poem published.

It is not difficult to relate 'a sleigh full of toys' to the unparalleled generosity of the saint, and 'the stocking . . . hung by the chimney with care' to the shoes that the children of Amsterdam and of New Amsterdam set in the chimney corners on the eve of 6 December; the 'sleigh and eight tiny reindeer' reflect Woden's horse, Sleipnir, upon whose back Saint Nicholas still makes his rounds in Holland. Santa's bells may have been suggested to the author as he drove home in his own sleigh one wintry night.

Herbert H. Wernecke

8: CAROL SINGING

A description from Laurie Lee's Cider With Rosie *of carol singing in and around the Gloucestershire village of Slad.*

The week before Christmas, when snow seemed to lie thickest, was the moment for carol-singing. . . .

By instinct we knew just when to begin it; a day too soon and we should have been unwelcome, a day too late and we should have received lean looks from people whose bounty was already exhausted. When the true moment came, exactly balanced, we recognized it and were ready.

So as soon as the wood had been stacked in the oven to dry for the morning fire, we put on our scarves and went out through the streets, calling loudly between our hands, till the various boys who knew the signal ran out from their houses to join us.

One by one they came stumbling over the snow, swinging their lanterns around their heads, shouting and coughing horribly.

'Coming carol-barking then?'

We were the Church Choir, so no answer was necessary. For a year we had praised the Lord out of key, and as a reward for this service, we now had the right to visit all the big houses, to sing our carols and collect our tribute. . . .

Steadily we worked the length of the valley, going from house to house, visiting the lesser and the greater gentry – the farmers, the doctors, the merchants, the majors, and other exalted persons. It was freezing hard and blowing too; yet not for a moment did we feel the cold. The snow blew into our faces, into our eyes and mouths, soaked through our puttees, got into our boots, and dripped from our woollen caps. But we did not care. The collecting-box grew heavier, and the list of names in the book longer and more extravagant, each trying to outdo the other. . . .

We approached our last house high up on the hill, the place of Joseph the farmer. For him we had chosen a special carol, which was about the other Joseph, so that we always felt that singing it added a spicey cheek to the night. The last stretch of country to reach his farm was perhaps the most difficult of all. In these rough bare lanes, open to all winds, sheep were buried and wagons lost. Huddled together, we tramped in one another's footsteps, powdered snow blew into our screwed-up eyes, the candles burnt low, some blew out altogether, and we talked loudly above the gale.

Crossing, at last, the frozen mill-stream – whose wheel in summer still turned a barren mechanism – we climbed up to Joseph's farm. Sheltered by trees, warm on its bed of snow, it seemed always to be like this. As always it was late; as always this was our final call. The snow had a fine crust upon it, and the old trees sparkled like tinsel.

We grouped ourselves round the farmhouse porch. The sky cleared, and broad streams of stars ran down over the valley and away to Wales. On Slad's white slopes, seen through the black stick of its woods, some red lamps still burned in the windows.

Everything was quiet; everywhere there was the faint crackling silence of the winter night. We started singing, and we were all moved by the words and the sudden trueness of our voices. Pure, very clear, and breathless we sang:

> As Joseph was a walking
> He heard an angel sing;
> 'This night shall be the birth-time
> Of Christ the Heavenly King.
>
> He neither shall be borned
> In Housen nor in hall,
> Nor in a place of paradise
> But in an ox's stall . . . .'

And two thousand Christmases became real to us then; the houses, the halls, the places of paradise had all been visited; the stars were bright to guide the Kings through the snow; and across the farmyard we could hear the beasts in their stalls. We were given roast apples and hot mince-pies, in our nostrils were spices like myrrh, and in our wooden box, as we headed back for the village, there were golden gifts for all.

Laurie Lee

9: MODERN NATIVITY

This modern version of the Nativity story appeared as a leader in The Guardian *when the Church of England was modernizing the language of its services.*

The position was that the colonial administration, headed in Syria by Cyrenius although overall control rested with Caesar

Augustus, had recently established a system whereby the provisions for personal taxation were to be progressively extended to make them universally applicable, and everyone was advised to contact his or her relevant local authority, in this particular instance Bethlehem, Judea. Consequently Joseph and Mary – she was pregnant at the time – were in transit from their Nazareth, Galilee home to Bethlehem when Mary began to have labour pains. The child – it was her first – turned out to be male. She dressed him in a romper suit but in the event she had to improvise an ad hoc cot in the form of an animal feed container due to the accommodation at the hotel all having been previously allocated to other clients.

As it happened some workers in the agricultural sector were in the neighbourhood supervising sheep on an overnight basis. It was to their considerable surprise, not to say alarm, that an angel suddenly materialized out of nowhere accompanied by startling lighting effects. 'Not to worry,' he told the workers. 'First, the good news, not just for you, but for all concerned – you know?' And he briefed them with the latest information about the child being born and then about the interim structure for child welfare arrangements involving the animal feed container. The child would, he added, become a nationalist leader. So the workers took time out to see what was happening.

Coincidentally with this, three intellectuals – they had been intrigued by the appearance of a super-nova – arrived in Bethlehem via an eastern route which meant a stopover in Jerusalem. They had been following the super-nova for some time, but as it transpired, it eventually stopped over the precise location of the child, which came as a relief. They went into the hotel service quarters, met up with the child and his mother, and knelt down as a gesture of respect. When they had had their baggage sent in they made him a donation of gold, spruce resin, and a substance known as myrrh, which is derived from shrubs of the genus *Commiphora*. But their anxieties were by no means over, and following an uneasy feeling in the night about their route for the return journey – the story is slightly complicated, but basically the local chief, Herod, had devised a plot to intercept them so that he could have the child killed as a threat to his own supremacy – the trio decided that in the general interest it would be prudent to make alternative arrangements.

The Guardian

10: CHRISTMAS NIGHT

In The Book of Witnesses *the Jewish actor and writer, David Kossoff, tells the story of Jesus through the eyes of real and fictional characters who knew or who might have known Jesus.*
The narrator in this passage is an elderly shepherd.

I was about nineteen at the time, and, although it's now about fifty years ago, I remember it like yesterday. I lived with my parents, not far from Jerusalem, and I was one of a group of shepherds who looked after the sheep owned by the Temple. We, our group, usually worked at night. On this night I'm talking about, we'd met up where we usually did, on the side of quite a big hill. We'd had a bite to eat and drink and were sitting talking. Around us, our hundreds of sheep. All normal and usual and quiet. Very restful and pleasant, those talks at night. It was a dark night.

Then there was a sort of stillness and a feeling of change, of difference. We all felt it. I had a friend called Simon, and he first noticed what the change was. It was the light. There was a sort of paleness. It was a dark night but suddenly it wasn't so dark. We began to see each other's faces very clearly in a sort of silvery shimmering light. We seemed surrounded and enclosed in a great glow. It was the purest light I ever saw. The sheep were white as snow. Then, as our eyes began to ache with it, just farther up the hill from us the glow seemed to intensify and take shape, and we saw a man. Like us but not like us. Taller, stiller. Though we were still enough, God knows.

He looked at us and we looked at him. We waited for him to speak. It didn't seem right (we all felt it) for any of us to speak first. He took his time – as though to find the right words – and then he began to tell us what he called good news of great joy. Of a new-born baby, born in David's town. A baby sent by God, to save the world, to change things, to make things better. He told us where to go and find the baby and how to recognize him. And to tell other people the good news. His own pleasure in telling us filled us with joy, too. We shared his pleasure – if you follow me. Then he stopped speaking and became two. Then four, then eight, and in a second there seemed to be a million like him. Right up the hill and on up into the sky. A million. And they sang to us.

'Glory to God', they sang, 'and on earth peace to all men.' It was wonderful. It came to an end and then they were gone. . . .

Well, we did as we'd been told, we spread the word, and people did get excited. But not for long. Nothing lasts. We shepherds were heroes for a while, but then everyone knew the story. It was old news. Soon we were just shepherds again.

David Kossoff

Spring Term

11: GOLD, FRANKINCENSE AND MYRRH

This is a second excerpt from David Kossoff's Book of Witnesses *(see also pages 202–3).*

In the Christian Church's year, Epiphany (6 January) commemorates the coming of the wise men to the infant Jesus. Tradition says that there were three wise men (perhaps astrologers), but the Bible simply says that 'there came wise men from the East' and that they brought three gifts.

Their story is told in Matthew 2; 1–12.

But what became of their gifts? In this story, the speaker is Ezra, a jeweller, working in Nazareth (which was the town in Galilee in which Jesus grew up). He remembers how, one day, a woman called Mary came to his house with a casket to be repaired, bringing her eleven year old son with her.

She carried the casket wrapped thickly in cloth. When I took off the cloth, it took my breath away. Quite superb. Worth a fortune. The woman listened to my rapture calmly. She was a calm, quiet person, with a look of great candour.

'Very few people have seen the box,' she told me. 'It was given to my son' (she put her hand on the boy's arm) 'shortly after he was born. By a wise man from far away who seemed to be very rich. There were three.'

'Three wise men?' I said.

'Yes,' she said, 'and three boxes. This one contains as you see small blocks of pure frankincense resin.'

It did, too. Quite full. The purest, whitest, I'd ever seen. I asked her about the other boxes, as she called them.

'One is of pure gold, without jewels,' she said, 'and contains gold. The other is like this one and also contains blocks of resin.

Of myrrh.' Then she paused. I remember it so clearly. 'Myrrh,' she said, 'which is used in the purification of women and the anointing of kings. It is used in wine to deaden pain. It is used in the preparation of the dead for the grave, and in the ointment of embalming.'

It was said strangely. Not to inform, to show knowledge, but in an even flat voice. Then, with more animation, she told me what she wanted done. To repair and make new again. The work I love. The workmanship of the casket was wondrous. I knew that, in putting right the damage here and there and in its renovation, I would learn much, and I made that my excuse for promising to do the work at a very low price. The woman, her name was Mary, I recall, told me that they had little money anyway, and that her plan was that her husband Joseph would pay me in work. He was a skilled carpenter, she told me, and they often paid bills that way. Also, she said, the boy would give his services in any useful way.

I found her honesty and simplicity most attractive, and agreed. And so it was. I worked on all three caskets and was paid in benches and shelves and cupboards – and a beautiful hardwood workbench, which I use to this day. And when the family took the boy to Jerusalem to be confirmed at the age of thirteen, I looked after the boxes for them.

He was a pleasant boy. We became good friends. I would see him nearly every day. He would call in to see me if I needed anything and I grew to trust him completely. A steady lad, with good sense, and initiative. His father was teaching him to work in wood and I added a few lessons in metalwork. He was quick and dexterous. He enjoyed the company of older people, I think. He always seemed a little apart with boys of his own age. He was a good reader and loved the Scriptures, as I do, so we had lots in common.

I left Nazareth about nine months after his confirmation in Jerusalem. I was sad to leave. I made him a belt buckle in silver and bronze with his name, Jesus, engraved on it.

I went far away to the North, and later to the East, and I lost touch with the family. Pity.

It is very sad to think that a pleasant boy like that should have come to such an end. He could have been no more than thirty-three or four.

David Kossoff

12: CHINESE NEW YEAR

In the Chinese calendar, the lunar New Year (now called the Spring Festival) falls in late January or early February and is the most important festival in modern China (as it was in the past).

Traditionally, the beginning of the New Year was considered a time for clearing up (paying off debts, spring-cleaning the house from top to bottom) in preparation for a prosperous year ahead. The first task was to make sure that the kitchen god (whose effigy or portrait stood in every house by the stove) was happy. It was believed that he went up to heaven every Spring Festival and reported on the household. If his report was good, then the gods would look after the family in the new year. Long strips of red paper with the words 'When you go up to Heaven, report favourably' and 'When you come back down to earth, bring good luck' were pasted on either side of the stove and the mouth of the god's effigy was smeared with honey. This was either to make sure that he would use 'honeyed' words or, perhaps, to stick his mouth together so he could not say anything bad – no one is quite sure. On the outside doors to the house pictures of fierce-looking guardian soldiers were pasted, to keep evil spirits away.

In China today, there are no kitchen gods, but the idea of spring-cleaning remains. In traditional-style houses, there is no glass in the windows but fine white paper stuck over a wooden lattice, and this window paper is renewed at Spring Festival. In some parts of China special window decorations are put up. In Hebei province red paper-cuts are stuck on to the new window paper, and in the town of Datong, in Shanxi province, hand-painted paper with flowers, birds and cats, is stuck up, instead of the usual plain white paper.

Spring Festival is a national holiday, though some people have longer off work than others. It is a time when all Chinese want to be with their families and those working away from home get a few weeks leave so that they can travel home. The trains are booked up and bursting for weeks around Spring Festival. Passengers carry bundles of bedding – everyone in China travels with his two brightly coloured quilts, and no hotel in China provides bedding since it is assumed that travellers will bring it along with them – and presents for children, or local delicacies like peanuts from Shandong, dried fruit from Beijing, tea from the Dragon Well near Hangzhou or biscuits and cakes in bright boxes.

On the day of the festival, families prepare a special meal together. One of the best things to eat is *jiaozi* – pronounced jow (*as in 'jowls'*) – tsa (*as in 'it's a'*). These are little pastry packets of minced pork flavoured with ginger and garlic. All the family sits round a table making the *jiaozi* and joking about how many they will be able to eat (up to fifty!).

After a family meal, everyone goes to call on neighbours and friends, to drink tea and eat sweets or nuts. The sidestreets and lanes are full of people going about their business at any time of the year, but at Spring Festival all you can see is families entering one courtyard after another, visiting friends. Children break the conversation by letting off fire-crackers in the courtyards. Fire-crackers are like long strings of bangers tied together so that they go off one after another like machine-gun fire. In the past they were let off at Spring Festival to frighten away any lurking evil spirits.

Frances Wood

13: WASSAILING

'Wassail' is an old word meaning 'Be well'. To go wassailing is to go round wishing people well. The custom was performed on different winter nights in different parts of the country, often on 17 January.

Almost as soon as the last of the Christmas decorations have been cast on to the fire, or the surviving glass ornaments and tangled fairy lights consigned to their summer abode, some people, particularly in rural, cider-making areas will be getting ready for another celebration.

In Somerset, (and in Kent where they do something similar), a bunch of folk will be preparing to go wassailing. Now many people think that wassailing is carol-singing, and in one sense, it is, but it has an older, and in this context, slightly different meaning. On the evening of 17 January (old Twelfth Night) a group of people prepares another activity concerned with warding off harm and ensuring peace and plenty, this time among the orchards of apple trees. In some places it is the villagers, in others Morris Dancers have taken on this task, but basically it is similar.

207

The idea is to go out this bitter winter night with barrels of cider, guns, and toast, and sing a song to an apple tree! Like many festivals it seems totally irrational, although there may run through it a thread of logic.

A short, torchlit procession goes out into the orchard at Carhampton in Somerset; the participants are dressed in a sort of medieval costume, and carry a huge tankard full of cider. Under an old orchard tree they all pause and sing:

Here's to thee, old apple tree,
Whence thou may'st bud and whence thou may'st blow;
Hats full, cups full, bushel basket, sacks full,
And all my pockets full, too. Hooray!

The slices of toast are dipped in cider and stuck up among the branches, shotguns are fired upwards through the trees to drive off evil spirits, libations are poured over the roots, and drink is shared by all the carollers, who may dance about the trees; or shout and sing to bring fertility and good luck.

Under these trees we have again a mixture of several streams of tradition running together. Wassailing dates back to the Vikings, the greeting given in *Beowulf* being 'Waes thu hal'. The Saxons would offer a guest a cup of ale, saying 'Was Hail', roughly translated as 'I wish you good health' (as in 'hale and hearty') 'and good luck'. The guest would reply 'Drinc Hail' – 'I drink, and good luck be to you'. This custom of drinking each other's health on Twelfth Night from a Wassail Bowl, decked with ribbons and containing mead spiced with sweet herbs, or a sort of punch, was well established by the fourteenth century. Initially this was indoors but later it was taken out into the open, and Wassail Bowls were carried about the streets. 'Here we come a-wassailing, among the leaves so green . . .' although sung at Christmas it may be more appropriate to another time of year for it continues '. . . God bless you and send you a happy new year' – which could equally apply to the new growth of plants.

Marian Green

14: CANDLEMAS
(2 February)

Candlemas is also known as the Presentation of Christ in the Temple and the Purification of the Blessed Virgin Mary.

Forty days after the birth of a Jewish boy, it was customary to take him to the Temple in Jerusalem to be 'offered' or presented to God in thanksgiving for his safe birth. His mother was 'purified' or blessed.

The story of the Presentation of Jesus is told in Luke 2: 22–40.

Because Jesus was described as a 'light', the celebration of the event became connected with candles (thought of in pagan times as offshoots of the life-giving sun).

Candlemas was held in commemoration of the Purification of the Virgin; it was an important festival of the Church and, on its day, the church bells were rung. Many devotional and ritualistic ceremonies were performed and a characteristic feature of the festival was the large number of candles used in its celebration. Several popular customs were celebrated, many Candlemas sayings, beliefs, and omens were current among the people, and Candlemas fairs were numerous.

From the earliest times, our English forefathers gathered together in their parish churches, on Candlemas day, for the blessing of the candles and for the procession with lighted tapers.

In olden times, parishioners attended church on Candlemas day, when wax candles and tapers were consecrated, lighted, distributed to the officers of the church and members of the congregation, and then carried in procession. The consecrated candles, when lighted, were believed to be protective against evil spirits and storms, and the larger the candle and the more brightly it burned the more powerful the protection. The custom was discontinued in the churches of London and in many churches throughout the country, on Candlemas Day, 1547–8.

It was customary to take down Christmas decorations on Candlemas Eve and replace them with box [a species of tree]. On Candlemas Eve, it was said:

Down with the Rosemary and Baies,
Down with the Mistletoe;
Instead of Holly, now upraise
The greener Box for show.

Laurence Whistler

15: SHROVETIDE

Shrove Tuesday (or Pancake Day) is the day before Ash Wednesday, the first day of Lent. Its date varies according to the date of Easter, Lent being the period of forty days that leads up to Easter.

Lent was traditionally a time of fasting: Shrovetide was therefore a period of celebration and 'carnival' before the fast. Until the Reformation, when the festival was reduced to one day, Shrovetide lasted for a week or more.

The derivation of the word 'carnival' is a matter for debate, but one theory is that it comes from two Latin words, 'carne' (flesh) and 'vale' (farewell).

The word Shrovetide derives in some way from Old English *scrifan*, to shrive. Shrove-tide, therefore, was the time for being shriven.

Good Catholics are still required to go to confession and communion at least once a year, 'at Easter or thereabouts'. Why these islands should have adopted Shrovetide as expressly 'the time for confessing and shriving' is not clear. But once duty had been done, however, the rest of the day was free for 'feasting and boisterous hilarity'. For centuries, Shrovetide was associated with 'the making and eating of pancakes, door to door visits by children and others who sung to obtain Shrovetide gifts, football, games and sports', including cock-fighting and the even more barbarous pastime of throwing at a cock. As with the Carnival, the height of Shrovetide revelry came in the thirteenth, fourteenth and fifteenth centuries. Some of the traditional merry-making 'survived the restraining efforts of the Reformers and the Puritans' and was 'observed with enthusiasm' till the nineteenth. But by the twentieth 'the making and eating of pancakes is one of the few customs left'.

We have eaten pancakes at least since the fourteenth century, though sometimes under other names – 'Pancake or fritter or flap-jacke' wrote John Taylor in 1634 and Pepys, who enjoyed his food, noted in 1664, 'Home to dinner. It being Shrove Tuesday, had some very good fritters'.

Yet though pancakes have been associated with Shrove Tuesday for centuries, the name Pancake Day is not recorded till 1825.

Pancake eating too has many origins attributed to it. One of the most interesting, coming from Sherwood Forest, takes us back again to the time of the Danish invasion. When the Danes, it is

210

said, reached the village of Linby in Nottinghamshire, the Saxon men 'ran into the Forest, and the Danes took the Saxon women to keep house for them: this happened just before Lent, and the Saxon women, encouraged by their fugitive lords, resolved to massacre the Danes on Ash Wednesday. Every woman who agreed to do this was to make pancakes for dinner on Shrove Tuesday as a kind of pledge to fulfil her vow. This was done, and the massacre took place the next day.'

Gillian Edwards

16: PURIM

The Jewish festival of Purim occurs one month before Passover and therefore falls within the Jewish month of Adar (February–March). It is a time of carnival and fancy dress parties.

Purim commemorates the story retold here. It comes from the Book of Esther and when it is read in the synagogue on this festival, children make as much noise as they can every time Haman (the villain) is mentioned. Besides hissing and stamping their feet, they use football rattles, whistles and even dustbin lids. The aim is to drown Haman's name with the noise.

After their captivity in Babylon, most Jews returned to Palestine. Not all did. Some settled in Susa, the capital of the Persian empire. At the time of the story of Esther, the king of the Persians (and Medes) was Xerxes. When his queen offended him in public one day, he decided to search for another.

Among the Jewish families living in Susa was a very attractive girl called Esther. Her parents had both died, so she was looked after by her cousin, a man named Mordecai. Along with several other girls she was taken to the royal palace when Xerxes was looking for a new queen. As soon as the king met her, he liked her more than any of the others and he decided to give her the crown once worn by Vashti. A great celebration banquet was held and she was proclaimed queen of the Medes and Persians. One thing the king did not know about her was that she was a Jew: that was a secret she kept from him.

Not long after this Mordecai, who had become a royal official, uncovered a plot to kill the king. He told Esther to inform Xerxes, who found that it was true, and the people responsible were put to death. Xerxes was so grateful that Mordecai's loyalty was noted down in the records of the empire.

Years later a man called Haman became the most important official in Persia, and Xerxes ordered everyone to bow to him in respect. Mordecai refused to do this and, as a result, Haman hated him and decided to punish not only him, but also every other Jew in the Persian empire. He persuaded the king to issue a degree ordering that all the Jews be killed on a chosen day. Mordecai was bitterly distressed when he heard this and he sent a message to Queen Esther asking her to plead with the king for the Jews to be spared.

Esther was afraid because the king had not wanted to see her for a month and no one could go to him without first being asked; also, the king still had no idea that she too was a Jew. Mordecai pleaded with her again. 'You're as much in danger as any other Jew. Go to the king. Who knows? God may have let you become queen to do just that.'

Esther asked all the Jews to pray for her and three days later she nervously entered the throne room. King Xerxes saw her at the door, and to her relief, he pointed his sceptre towards her as a sign that he welcomed her. She went forward, and as she knelt in front of him he asked her what she wanted. She replied by inviting the king and Haman to a banquet which she was going to prepare that very night.

Xerxes accepted her invitation and went along with Haman, who was pleased to be the queen's special guest. She invited them to another banquet the next evening. They both agreed to return and, as they were leaving, Haman spotted Mordecai near the palace gate still refusing to bow to him. In his rage Haman had a tall gallows built the next day, hoping to have Mordecai hanged on it.

That night King Xerxes was unable to sleep, so he asked for some of the official records to be read to him. To his surprise he heard Mordecai's name read out: he had forgotten that Mordecai had saved his life some years earlier. Xerxes decided to reward him, so in the morning he told Haman to dress Mordecai in royal robes and let him ride through the city on the king's horse. Haman was angry and humiliated, but had to carry out the king's orders.

The king and Haman went to Esther's second banquet as planned and during the meal Xerxes asked her to make a request.

He promised to give her anything. 'Your majesty,' she courage-
ously replied, 'my request is that I and my people should be
allowed to live! We are about to be destroyed!'

'Who dares to do such a thing?' Xerxes asked.

'There is the man, your majesty,' Esther said, pointing at
Haman. 'He is our enemy!'

Haman went pale with terror as the king stormed out of the
room in a rage. Soon he returned and commanded that Haman
should die on the very gallows that had been built for Mordecai.

Unfortunately the order had already gone out, signed with the
king's seal, to kill all the Jews in the empire. The laws of the
Medes and Persians could not be altered, but the king issued
another decree telling Jews everywhere to defend themselves
against anyone who attacked them. That is what happened and
the Jews managed to destroy all their enemies.

Geoffrey Marshall-Taylor

17: ST PATRICK
(17 March)

In the library of Trinity College, Dublin, there is a book more than
a thousand years old, and the scribe claims that he copied St
Patrick's own handwriting from 500 years before that. It is in
Latin, not very good Latin. The author confesses, 'I am the most
uneducated and least of all the faithful' and he ends with these
solemn words, 'This is my confession before I die.' There is no
reason to doubt that this is Patrick telling his own life-story.

He says the name of his village was 'Banavemtaberniae'. Every
attempt to identify it has its difficulties. An eleventh-century
writer says it means 'Ail Cluad', which is 'The Rock of the Clyde'.

*Patrick may have been born near the Clyde, but we do not really know
where his home village was. It could have been anywhere between the
Clyde and the Severn Estuary. What we do know is that Patrick was
captured by raiders.*

The year was 405. Patrick was a lad of sixteen, just the sort they
wanted. With two of his sisters and many of their neighbours,
they took him back to Ireland, a slave.

His father was a deacon, his grandfather a presbyter, yet he says, 'I knew not the true God.' He means that religion did not mean much, till now when he was in trouble. 'Day by day as I went, a shepherd with my flock, I used to pray constantly, a hundred prayers, and as many in the night again.' He was there for six years, and the most formative in a man's life, from sixteen to twenty-two. Then he escaped, worked his passage on a ship, nearly died of starvation when he got ashore, and at last got back to his own folk, 'who received me as a son, and besought me after all I had been through, not to leave them to go anywhere at all.'

But he was not to be left in peace.

'I saw in the night visions' (*Daniel 7: 13*). A man whose name was Victoricus coming, as it were, from Ireland with countless letters and he gave me one. And I thought I heard the voice of them who lived beside the wood of Foclut, which is near to the western sea. And they cried as with one voice, 'We beseech you, holy youth, come and walk among us once more.' And I was exceedingly 'broken in heart' (*Ps. 109: 16*) and could read no more.

And so I awoke. Thanks be to God that after many years the Lord granted to them according to their cry.

He went to Ireland in the year 432. Before going he needed training. He spent many years at the monastery of Auxerre in France. He says that those who advised him thought his idea of a mission to Ireland venturesome, and doubted his fitness. In those formative years when he should have been learning, he had been a slave. But if his Latin style never came up to standard, he did learn one thing. In those sentences about his dream, he begins with words from Daniel, and goes on to the Psalms. Everything he has left in writing is like that, full of Bible quotations. Bibles were few, hand-copied, bulky. You could not carry one in your pocket, nor often stop to look one up. He must have carried great stretches of it in his memory, taking back to the land of his slavery the truth that makes men free. 'I am ready', he wrote, 'to give even my life for his name's sake. . . . I owe so much to God.' But he does not magnify his attempt to repay. Surveying the achievements of the mission, the Church planted all over the country, the sons and daughters of kings converted to the Faith, he ends with this:

How is it that in Ireland, where they knew not God but worshipped idols, there has come to be a People of the Lord? Say not that it was through ignorant me. It was the gift of God. And this is my confession before I die.

John Foster

There is a legend that when Patrick was explaining that God is one, but also three in one – the mystery of the Holy Trinity – to illustrate the point, he picked up a shamrock and demonstrated that it had one leaf but that three parts made up the one leaf. This, it is said, is why the emblem of Ireland is the shamrock.

His best-known words are a prayer, known as Saint Patrick's breastplate:

> I bind unto myself today
> The power of God to hold and lead
> His eye to watch, His might to stay
> His ear to hearken to my need
> The wisdom of my God to teach
> His hand to guide, His shield to ward,
> The Word of God to give me speech
> His heavenly host to be my guard.

18: PASSOVER

The Passover occurs in the Jewish month of Nisan (March–April) and lasts seven or eight days.

In late March or early April the most famous of all Jewish festivals is held: *Pesach*, or Passover. This marks the escape of the Jewish people from their slavery in Egypt – and in particular, the night when the angel of death 'passed over' the homes of Jewish children, killing only the children of the Egyptians, as God had promised.

Passover is preceded by a thorough cleaning of Jewish homes, to remove every crumb of old food. This is because it is the festival of *matzot* (unleavened bread), and the usual bread and rolls will not be eaten for a week. Any other food which may contain yeast is also forbidden.

The most important and popular part of the festival occurs on the first two evenings. It is a home celebration, attended by many members of each family, and friends are also invited. It is known as the *seder*, and during it a special book called the *Haggadah* is read. This tells the story of the exodus from Egypt, and God's delivery of the Jews from slavery to freedom. Many versions of the *Haggadah* have been compiled through the centuries, some with beautiful illustrations. . . .

The *seder* plate contains a number of foods which remind everyone at the table of the festival's meaning:

* A roasted or baked egg; a reminder of the festival sacrifice brought to the Temple in ancient times.
* A roasted lamb bone; which represents the Passover lamb which used to be sacrificed in the Temple.
* Bitter herbs; a reminder of the bitter lives of the slaves in Egypt. Horseradish is often used for this.
* One or two other fresh vegetables (such as lettuce, watercress or cucumber); reminders that this is a spring festival.
* A mixture of chopped apple, nuts, cinnamon and wine; a symbol of the mortar used by the slaves to make bricks in Egypt.
* Finally, a dish of salt water is placed on the table. This represents the tears shed by the Jews during their long years of captivity.

In this way Jews relive the experience of slavery and freedom, through the eating of these foods and the drinking of wine (everyone drinks four cups of wine). A cup of wine, and sometimes a chair, are also provided for the famous prophet Elijah. It is Elijah whose return to the world, it is said, will herald the Messiah's arrival.

The youngest child present at the *seder* will ask the Four Questions from the *Haggadah*, which begin: 'Why is this night so different from all other nights?' The rest of the *Haggadah* answers the questions – in stories, riddles and songs. It is certainly a night to remember, for adults and children alike.

Douglas Charing

The first Passover is described in Exodus 12. *Sometimes Passover coincides with the Christian festival of Easter, as of course it did on the first Easter. The gospels of Matthew, Mark and Luke suggest the Last Supper was a Passover meal. The gospel of John does not.*

19: MAUNDY THURSDAY

After the last supper Jesus led his disciples to the Garden of Gethsemane. The garden was an orchard enclosed on two sides by a high wall, with the other two sides bounded by a deep ravine. There was almost a full moon, and its brilliancy lit up the scene as though it were daylight.

William Barclay

The story of the first Maundy Thursday when Jesus was betrayed in the Garden of Gethsemane. It can all sound really rather romantic — something from a fairy tale maybe. Perhaps we can get a new understanding of what it was all really about if we bring the story up to date, and hear about the events as if they were being reported by a journalist.

There has been great excitement in this famous city over the past few days. It began with the arrival of the man everybody is talking about in these parts. His name is Jesus Christ.

Although just a carpenter's son this man has built up a great reputation in a very short time and there are many people who will tell of his sensational powers.

The other day Jesus Christ arrived at the gates of the city, riding on an ass.

Never in my years of reporting have I seen anything like it. There was a tremendous crowd to greet him, and his welcome was like that of a popular hero. He showed something of his personal charm too. Within a short time of entering the city he had befriended one of the most unpopular men here, a notorious tax collector.

Since that momentous first appearance the city has been full of rumours, sensational events and intrigue, all of which seem to surround Jesus Christ. There was a violent scene in the temple when he was quick to anger at the sight of the customary market place activities. Wherever he goes in the city there are crowds and excitement and a feeling that unusual things are going to happen. The government have remained very quiet during all this activity. I have it on good authority however that the members of the Supreme Council, the Sanhedrin, consider this man a troublemaker, a disturber of the peace and a revolutionary. There are rumours that spies are collecting information about Christ's deeds and that he will soon be arrested.

And tonight, apparently there was a plot to make sure that Jesus Christ was arrested. Tonight he was having a meal with a group of his special friends. During the meal one of these so-called friends left the group and went to see the members of the Sanhedrin. It is said that he provided them with 'helpful information' and will receive a reward for his services. The name of this man has been released. It is Judas Iscariot.

20: CRUCIFIXION

Strapped to a post,
clothes ripped off his back
he smiled
for they could not hurt him –
he was Christ.

But they whipped him and it hurt

Then came the cross
all shiny and clean
and he said to himself,
'This can't be real. For
my angels will come and take me away.'

But the angels in heaven
were asleep at the time

And he dropped his cross
three times in a mile

Till another Jew had to help him
up the last slope

And he stood there alone
a man without hope.

They nailed him that day
on to the cross, two men-thieves
beside him, the sheep of his
flock.

He was right about one thing, though,
for the angels that day
did come down
and take him away.

Erno Muller

(See pages 264–6.)

Summer Term

21: EASTER

Something happened to convince the disciples that the story of Jesus did not come to an end on the cross. The evidence of the empty tomb and the appearances of Jesus prompted them to claim that Jesus had been resurrected from the dead. It was this event more than any other that convinced the disciples that Jesus was God's promised Messiah . . . .

Can the stories of the empty tomb and Jesus' appearances be explained in other ways? To try to answer these questions, it is important to look at the evidence and the possible explanations. What follows are some theories; you may already be able to work out arguments for or against these theories.

Theory 1 The women went to the wrong tomb on the Sunday morning.

Theory 2 Jesus did not actually die on the cross and managed to escape from the tomb.

Theory 3 The disciples stole the body and later told people that Jesus had been resurrected.

Theory 4 Some other person or persons stole the body, e.g. the Jews or Romans.

Theory 5 The disciples only imagined they saw Jesus, they were suffering from hallucinations.

Theory 6 Jesus did, by some miraculous means, rise from the dead, as Christians claim.

Ray Bruce and Ian Wilson

The following sketch imagines the man who brought Jesus to trial, Caiaphas, having to answer questions about 'the alleged resurrection of Jesus Christ'.

MASTERMIND

The questioner sits at a desk. There is a black leather armchair in the centre of the stage.

Questioner: [*Sitting at table*] Will the next contender take the chair, please.

[*Caiaphas enters and sits in the chair.*]

Your name, please?

Caiaphas: Joseph Caiaphas.

Questioner: Occupation?

Caiaphas: Retired High Priest of Jerusalem.

Questioner: And what is your specialist subject?

Caiaphas: The alleged resurrection of Jesus Christ, AD 33.

Questioner: Mr Caiaphas, you have two minutes to answer questions on the alleged resurrection of Jesus Christ, AD 33; starting *now*: It has been argued that the so-called empty tomb was, in fact, the *wrong* tomb; if this were correct, why didn't the authorities try and find the *right* tomb?

Caiaphas: [*After a moment's perplexing thought.*] Pass.

Questioner: If, as the authorities said, Jesus' disciples *stole* his body, who organized that disorganized group into doing so?

Caiaphas: Pass.

Questioner: And why did the authorities have to *pay* people to say that the disciples had stolen the body?

Caiaphas: Pass.

Questioner: And, if they *had* stolen it, why did so many of them die still claiming the resurrection was true?

Caiaphas: Pass.

Questioner: Others have said the *authorities* stole the body: if they did, why didn't they produce it and stop the resurrection rumours?

Caiaphas: Pass.

Questioner: If anybody *had* tried to steal the body, why didn't the guards stop them?

Caiaphas: [*Tries to think of an answer, but fails.*] Pass.

Questioner: What explanations can be offered for the alleged appearances of the risen Christ?

Caiaphas: Pass.

Questioner: Why was there such a change in the disciples' lives following the alleged resurrection?

Caiaphas: Pass.

Questioner: What other explanation . . .

[*A buzzer or bell is sounded.*]

I've started, so I'll finish: what other explanation can be offered for the alleged resurrection of Jesus Christ? [*Pause*] I'm afraid I shall have to ask you to answer . . . [*Pause*]

Caiaphas: [*Slowly and quietly*] Pass . . .

Questioner: And, at the end of your specialist round, Mr Caiaphas, you have scored – nothing . . . .

Brian Sibley

The 'Mastermind' theme is called 'Approaching Menace' and is available on various LPs, including BBC Records REH 3655 and KPM Records, KPM 1055.

22: BAISAKHI
(13 April)

Baisakhi is both a Hindu and Sikh festival. On it (13 April), Sikhs celebrate the 'birthday' of the Khalsa, the brotherhood of all Sikh men and women. This dates from when the tenth Guru summoned the Sikhs to Anandpur.

The following are the names of the Sikh Gurus. The Gurus were ten in number. Out of respect for their Gurus the Sikhs add 'Siri' before and 'Ji' after the name of each Guru. This is their order of appearance:

1	*Siri Guru Nanak Dev Ji*	1469–1539
2	*Siri Guru Angad Dev Ji*	1504–1552
3	*Siri Guru Amar Das Ji*	1479–1574
4	*Siri Guru Ram Das Ji*	1534–1581
5	*Siri Guru Arjan Dev Ji*	1563–1606
6	*Siri Guru Hargobind Ji*	1595–1644
7	*Siri Guru Har Rai Ji*	1630–1661
8	*Siri Guru Har Krishan Ji*	1565–1664
9	*Siri Guru Tegh Bahadur Ji*	1621–1675
10	*Siri Guru Gobind Singh Ji*	1666–1708

After the death of Guru Gobind Singh Ji, the Sikhs were asked to accept no other Guru except the Holy Book (The Granth). The Sikhs, therefore, call the Holy Book not simply the Granth, but 'Siri Guru Granth Sahib Ji'. The Sikhs bow to the Holy Book because it contains hymns in praise of God. They keep it with great care and wrap it in fine cloth.

The Sikhs were summoned to gather at Anandpur on Baisakhi day, 1699 CE. After morning prayer the Guru addressed the assembly. By now this month, when Indian wheat harvest celebrations were held, had become an occasion upon which the Sikhs assembled together. Sword in hand he made a strange request – the head of a Sikh. The horrified crowd, living in fear of the Mogul armies, had not expected their own leader to make such a demand. Daya Ram at last came forward saying, 'My head is at your service, my true Lord. There can be no greater gain than to die under your sword.' He was taken by the Guru to his tent from which, a few minutes later, Guru Gobind Rai returned alone, his sword dripping blood, to repeat his demand. Amid distressed murmurings Dharam Dass offered his life and was led to the tent. Again the Guru returned alone with his blood-stained sword and again he asked for the life of a Sikh! By the time this had happened five times many Sikhs had fled the assembly, all who remained failed to appreciate the meaning of the Guru's actions, even when he returned at the end of the drama with the five Sikhs alive and well and the blood turned out to be that of a goat.

He had demanded complete self-sacrifice, not to himself as a person Gobind Rai, but to himself as Guru, the one in whom the spirit of truth lived. He had stated in action the belief that the survival of the Sikh faith depended upon the complete trusting obedience of Sikhs.

Now he declared his intention of forming into a distinct brotherhood those Sikhs who were willing to commit themselves totally to the key principle of Truth (*Nam*) and service (*seva*). They were to be the Khalsa, the Pure Ones, a casteless brotherhood.

The first five members were Daya Ram, a Kshatriya, Dharam Dass a Jat or peasant, Mukham Chand a washerman, Himmath a water-carrier and Sahib Chand a barber (the last three were all of the servant caste). The five were initiated into the Khalsa by Guru Gobind Rai and given the surname Singh, which means 'lion', first to remove the caste distinction carried by their former surnames, second to give them a common surname signifying that they were brothers and finally to give them self-respect, hence the choice of the name Singh.

He then laid upon them certain rules of discipline which they vowed, as men who had been reborn, to keep.

Finally, he asked the five brothers (*panj pyares*) to initiate him into the Khalsa, consequently the tenth Guru is best known by the name Guru Gobind Singh. In submitting to initiation the Guru was asserting that in future authority lay not with an individual but with the community and was preparing for the day when, after his death, the Khalsa and the Guru Granth Sahib were to replace the human succession of gurus.

W. Owen Cole and P. S. Sambhi

23: MAY DAY

In pre-Christian times, the Celts celebrated the return of summer in the Feast of Beltane on 1 May with bonfires, song and dance. It is one of the few pagan festivals that the Christian Church failed to transform into one of its own celebrations.

In the olden days the month of May also had its sinister side. 1 May was the start of the second half of the Celtic year, and people feared that witches and evil spirits would try to take advantage of this halfway stage. Gorse was set alight to smoke them out, and branches of rowan (mountain ash) and buckthorn festooned homes and cattle stalls to protect the occupants.

Because her feast day was 1 May, St Walburga, who founded a monastery in Germany in the eighth century, inadvertently became mixed up with the unholy superstitions connected with that date; on Walpurgis Night (the Eve of May) witches rode on broomsticks to ancient places of sacrifice, to hold revels with their master, the Devil. The best known of these 'witch-hills' was the highest point of the Harz mountains in Germany, famous as the scene of the witches' Sabbat in Goethe's *Faust*.

For many years the whole month of May was considered unlucky, not good for weddings – 'Marry in May, rue for aye' – nor for having a baby. Even kittens born this month were suspect – 'May chets (cats), bad luck begets' – and were usually destroyed at birth.

Peter Watkins and Erica Hughes

Perhaps because May was thought to be an unlucky month, many of the traditional customs of May Day are connected with the seeking of good luck.

At this time many villages would seek their share of good luck by dancing round the maypole on the village greens. In some Kentish and Sussex villages the custom is still kept, usually towards the end of May or even early June, when there are plenty of flowers. Traditionally, there is the May Queen, chosen from the pupils at one of the junior schools, who is crowned and decked out in a long white cloak and carries a garland of flowers. Usually she has a number of attendants, even a May King in some places, although it really is her day. She (though she may well not be aware of it) is a representation of the White Goddess, the Earth Mother in her Maiden aspect. In ancient times there was a sacred festival with the Spring Queen and the Corn King, who went into the fields and by their own mating, made them fertile. The ordinary folk would spend the night before the feast in the woods, gathering green branches and flowers to deck a bower for the Queen and King, among other things! When the dancers circle the maypole with its coloured ribbons and bright flower crown they are celebrating the very force of life, and magically binding it into their land. Sometimes after this dance everyone would go out into the fields with garlanded sticks or broomhandles covered in flowers and leap high, singing and dancing, to make the corn grow tall, and the beasts become fertile. Today we have forgotten our pagan past and rely on artificial fertilisers in plastic sacks to make our crops successful.

Marian Green

Labour Day

In July 1889, on the centenary of the storming of the Bastille, European labour and socialist leaders, meeting in Paris, decided to join the American Federation of Labor in pressing for an eight-hour working day. Mass demonstrations in support of this claim were held at the beginning of May 1890. From then on, May Day was used to demonstrate the strength and solidarity of the international labour movement– in other words, working people all over the world.

24: ROGATIONTIDE

Ascension Day, which also used to be known as Holy Thursday, is one of the great festivals of the Christian Year. The Paschal or Easter Candle is extinguished as a sign that on this day Jesus Christ made his last earthly appearance to his disciples, before 'He ascended into Heaven'.

The three days before Ascension Day are Rogationtide – from the Latin 'rogare', to ask or beseech.

On these three days (and on the Sunday before them, Rogation Sunday), prayers are made in Christian churches for God's blessing on the crops. Seaside parishes often pray for fisheries and in city parishes prayers are offered for factories, shops and industries.

Traditionally, in country parishes, the congregation walked (and, in some, still does walk) around the different fields, stopping to pray for each field. This custom was derived from an older one called 'Beating the Bounds' when priest and people walked around the boundary of the parish.

'Beating the Bounds' was introduced into England early in the eighth century, and has remained with us ever since. During Rogationtide, at any period in history, including our own, a party might be seen setting out to trace the boundaries of the parish. At the head marched the bishop or priest, with a minor official bearing the Cross, and after them followed a crowd of persons, including the schoolboys of the parish, led by their master. Most of them held slender wands of willow, like those of May Day, peeled white, and sometimes crowned, a little below the top, with a knot of flowers. At certain points along the route, at certain well-known landmarks – bridge or stile, or oftenest an ancient tree – the Cross halted, the party gathered about the priest, and a litany or rogation was said, imploring God to send seasonable weather, keep the corn and the roots and the boughs in good health, and bring them an ample harvest. At one point beer and cheese would be waiting, provided out of small endowments made for that purpose. A rogation is no more than an 'asking', appropriate to any emergency, war, plague, drought or foul weather. The heathen perambulations of Spring had merely suggested a rogation of a fixed and perennial sort.

Then, beneath the 'Gospel Oak', or at the boulder on the hill, a curious duty was performed. The wand-bearers set to work to beat the landmark with their clashing wands. Suddenly, amid shouts of amusement, they transferred their attack to one of the boys, who offered himself, half-willing and half-reluctant. They rolled him in a briar bush, flung him in a pond, or, seizing him by shoulders and heels, bumped him several times against the boundary stone. Though lucky to escape without a scratch, a bruise or a wetting, the sacrificial victim did not show any great reluctance, for a new shilling was likely to be his reward.

Laurence Whistler

25: WESAK: A BUDDHIST FESTIVAL

Because Buddhism has tended to merge into the everyday life of the countries where it has taken root, few purely Buddhist festivals are to be found. Instead Buddhism has tended to adopt or adapt itself to existing festivals, and in some countries (e.g. Nepal) these are numerous and very colourful. The highpoint of the Buddhist calendar in countries such as Thailand and other South-East Asian countries is 'Wesak', when the birth, enlightenment and death of the Buddha are celebrated. This generally falls on the full moon day of the month of May each year.

'Buddhism' is the word we use to describe the teachings of Siddhartha Gautama, the Buddha.

Gautama was born in northern India about 2500 years ago. The exact place of his birth is said to be the Lumbini Garden, which nowadays lies just inside the border of the little Himalayan kingdom of Nepal. Gautama's father, Suddhodana, was the ruler of the tiny kingdom of the Shakyas. Naturally, he was delighted to have an heir who could follow him on to the throne. And naturally he was not very pleased when a wise man predicted, upon seeing the new arrival, that if he did not become a great world ruler he would become a great religious teacher.

Suddhodana knew that it would be experience of the hard, painful things of life that would turn Gautama's mind in the direction of religion, so he did everything in his power to keep them out of the young prince's life. Gautama was thus brought up in a sealed world of security and luxury. He lived in beautiful palaces, wore clothes of the most splendid materials, ate only the finest foods, and was generally entertained and waited upon in the best style.

Gautama grew up and eventually married a young princess,

Yasodhara, who bore him a son, Rahula. One day, however, he persuaded his groom, Channa, to drive him down to the local village, where he had not been up till then. In all, he was to make four trips to the village which were to change his life totally. On the first trip he met an old man, on the second a sick man, and on the third he met a party of people carrying a corpse to the cremation ground. Not having seen old age, sickness and death before, he was naturally deeply shocked. In fact so shocked that palace life was no longer pleasant or even bearable for him. He became obsessed with the fact of suffering, and obsessed with finding a way of ending it. On a fourth trip to the village, he came upon a possible way of finding an answer to his problem. He met an ascetic, a holy man: one who had given up everything to follow the religious life. Despite having nothing, this man radiated a calmness that suggested to Gautama that he had somehow come to terms with the unpleasant fact of suffering.

So Gautama decided to follow the example of the ascetic, that is, a person who denies himself physical pleasure and comfort. He slipped out of the palace in the dead of night, exchanged his splendid silken robe for the simple orange one of a holy man, and cut off all his beautiful black hair. Then, carrying nothing but a begging bowl for people to put food in, he set off on his great search.

Gautama went to all the most famous religious teachers of his day and learned all they had to teach. In the process, he subjected his body to great hardship and torment. He lived in terrifying forests, burning in the heat of the midday sun and freezing at night; he slept on beds of thorns; sometimes he lived in cemeteries; he starved himself until he became so thin that if he touched his stomach he could feel his backbone. But still he could not find an answer to his basic problem – and he realised that if he kept on that way he would probably die before finding one.

He therefore took a little food – much to the disgust of his fellow ascetics, who promptly left him. Then he sat himself on the 'immovable spot' under a great Bo tree at a place nowadays called Bodh Gaya. He was determined to sit there until he found an answer – or die trying.

During the night of the full moon of May, Gautama passed into deep meditation and gain various kinds of new knowledge. For instance, he saw how to overcome desire, attachment to existence and clinging to false or fixed views. Finally, as the morning star rose, he awakened as from a dream.

He was Gautama no more but The Buddha – 'The Awakened One'. He had seen things as they really are. Sometimes he is spoken of as having entered *'Nirvana'*. *Nirvana* is 'the extinction of greed, the extinction of hate, the extinction of delusion'. Its true nature cannot be put into words; a person must know it for himself in his own heart.

At first the Buddha was reluctant to tell other people about what he had discovered. He felt they would not understand. He was persuaded, however, that there were some 'with but a little dust in their eyes' who might benefit from being told. Thus began a forty-five year teaching career.

The Buddha taught all classes, conditions and types of men and women. The way that he taught is often called *The Middle Way*, because it teaches that we should try to keep to a middle path between all extremes. Soon the Buddha gathered around himself followers ready to give up everything to hear his teachings and put them into practice.

Buddhist Society

26: PENTECOST

In the Jewish faith, the Festival of Pentecost (from the Greek word meaning 'fiftieth') or Festival of Weeks ('Shavuot') is celebrated fifty days after the second day of Passover. It commemorates the giving of the Law by God to Moses on Mount Sinai. (See Exodus 19.)

Pentecost is also the 'Feast of the First Fruits'. The synagogue is decorated with flowers and plants and dairy foods are eaten.

In the Christian faith, the Festival of Pentecost commemorates the coming of the Holy Spirit to the disciples. (See Acts 2.) Pentecost or Whitsunday is sometimes called the birthday of the Christian Church.

'The Big Fisherman' (which might be described as a 'romantic yarn') is a novel by an American clergyman called Lloyd C. Douglas. It tells the story of St Peter and includes this lively account of that particular Pentecost, and should perhaps be read in conjunction with the account in Acts.

It begins with the disciples assembled in an upper room . . .

The massive oaken door flew open and banged hard against the wall. There was the deafening roar of a mighty tempest that swept through the hall. The startled men held to their seats and clung to one another as the rushing wind lashed to and fro. It was as if the world had come to an end! Now tongues of flame stabbed through the storm, coming to rest– torch-like– upon the heads of all present! The glow of the fire possessed exhilarating properties. Some of the men shouted ecstatically. Some wept for joy. Strangers grasped the hands of strangers and gazed at one another in wonderment. Jairus put his arm round Joel, who was weeping. Mencius put both hands over his eyes and shook his head. Joseph of Arimathaea clutched Hassan's arm.

Now the torch-like flames departed and the tempest roared out as suddenly as it had come. Every man was on his feet, all talking at once, loudly, as if the tempest still raged. Mencius, not one to be easily discomposed, was so utterly stampeded that he turned to Jairus and shouted – in Greek: 'This is a most amazing thing, sir!' And Jairus, who didn't know a word of Greek, instantly replied, in that language, 'Surely the Lord has visited us!' Young Joel, listening intently, nodded his head; and when Jairus asked him if he had understood what they were saying he said he had, and added, in his own Aramaic, 'It is true, sir! God Himself has been in this place!'

The roar of the storm had been heard throughout the city. The urbane guests at Levi's Inn had rushed out into the street to see what was happening. They ran up the stairway, arriving when the tornado had spent itself and all the men were shouting joyfully. Crowding into the room they stared at the strange scene.

A tall, haughty man from Crete remarked sourly to his bodyguard, in the outlandish dialect of that country, a curious composite of Greek and Egyptian, 'Bah! They're all drunk!'

Peter, striding toward the door, answered him in Crete's gutteral patois, 'These men are not drunk! They are rejoicing because the Kingdom of God is at hand! The world shall have peace! The slaves shall be freed! The Lord has proclaimed a new day!'

'How do you happen to be speaking our language?' demanded the stranger. 'You are not a citizen of Crete!'

'I am a citizen of the Kingdom of God!' declared Peter. 'And from henceforth that Kingdom includes Crete!'

'You say – all the slaves are to be set free?'

'Yes – and their masters, too. No men can be free while other men are slaves!'

'You should be locked up!' growled the Cretan. 'You are speaking treason!'

230

The controversy was attracting attention . . . .

The street was packed with a huge crowd of bewildered people. The newly-commissioned men, radiant, confident, infiltrated the throng, shouting, 'The Kingdom of God has come for all who believe in Him!' They scattered through the city, spreading the news. They were unafraid. They stopped Roman legionaries on the street to announce the new Kingdom; and the legionaries, stunned by their audacity, did not detain them.

That day, three thousand men in Jerusalem said they believed it and would join the disciples in preparing for the reign of peace.

Lloyd C. Douglas

27: OAK-APPLE DAY
(29 May)

This day is the anniversary of Charles II's entry, amid great rejoicings, into Whitehall in the year 1660; on this account, the day is believed by many to commemorate the Restoration, but it is probably best known as Oak-apple day, commemorating Charles's adventure in the famous oak tree at Boscobel, early in September, 1651. The custom of wearing, on the 29th of May, oak branches, twigs and leaves and also oak galls or apples, when these were obtainable, became very popular.

Twigs and leaves of the oak and oak apples were worn in button-hole, hats, caps and other articles of personal wear or were carried in the hand.

The duration of the celebration of the custom was regulated by a 12 o'clock rule, similar to the 12 o'clock rule applied on the 1st of April.

A. R. Wright

In September 1651 Cromwell's forces defeated the Royalists (including Charles II) at the Battle of Worcester.

Charles II escaped, and, after cutting off his long hair and donning peasant's clothes, wandered among the Midland Counties for more than a month. A reward of a thousand pounds was offered for his apprehension; but, though he confided his safety to the care of more than forty persons, no one was ever found to fail in fidelity, in loyalty, or in caution. His chief hiding place was

Boscobel Wood in Shropshire, and here he one day – a trembling fugitive – lay on the top of a pollard oak (the 'Royal Oak') with a supply of bread and cheese and beer, while beneath he caught glimpses of the soldiers of Cromwell looking about for signs of his presence.

J. M. D. Meiklejohn

He hid for a whole day in the famous oak tree at Boscobel, while his pursuers passed by. On every side were men who would have rejoiced to win the price of catching him. But also on every side were friends, if they could be found, secret, silent, unflinching. Nearly fifty persons recognized him, and thus became privy to his escape and liable to grave penalties.

Winston Churchill

After this adventure, Charles II escaped to the Continent. He returned to London nine years later on 29 May 1660. 29 May was also his birthday.

28: ST JOHN THE BAPTIST
(24 June)

In the Christian calendar, 24 June marks the birth of John the Baptist, six months before the birth of Jesus. The story of John's birth is told in Luke 1: 5–25. *Verse 26 indicates the six months' difference in their ages.*

His preaching is described in Matthew 3: 1–12; Mark 1: 1–8 *and* Luke 3: 1–18.

John was eventually imprisoned by Herod Antipas, governor of Galilee. John had criticized Antipas for marrying Herodias, previously wife of Philip who was the brother of Antipas.

Herodias developed a strong hatred for John the Baptist.

The following extract is from David Kossoff's Book of Witnesses *(see pages 202–5). The witness telling the story in this case is Hesseth, supposedly a retired palace official. He first remembers visiting John in prison, the day before a party at the palace.*

I was curious about John the Baptist. My son had heard him speak a number of times, and had become a sort of follower. Very little impressed my son, who was a regular soldier and a tall, powerful, outdoor sort of man. 'John makes you uncomfortable,' he used to say to me, 'stops you being self-satisfied, and too

232

complacent.' I'd heard how thin and sunburned John was, how he dressed like a beggar-monk, how he had lived most of his life in the desert, in caves or tents.

When I met him he'd been in prison some time. Not so much in a cell or dungeon, as just locked up, to keep him quiet. I was taken down by a young warder. What I didn't expect was the stillness of John. And the remarkable eyes. They burned. They were more open than most people's, and you got the impression that they saw more. My son was right, he made you uncomfortable . . . .

Suddenly he asked me about Jesus, of Nazareth. 'My kinsman,' he said, 'a great man, a prophet sent by God. Jesus, whose birth and coming were foretold in the Scriptures. 'I told him that I had heard of Jesus, that he was preaching regularly, that he was becoming well known, that he was said to be able to heal the sick and cure disease. He listened to me with his whole attention, without blinking. 'Then I am content,' he said.

The next evening was the great party. The biggest ever. Herodias had a great flair for such things. Every kind of rare food and drink, and between courses the most unusual and exotic entertainers. Drugs and aphrodisiacs were in the food and drink. The most sensual music was played, the heaviest incense perfume was burnt. 'There is no such thing as an orgy,' she used to say, 'only freedom. At my parties no one must wish, or desire, or want. Every wish and desire and want must be gratified.' She was decadence itself, a whore-mistress, a witch – for she knew men's minds. In the main, people, in her company, became as rotten as she was. She could bring out the worst.

Well, you know the story of how the night ended. Salome (her daughter by her first marriage) danced for the guests and Herodias told Antipas that the dance was his gift. She hinted that the dancer, her daughter, might also be his for a while. The company roared, although it was not a joke, and Antipas, who was more drunk and inflamed than his guests, told Salome she could have anything she desired. Then there was a silence, and the girl stood staring at her mother, who looked like a mad sorceress. The girl, I swear, was bewitched. She asked for the head of John. Then Herodias turned her eyes on Antipas and gestured that an officer swordsman should be sent to do it immediately.

Antipas, too drunk with wine and pride to retreat, gave the

order and the officer left. Some people started to sober up and wanted to leave, but Herodias forbade anyone to go. 'Not until my husband's order has been obeyed!' she screamed. 'Antipas, son of Herod the Great, must be obeyed!'

So we sat and waited. Then the main doors were flung open and the officer came in with four soldiers, marching. He carried in a shallow silver dish the severed head of the Baptist. The eyes were open. The officer strutted round showing the ghastly head to everyone . . .

John's body was buried by some of his followers.

David Kossoff

29: HINDU PILGRIMAGES

At the times of the great Hindu festivals, many Hindus undertake a pilgrimage. Special merit is obtained by going to some particularly holy place, either a temple or a place hallowed by association with some deity. One writer has described the reason for such pilgrimages:

Pilgrimages to the shrines of India are undertaken for the completion of vows, for the appeasing of the deity in terms of misfortunes, to gain prosperity and good fortune, and as simple acts of devotion to the Lord. Toward the end of life when people are expected to be more godly minded, when the pettiness of earthly life seems to fade away, they are more inclined to go on pilgrimages to sacred spots. After the death of a parent, the son longs for the opportunity to visit Gaya, Benares, and Allahabad to perform there the ceremonial rites for his father and mother.

Benares or Banaras is now known as Varanasi. This sacred Hindu city is on the River Ganges and for about three miles along the river, the left bank is lined with steps (known as 'ghats') where tens of thousands of pilgrims bathe every year. In the city there are about fifteen hundred temples and several mosques.

Indians undertake pilgrimages to holy places such as Benares in order to fulfil vows, to appease deities and so gain prosperity, to accumulate merit, and to show devotion. It is the ambition of every devout Hindu to have his sins washed away in the River Ganges, and at death to be cremated there and to have his ashes scattered on the water.

In *Slowly Down the Ganges*, Eric Newby explains the importance of the river:

It is great because, to millions of Hindus, it is the most sacred, most venerated river on earth. For them it is Ganga Ma – Mother Ganges. To bathe in it is to wash away guilt. To drink the water, having bathed in it, and to carry away bottles for those who have not had the good fortune to make the pilgrimage to it is meritorious. To be cremated on its banks, having died there, and to have one's ashes cast on the water, is the wish of every Hindu. Even to ejaculate 'Ganga, Ganga' at the distance of fifty-five kilometres from the river may atone for the sins committed during three previous lives.

Little bands of men and women who had travelled here together from their villages, some of them very old with skin like crumpled parchment, the women singing sadly but triumphantly, lurched barefooted across the silt. The women dressed in saris, the men in loincloths, they entered the river, dunking themselves in it, drinking, taking it in their cupped hands and letting it run three times between their fingers with their faces towards the still invisible sun.

(See also pages 90–5.)

30: MUSLIM FASTS AND FESTIVALS

Because the Muslim year is roughly eleven days shorter than the Western year, Muslim months do not occur in the same season every year. The dates of Ramadan and the various festivals are shown at the front of most diaries. See also page 16.

Ramadan

Ramadan is the ninth month of the Muslim calendar and special because it was the month in which the Prophet first began to receive revelations from God. To remind them of this Muslims are supposed to fast for every one of the thirty days of Ramadan from dawn (when one can first tell a white thread from a black one) to sunset (when one can no longer do so). This means that they should not eat or drink anything at all, nor smoke, nor have sexual relations during this time.

During this month they should also say extra prayers and try to read the whole of the Quran. They should be particularly careful not to quarrel with friends and neighbours but should try to be particularly kind and helpful.

Fasting

Fasting in Ramadan teaches Muslims to value the good things God has provided for their enjoyment and to remember the sufferings of the poor and the hungry. Fasting is held to develop self-discipline and an attitude of generosity toward others.

All adult Muslims must keep the fast but very old people, the sick and women who are pregnant or feeding a baby are excused. Travellers may eat while they are on a journey but must make up the lost days later on.

Festival of Eid ul-Fitr

At the end of Ramadan comes the festival of Eid ul-Fitr. Muslims put on their best clothes and go to the mosque to pray together. Elaborate meals are prepared and served and visits made to relatives and friends. Children are given sweets and presents and new clothes to mark this happy occasion.

Festival of Eid ul-Adha

The other main festival of Islam is Eid ul-Adha, the festival of sacrifice, which celebrates Abraham's willingness to sacrifice his son Ishmael on God's orders. Through this festival Muslims record their willingness to sacrifice what they hold dear in order to carry out God's commands.

Eid ul-Adha occurs in the month of Dhul-hijja and coincides with the pilgrimage to Mecca. It is celebrated on the anniversary of the day when the Quran, God's revelation through Muhammad, was finally declared complete. Eid ul-Adha is also marked by the wearing of one's best clothes and prayer at the mosque. Muslims who can afford to do so sacrifice an animal and share the meat with their friends and relatives and the poor.

In Muslim countries these two festivals are celebrated as public holidays and shops, offices and schools are closed. Other Muslim festivals include the anniversary of the birth of the Prophet, the death of Ali's son Hussein at the battle of Kerbala and the anniversary of the Hijra (the Muslim New Year).

Richard Tames

PRESENTATIONS

All the following scripts may be used in the form in which they stand. It is hoped, however, that assembly leaders will adapt them to local needs and circumstances, increasing or decreasing the number of participants as required and adding to the visual impact (by means of posters, slides, 'props' and costumes, etc.) where time and facilities make this a possibility.

(See also page 13.)

1: A HUNDRED YEARS AGO

This presentation is adapted from Ordinary Lives, *a vivid picture of life a hundred years ago.*

By encouraging thoughts about education in the last century, it may promote constructive thought about contemporary education.

It is arranged for two narrators, a pompous school inspector, teacher, pupil, woman and reader. It may be more effective if Narrator 1 is male and Narrator 2 is female, but it can be easily adapted for any number and combination of voices.

Narrator 1: From 1870 onwards, all children in Britain were supposed to go to school from the age of 5 to 13. By no means all children attended school regularly, but those who did attend the Board schools (the local state schools) often shocked teachers, inspectors, and visitors alike:

Pompous Inspector: One or two are tidy-looking boys; one has a clean, washed face and a white collar on. The rest are ragged, ill-kempt, and squalid in appearance. Some are filthy dirty, others sickly looking with sore eyes and unwholesome aspects. One or two seem hopelessly dull, almost vacant. In the girls' department it is the same. Everywhere we are met by tokens of poverty and bad conditions at home. Children are pointed to us stunted in growth, with faces old beyond their years.

Narrator 2: Many parents could ill afford to lose their children's earnings and help at home, let alone pay the school fees. (A penny to fourpence a week. This was abolished in 1891.) Some protested by attacking the teachers:

Teacher: I well remember how, early in my career as a teacher, I had to evade sundry missiles thrown at me by irate parents

239

who would rather have had their children running errands and washing up things in the home than wasting their time in school on such a thing as learning.

Narrator 2: The children were unused to the discipline of school life and the first job for the teacher was to instill some obedience and order:

Teacher: Tens of thousands of children in our schools are, I regret to say, grossly ignorant and utterly uninstructed, and the only thing we can do is to look to their cleanliness and give them habits of order, and promote their regular attendance.

Narrator 1: Classes were very overcrowded and noisy:

Inspector: Seventy or eighty pupils in a class are common. Sometimes there is more than one class in a room . . . many of the schools are in noisy thoroughfares . . . the teachers soon acquire the habit of shouting or, as is frequently admitted, of screaming at their pupils.

Narrator 1: One London doctor saw so many teachers who developed bad throats from shouting that he called the complaint 'Board school laryngitis'.

Narrator 2: Most Board schools were mixed, with the same basic lessons for girls and boys. These were the 'Three R's' – reading, writing and arithmetic; the whole class would chant the lesson together under the teacher's instruction.

Reader: The chief business of the infants was to learn to chant the alphabet and the numbers to 100. In the next class they chanted tables and recited even numbers and the odd. When the children were unbearably fidgety, the teacher would tell them to sit up straight; when he could hear a pin drop they would say their rhyme again.

Narrator 1: History and geography lessons also meant learning by heart, and text books provided set answers to be memorised. For example, a lesson on English history to be recited went like this:

Teacher: Who was Henry VIII?

Pupil: Son of Henry VII.

Teacher: What was his character?

Pupil: As a young man he was bluff, generous, right royal and very handsome.

Teacher: How was he when he grew older?

Pupil: He was bloated, vain, cruel and selfish.

Narrator 1:   And so on.

Narrator 2:   Later schools had to introduce additional subjects to qualify for a government grant, and for these subjects girls and boys were taught separately. First, needlework was introduced for the girls. In 1873 school inspectors in London found that girls spent one-quarter of school time sewing. The boys spent this extra time doing more arithmetic, which, from their point of view, seemed most unfair.

Narrator 1:   As a result of this division, as the inspectors reported in 1878, girls could not be expected to reach the same standard in arithmetic as boys. From the pupils' point of view, needlework lessons were not always useful or practical. One woman who went to school in the 1890s remembered:

Woman: We learnt hemming, gathering and cross-stitch. We had to practise these stitches on pieces of material, but we never learnt to make a single garment, nor to use a sewing machine.

Narrator 1:   By the 1890s practical subjects were introduced for boys too – carpentry, farmwork, gardening, shoemaking, drawing, handicraft. All were aimed at training them for a job. Boys were allowed to do cookery only if they lived in seaside towns where they might get a job in catering, but it was not considered necessary for them to learn domestic skills for the home. They were educated to be breadwinners while girls were trained to be housewives. New subjects were introduced to the higher forms of the Board schools, giving boys a far wider scope than girls. Boys could take animal physiology, physical geography, mechanics, algebra, chemistry and physics.

Narrator 2:   Girls were limited to domestic economy and botany. When science was introduced in the 1890s, three times as many boys as girls attended the lessons. The domestic bias in girls' education continued if they trained as 'pupil-teachers' while at school, which meant they could qualify as teachers. Girls had to pass a needlework test, while boys had to reach a higher standard of arithmetic. Girls were expected to reach the same standard in arithmetic by the end of their third year as boys were by the end of the first. As one headmistress said: 'I do not think that the mathematical powers of women enable them generally (their physical strength I dare say has a great deal to do with it) to go so far in the higher branches of mathematics as boys.'

Narrator 1: By the end of the century the opportunities for middle-class girls to get an education had improved. The suffragettes and suffragists, who fought for women's votes and other rights, and the pioneering work of the educational reformers, contributed a good deal to this change.

There were, however, still differences in the education provided for girls and boys. Few girls' schools had science laboratories and government grants for science education before this century all went to the boys' schools; middle-class girls did not learn domestic science because they had servants to do the housework, but they still learnt needlework. Music, singing and dancing were still common in girls' schools, but not in boys'. And in the upper and middle classes still far more boys than girls went to school. Girls made up less than a quarter of pupils in private schools at the turn of the century.

Pupil: But that was last century. Things have changed now.

Narrator 2: The Sex Discrimination Act has, in theory, abolished the distinction in education based on sex. In practice, as a recent report on physics textbooks illustrates, they are still much in evidence.

Reader: 'Physics has no room for girls. That is the message of most modern physics textbooks which promote a clearly masculine image for the subject and positively discourage girls from taking it. In textbook pictures with people in them, men outnumber women often by as much as ten to one.

Where women are pictured, they are invariably doing something trivial, looking pretty or working at the kitchen stove rather than involved in real physics like the men.

Narrator 2: Even today, twice as many boys as girls go to university.

Carol Adams

2: HARVEST: MORE THAN WE NEED?

A presentation for Harvest time, to encourage gratitude for plenty and an awareness of the needs of others.

It is here arranged for four readers, but can be easily adapted for a smaller or larger number.

Reader 1:   In the first edition of Mrs Beeton's famous cookery book (published in 1861), we are told what you need for a picnic.

Reader 2:   A joint of cold roast beef, a joint of cold boiled beef, 2 ribs of lamb, 2 shoulders of lamb, 4 roast fowls, 2 roast ducks, 1 ham, 6 medium-sized lobsters, 1 piece of collared calf's head, 18 lettuces, 6 baskets of salad, 6 cucumbers, stewed fruit well sweetened and put into glass bottles well corked, 3 or 4 dozen plain pastry biscuits to eat with the stewed fruit, 2 dozen fruit turnovers, 4 dozen cheese cakes, 2 cold cabinet puddings in moulds, a few jams puffs, 1 large cold Christmas pudding (this must be good), a few baskets of fresh fruit, 3 dozen plain biscuits, a piece of cheese, 6 pounds of butter (this, of course, includes the butter for tea), 4 quartern loaves of household bread, 3 dozen rolls, 6 loaves of tin bread (for tea), 2 plain plum cakes, 2 pound cakes, 2 sponge cakes, a tin of mixed biscuits, half a pound of tea.

Reader 1:   Even if we don't eat so much today, we still enjoy our food. Think what we might eat on a day out today.

Reader 3:   Hamburger, Mars bar, salt and vinegar crisps, milk shake, another Mars bar, fish and chips, cheese sandwich, salted peanuts, coke, another Mars bar, dry roast peanuts, sausage roll, cheese and onion crisps, another Mars bar . . .

Reader 1:   What some people might call junk food. But still food. Few of us go really hungry for any length of time. And, when we stop to think, most of us are grateful for our food. Nowadays, we may not often say grace before a meal:

Reader 4:   For what we are about to receive, may the Lord make us truly thankful. Amen.

Reader 1:   But we are grateful. Especially at times of the year like Harvest, when Christians give thanks for all the crops that have been 'safely gathered in'. At Harvest Festival, churches are decorated with sheaves of corn, fruit and vegetables – part of the crop being offered to God as a thank-you. In a similar way the Jews give part of their crops to God in thanksgiving for having been saved from slavery in Egypt.

Reader 2:   Each of you must place in a basket the first part of each crop that you harvest and you must take it with you to the one place of worship. Go to the priest in charge at that time and say to him, 'I now acknowledge to the Lord my God that I have entered the land that he promised our ancestors to give us.' The priest will take the basket from you and place it before the altar of the Lord your God. Then, in the Lord's presence you will recite these words: 'My ancestor was a wandering Aramean, who took his family to Egypt to live. They were few in number when they went there, but they became a large and powerful nation. The Egyptians treated us harshly and forced us to work as slaves. Then we cried out for help to the Lord, the God of our ancestors. He heard us and saw our suffering, hardship, and misery. By his great power and strength he rescued us from Egypt. He worked miracles and wonders, and caused terrifying things to happen. He brought us here and gave us this rich and fertile land. So now I bring to the Lord the first part of the harvest that he has given me.' Then set the basket down in the Lord's presence and worship there. Be grateful for the good things that the Lord your God has given you and your family; and let the Levites and the foreigners who live among you join in the celebrations.

Deuteronomy 26: 2–11

Reader 1:   But giving thanks for what *we* have is not enough.

Reader 3:   Twelve million children under five died from starvation during 1978; and then in 1979 – the so-called 'Year of the Child' – the death rate was just as bad. The first task must be to eliminate hunger; for 'while hunger rules peace cannot prevail. He who wants to ban war must also ban mass poverty'.

Reader 1:   We are responsible for other people's welfare, not just our own. In the New Testament, Paul tells us to share what we have. Then the whole world will have a reason to praise God.

Reader 4:   Remember that the person who sows few seeds will have a small crop; the one who sows many seeds will have a large crop. Each one should give, then, as he has decided, not with regret or out of a sense of duty; for God loves the one who gives gladly. And God is able to give you more than you need, so that you will always have all you need, for yourself and more than enough for every good cause. As the scripture says, 'He gives generously to the needy; his kindness lasts for ever.' And God, who supplies seed to sow and bread to eat, will also supply you with all the seed you need and will make it grow and produce a rich harvest from your generosity. He will always make you rich enough to be generous at all times, so that many will thank God for your gifts which they receive from us.

2 Corinthians 9: 6–11

Reader 1: And elsewhere in the New Testament, we are told to use what we are given responsibly.

Reader 3: Then Jesus told them this parable: 'There was once a rich man who had land which bore good crops. He began to think to himself, "I haven't anywhere to keep all my crops. What can I do? This is what I will do," he told himself, "I will tear down my barns and build bigger ones, where I will store my corn and all my other goods. Then I will say to myself, Lucky man! You have all the good things you need for many years. Take life easy, eat, drink, and enjoy yourself!" But God said to him, "You fool! This very night you will have to give up your life; then who will get all these things you have kept for yourself?"' And Jesus concluded, 'This is how it is with those who pile up riches for themselves but are not rich in God's sight.'

Luke 12: 16–21

Reader 1: For what we have received, may the Lord make us *truly* thankful.

All: Amen.

3: A CRUSADE FOR LITERACY

This assembly is focused on the very necessary struggle to improve literacy in the world.

Leader: Most of us take literacy for granted but it's a fact that millions of young people are still denied the chance to read and write – either because there are no schools in their area or they simply cannot afford to go to school.

Voice 1: [*Indicating a picture or slide: an advertisement with a slogan would be suitable.*]

What's in a picture? – what's in a word? We are surrounded

by pictures and words – on TV, in magazines, on posters, in comics, on adverts – for most of us the world is full of clever, colourful messages.

Various voices:	Eat this!	Fly there!
	Cook that!	Try this!
	Buy here!	Drink that!
	Grow this!	Drive there!
	Wear that!	Read this!

(NB   *These might be replaced with actual advertising slogans*)

Leader: Images and words are used to stimulate us:
    to buy
    to desire
    to love
    to think
    to generosity
and to compassion

Voice 1:   The image and the word are designed to have an impact on us – to get a reaction from us. Here is one person's reaction to an advertisement. The advert showed a pitiful child from Asia and asked people to show compassion and support for children like her. Elizabeth Gordon wrote this poem after she had stared at the poster for many mornings while waiting for the bus to school.

Voice 2:   *To a Charity Poster*
Every morning the bus is late;
so every morning,
for perhaps five minutes,
we look at each other across the traffic.
You,
in your far-off, third world land,
looking out of a poverty so utter
that I can scarcely realise
the thousand subtle miseries
the lie behind the word;
and I,
vaguely uncomfortable . . .
not because of what I have,
but because I can't react
to your appeal to my compassion,
but with pitying indignation

at your final exploitation.
I don't suppose you knew – or cared –
that by the click of a shutter
you were transformed
into a million posters
complete with slogan
designed to flaunt your wasted limbs,
your agony, before countless
careless
incurious
vaguely uncomfortable people,
into
just another hypodermic
in the numb and blackened arm
of the first world public conscience.

Elizabeth Gordon

Leader: Something not mentioned by the poet is the fact that almost certainly the person in the poster couldn't read it even if it had been printed in the local language.

Voice 1: In many developing countries most people can't read and write. Even in 1983 children don't have the opportunity you have had of a free education from the age of five.

Voice 3: In Zimbabwe plans are well in hand to eradicate illiteracy by 1988. The government hopes to train 150,000 volunteer teachers from churches, companies and schools.

Voice 1: Meanwhile almost two-thirds of India's population of 650 million are illiterate in their local language. And in many other countries illiteracy rates remain very high: Guatemala, 54 per cent; Senegal, 75 per cent; Tanzania, 30 per cent, Pakistan, 75 per cent.

Voice 2: And in Britain it is estimated that 6 per cent of the adult population is functionally illiterate – that's about two million adults.

Voice 1: Yet article 26 of the United Nations Universal Declaration of Human Rights says the following: 'Everyone has the right to education. Education shall be free, at least in the elementary and fundamental stages.'

Voice 3: More and more countries are making education possible. For example in 1980, Nicaragua in Central America completed a huge campaign where one million people learned to read in six months.

Voice 2:   The whole country was turned into a great school – the government asked anyone who could read and write, however young and however old, to join up as volunteer teachers – thousands were needed for the one million students: on the farms and in the forests, on the coffee plantations and in the factories. A quarter of a million helpers were trained. Many were teenagers. Learning kits, blackboards, chalk, books, lamps, paper and pencils were provided using money from all over the world by governments, churches and groups including Christian Aid.

Voice 3:   The campaign cost £10 million – the price of just one new Tornado RAF combat aircraft – but after just six months, over 75 per cent of the population could read and write.

Leader: In Zimbabwe
In India
In Brazil
In Britain

thousands of adults are learning to read and write – in voluntary groups at local centres. Christian Aid is helping some of these groups, especially those in refugee camps, by sending books, pencils and paper, essential for people who are working to help themselves.

A reflection

Words are like weapons – they are dangerous when misused.
Let us learn to use the power of words
For the benefit of others.
Let us learn to use the wisdom of our traditional books.
Let us help others to share in the excitement and adventure of
   being able to read.

Christian Aid

4: HUMANISM

Humanism is not 'another religion'. It does not have a creed. Not all humanists take the same moral or philosophical stance, nor do they all regard religion in the same way. Some, like Marx, are critical. Others are

248

tolerant, and say they have no wish to entice people away from sincerely held beliefs.

The presentation of a humanist stance in school can be controversial. Many would say that it has no place within a religious education syllabus or an assembly within the meaning of the 1944 Act. However the following is offered for use by those who feel that it is only honest or fair to show that, for many people, there is an alternative to seeing the world in a religious way.

Reader 1: Humanists believe that if human problems are to be solved at all, they will be solved by human beings.

Reader 2: Humanists do not believe – in God. Some describe themselves as *atheists*; they say there cannot be a God. Others are *agnostics*; they say nobody can really know whether there is a God or not.

Reader 1: Humanists believe that life should be joyful and satisfying for every individual.

Reader 2: Humanists do not believe in life after death. But they DO believe that the effect of a person's life can be felt long after she or he has died.

Reader 1: Humanists believe that humans have evolved from simpler forms of life through natural processes taking millions of years.

Reader 2: Humanists do not believe that there is a supernatural power.

Reader 1: Humanists believe that people can now influence for better or worse, the future of life on this planet.

Reader 3: Some humanists play an active part in local Humanist groups which hold discussions and social events.

Reader 4: Many are active in their local areas in such things as getting more attractive Register Offices for people who don't want to marry in church and trying to get better nursery school provision.

Reader 3: Some work for bodies such as The Independent Adoption Society – for people who do not practise a religion who wish to adopt children.

Reader 4: Humanists support and join organisations such as Shelter, Friends of the Earth, Oxfam, Age Concern, National

Council for Civil Liberties, Amnesty International, Howard League for Penal Reform.

Reader 3: Some work as individuals in marriage guidance counselling; as prison and hospital visitors; as local councillors; as social workers, teachers, nurses and doctors; as magistrates; as officiants (the person in charge) at funerals where no hymns or prayers are included.

Reader 1: But why should you help anyone else, if you're not a Christian?

Reader 3: An old lady, a humanist, living in an old people's home, explains in the following way:

Reader 4: 'The brutal fact is, because it helps us. The moment a baby is born it cries for breath, thus starting the battle for existence which continues throughout life. And that baby's existence depends on people. We all *need* people in order to survive. And we all *need* to be needed. Just think what it would be like if nobody ever needed you.'

Reader 3: So humanists help other people for various reasons, but one is almost certainly because they would want others to do the same for them.

Reader 2: Humanists have a great regard for sincerity and fairness. They try to behave responsibly and thoughtfully, and not to reject or exploit anyone.

Reader 3: They use their own reason, and try to think out all the possible consequences of their actions. The main questions they ask themselves are 'Will it make him/her feel better (happier, relieved, more loved)?' and 'Will it hurt anyone?'

Reader 1: Isn't it rather hard work always having to make up your own mind?

Reader 4: It is hard to think out the answers to your own problems, instead of just obeying a set of rules or commandments. But we live in a world which is changing fast, and any set of hard-and-fast rules may soon get out-of-date. It seems a good idea to get into the habit of making one's own decisions quite early in life, starting from a few *really basic* principles. The only 'fixed' point of humanism is happiness, and that's as variable as human beings.

Reader 1: But I still don't see the point in Humanism: what's the end product?

250

Reader 2:   Freer, happier people. A more rational, secure and understandable world. Humanism is a flexible philosophy, always evolving to meet new challenges. It's a method of living, a way of using reason and concern to ensure a better life.

Reader 3:   Humanists value *people* and their *happiness*.

Reader 4:   They value the *power of reasoning* and they value *love* because these make us distinctively human. Humanists try always to give reasons for the values they live by, such as:

Reader 2:   *Fairness* and *justice* because they regard each person as valuable and entitled to a happy and satisfying life.

Reader 3:   *Tolerance* because they accept people's right to hold differing opinions, so long as they don't hurt anyone.

Reader 4:   *Sincerity* because understanding one another is important. Only if feelings are expressed sincerely can people learn how to help each other and to appreciate another point of view.

Reader 2:   *Curiosity* and *creativity* because they extend man's understanding and enjoyment of the world.

Reader 3:   *Independence* because humanists learn to rely on themselves, and to be responsible for their own actions.

Reader 4:   *Freedom* – as much as possible for each, so long as it does not interfere with other people's freedom, happiness and security.

The Humanist Dipper (adapted)

5: FORGIVE-ME-NOT

In the parable of the prodigal son (Luke 15: 11–32), the elder brother's viewpoint might be said to be, 'I longed to forgive, but . . .'

This presentation consists of a number of sketches on the essentially comic situation of longing to forgive or be forgiven but being prevented from doing so by pride.

The characters suggested are a farm lad (overalls, hat and pitchfork), two teachers, two pupils (one with an LP record), a man and woman, another pupil and a games teacher (both in suitable kit). The characters may be altered to suit local circumstances and the farm lad scene used either at the beginning or the end to link with the parable of the prodigal son.

Enter a farm lad

Farm lad: So my brother leaves the farm, runs off to the smoke, gets up to things that 'ud turn my old mother grey, wastes a fortune. Meanwhile, here am I, shifting muck, cleaning the pig-sty, being a good little farmer's son. Bored rigid. Thinking at least one day the farm'll be mine – then he comes home! And I'm supposed to be glad. (*Pause*)

Farm lad: Well I am of course. Glad he's all right. Glad of the help. But if I take him down the pub, what'll me mates think? Working myself inside out and then welcoming him back! I'll look a right prat. (*Pause*) Won't I?

Exit

Enter two teachers, one with two cups of coffee, the other with a pile of books.

Teacher 1: Coffee?

Teacher 2: I thought it'd never be break.

Teacher 1: You look shattered.

Teacher 2: 3L Maths. I'm sure they've got it in for me. Especially that little Gary Tomlinson. Can't think why he's so popular with the rest of them.

Teacher 1: Sorry – this milk stuff's congealed. Was that the kid there was all the fuss about?

Teacher 2: Aerosol on the main corridor wall.

Teacher 1: You said he'd done it.

Teacher 2: Yes.

Teacher 1: And it was really that gang of louts in 4C?

Teacher 2: Well, it still might have been him.

Teacher 1: Did you ever apologize?

Teacher 2: You what?

Teacher 1: Apologize. For wrongly accusing him.

Teacher 2: Are you daft?

Teacher 1: (*affronted*) Pardon?

Teacher 2: Well, I mean, I have enough trouble keeping that lot in control anyway. What would they think if I stood up in front of them and said, 'Look, 3L, I'm sorry for what I said about Tomlinson.'?

252

Exeunt, separately

Enter two pupils

Pupil 1: You don't have to listen to it. Look at it. Scratched right from the middle to the edge.

Pupil 2: I know. I saw it happen.

Pupil 1: You can't play a record like this. Click . . . click . . . click!

Pupil 2: Was an accident. I saw.

Pupil 1: Don't care what it was. It's a valuable record. It's 'unobtainable'. That's what they said at the shop.

Pupil 2: He did say he was sorry. Gave you the money.

Pupil 1: Fat lot of good that is.

Pupil 2: He feels bad about it.

Pupil 1: Good.

Pupil 2: But can't you . . . accept his apology? He wouldn't feel so bad.

Pupil 1: He wouldn't? What about me?

Pupil 2: You'd feel good if you . . . you know . . . forgave him.

Pupil 1: Oh yeah?

Pupil 2: Well, is there any point you both being miserable?

Exeunt

Enter a man and woman, together, arguing

Man: Look, I don't want her to forgive me! It wasn't my fault.

Woman: It was very good of her. She was upset.

Man: Look, if her stupid cat runs straight into the middle of the road, I can't help driving over it, can I? What was I doing? 35? 40? It's not even a built-up area.

Woman: It took a lot for her to say that. She was upset. She thought you were too. *(Pause)* You are, anyway.

Woman: Look, if she makes you the . . . the gift of forgiving you, saying she doesn't blame you, it's the least you can do to thank her. Turning that back in her face, that was cruel.

Man: If I let her forgive me, it's saying I'm guilty.

Woman: You aren't. But it would help her.

Man: Get back in the car.

Woman: Not until you've spoken to her. Thanked her, for what she said.

Man: Even though I'm not guilty, you want me to put myself in the wrong? Huh?

Exeunt

Enter a boy in rugby kit and games teacher in tracksuit

Boy: So I gave away a scrum.

Games teacher: Under the posts.

Boy: And they got the heel.

Games teacher: And touched down.

Boy: And converted. It was my fault. I know that.

Games teacher: Good.

Boy: But I didn't mean to. *(Pause)* And if I want to play for the team next week, I've got to cringe and say I'm sorry? 'Please forgive me sir, I won't give away a penalty next time, sir, please sir'? Is that what I'm supposed to say? Is that what forgiveness is all about?

Exeunt, separately *David Self·*

6: GIVING: ZAKAT

Charity, or the giving of money or time to those in need, is a prominent feature of most faiths. This, the first of two presentation on the theme of giving, considers zakat, *the third 'pillar' or duty of Islam. It has been written so that it can be read by Muslims or non-Muslims. Obviously a Muslim speaker could add to the sequence.*

Narrator: The third pillar of Islam is *Zakat*. The gist of *Zakat* is that every Muslim man and woman, who has any assets, should give two-and-a-half per cent of those assets to charity, and of those who deserve that charity – there is a priority list. The first are the poor, orphans, widows and others in need. That charity can be spent on hospitals, on schools, but it cannot be spent on building mosques. For mosques (places of worship), Muslims have to find funds from elsewhere. Zakat is both a tax and a kind of charity. As the Quran says, Zakat blesses the one who gives, as well as the one who receives. Imagine a very rich man. In front of him kneels a poor man, who owes him money.

Sheikh: So, you have come.

Debtor: *(Bowing low)* Noble master.

Sheikh: You know that you owe me much silver. Much silver.

Debtor: Master, yes. And you know I . . . cannot pay.

Sheikh: So I had heard – which is why I sent for you.

Debtor: Master, if I had but time, I should pay you all that I owe.

Sheikh: If you had time, you would pay me. *(He pauses)* Yes, I believe you. I will give you time. Yes, you may pay me what you owe . . . when you can.

Narrator: And that rich man believes he will be rewarded by God, because he was generous to the man who owed him money – but how much better might it have been:

Sheikh: So, you have come.

Debtor: *(Bowing low)* Noble master.

Sheikh: You know that you owe me much silver. Much silver.

Debtor: Master, yes. And you know I . . . cannot pay.

Sheikh: So I had heard – which is why I sent for you.

Debtor: Master, if I had but time, I should pay all that I owe.

Sheikh: But you have no money. No silver.

Debtor: No, but if I had time –

Sheikh: But you have no money. You are poor. Forget the sum. It will be my alms-tax, my zakat.

Narrator: Indeed, as the Quran teaches, those that do good works and pay the alms tax will be rewarded by God and will have nothing to fear.

7: GIVING: CHRISTIAN STEWARDSHIP

To Christians, 'stewardship' means regarding their time, talents and money as being given to them in trust by God. They are to be used for His work in the world.

This presentation has been adapted from a pamphlet published by the Norwich Diocesan Committee for Christian Stewardship and was designed for delivery by Christians.

Reader 1: We all have the same amount of *time.*

Reader 2: Seven days a week, twenty-four hours a day, sixty minutes in an hour. How we use it is different.

Reader 3: Time must be the most valuable thing we have. We can never replace the time we give.

Reader 4: Each day, do you sleep for eight hours?

Reader 1: Work for nine hours?

Reader 2: Eat for one hour?

Reader 3: Relax for three hours?

Reader 4: How much time do we give to Worship, to Prayer, to reading the Bible, to the work of our church and community?

Reader 3: Doing things for others is a Christian duty. There are always needs in every community for someone to give a little time. There are opportunities for helping the local church as well.

Reader 2: Our Time is a gift from God, given to us in trust to use. We are answerable to God for our use of his gifts. A Christian Steward learns to be definite and disciplined in Time given to worship, prayer and study.

Reader 4: Besides Time, God gives us Talent.

Reader 1: Most of us think of *talent* as something that the other person has got. We think of the great artists, footballers, political leaders, musicians. But we all have talent, even though we may think it very ordinary. God gave us all our talents to use. Our task is always to use our God-given talents in the best way we can to the glory of God.

Reader 2: But do we always do our work to the best of our ability?

Reader 3: Can you read or write, sew, build, garden or one of a hundred other things?

Reader 4: Is yours the ability to listen, to talk, to sing, to smile, to make someone happy?

Reader 3: All these are your talents. It is possible for you to help God's work and the church.

Reader 2: When we work, when we use our Time and our Talents, for others, we may be given MONEY in exchange.

Reader 1: The Church needs money so that it may in turn buy goods and time from others. Much of the work of the church can be done only if the financial resources are provided.

Reader 3: Think about these things:

Reader 1: Do you know how you spend your money?

Reader 2: How much do you spend on essentials?

Reader 4: How much do you spend on pleasure?

Reader 1: How much do you give to others?

Reader 2: If you gave 5p out of each pound to the church, how much would that be?

Reader 3: 25p might buy a bar of chocolate, or a Sunday paper, or it could buy food to save a child from dying.

Reader 1: Listen to what the Bible says about stewardship.

Bible readings related to stewardship: Parable of the talents (Matthew 25: 14–30); *The widow's mite* (Mark 12: 41–4) *The good Samaritan* (Luke 10: 30–7); *The treatment of money* (Luke 16: 1–15).

8: UP AGAINST THE LAW

A sequence designed to inform young people about their legal rights and to provoke thought and discussion about the role of the law (and especially the police) in society. It may be possible to invite a police schools' liaison officer to talk at the assembly that incorporates this presentation, or on another occasion.

This presentation requires two narrators and the following characters:

Upset housewife (slippers, apron)
Police constable
Police sergeant
Youth

Enter the upset housewife, running.

Housewife: Help! Help! Somebody help.

Enter, at a dignified pace, the police constable.

Housewife: Oh, please help. You must help me.

Constable: Don't you flap yourself. I'm here, missus. At your service. That's what the police are for. Ready to help whenever you need us.

Housewife: There's a man in there. In my house. And he's got the children. And a knife. He's going to do something terrible –

257

Constable: Now it's all right missus. You calm down and tell me what it's all about.

Housewife (*still worked up*): I'm telling you. He's in there. He came bursting in, I was slicing some bread, and he pushed me out of his way, grabbed the knife and then he, somehow, he pushed me out of the door and bolted it, and the children, they're still in there. (*She begins to cry*)

Constable: Is there anybody else in the house? Besides the children?

Housewife: No. No. Just the two youngest.

Constable: Do you know the man?

Housewife: No, I've never seen him before . . .

Constable: Well, it's lucky I've got my little radio, isn't it?

He leads her off. Enter the two narrators.

Narrator 1: When trouble happens, we expect that there will be someone around to protect us, to help us. Very often, in an emergency, it *is* the police that we turn to. The law.

Narrator 2: The law protects us in other ways. If you're eating out in a restaurant, you're entitled to a 'reasonable standard' of food and service.

Narrator 2: If the food or service isn't of a standard 'you might reasonably expect', you don't have to pay the full amount of the bill.

Narrator 1: And in England and Wales there are laws about people who work in food shops. They mustn't work there if they have any infectious disease.

Narrator 2: And if they have a cut or sore on their hand, it must be covered with a proper waterproof bandage.

Narrator 1: And all this is so that you, the customer, are protected against disease and infection.

Narrator 2: The law protects you in other shops, as well. If a handbag or wallet marked 'leather' turns out to be plastic, the law will protect you.

Narrator 1: If a new washing machine breaks down the first time you use it –

Narrator 2: If the food doesn't weigh as much as it says on the packet, the law will protect you, the customer.

258

Narrator 1:   And if someone attacks you or steals from you, the law will do its best to protect you and put right any damage.

Narrator 2:   Which means of course that other people are protected by the law if you do anything wrong against them.

Re-enter the Constable.

Constable: And it's my job to see the law is obeyed.

Narrator 2:   But the police do not make the laws. Parliament makes the laws. The policeman only sees that they are obeyed.

Enter the police sergeant.

Sergeant: The law lays down what's right and what's wrong. We have no say in that. We just enforce it – and we have to be fair.

Narrator 1:   Which means that the police must obey the law as much as anyone else.

Enter the youth, with bulging plastic bag and bike.

Constable: Ah ha!

The constable moves to the youth and places one hand on his shoulder.

Constable: Now then, where are you going?

Youth (*putting the bike down*):   Mind your own business.

Sergeant: But it *is* the constable's business.

Presenter 2:   The police work for all of us. They cannot stop crime without information. They must ask people questions.

Youth: Buckingham Palace.

Constable: You what?

Youth: You asked where I was going. I told you.

Presenter 1:   Don't give false information. That only puts you in the wrong. Give your name and address if you're asked. Apart from that, you don't have to answer any other questions, but you should try to be helpful.

Constable: Come on then. Shift yourself.

Youth: Must I?

Presenter 2:   The police do have the power to ask you to move on when you're in the street. And it is best to keep cool and move on.

Narrator 1: Otherwise you can be arrested, for example, for breach of the peace. And there are a number of times when the police have the right to stop and search people.

Sergeant: Exactly. If we think a person has or might have drugs, stolen goods or an offensive weapon about their person.

Narrator 1: It's best to agree to the search.

Narrator 2: But do ask why you're being searched, and remember the answer. It may be important later.

Constable: But so far as you're concerned, m'lad, you're coming down to the station.

Youth: Me? What've I done?

Narrator 2: If you are asked to go to a police station, ask if you're being arrested or detained. Take care you remember the answer. If you are being arrested or detained, you must go.

Narrator 1: If you're told you're being asked to help with enquiries, it is not against the law to refuse, but it may be best to go. Most important is that you keep cool and polite.

The constable escorts the youth off stage.

Narrator 2: If you are arrested and taken to a police station, you are allowed to ask for someone to be told of your arrest and where you are as soon as possible.

Sergeant: For example, you can send a message to your parent.

Narrator 2: Or a solicitor.

Narrator 1: You don't know a solicitor? Ask for the duty solicitor.

Narrator 2: You'll be searched and interviewed.

Narrator 1: But you do have certain rights. One is to say nothing (except giving your name and address). Remember, it's easy to get frightened in a police station and say something that may be misunderstood.

Sergeant: And remember, when interviewing a suspect, we keep to what are known as 'The Judges' Rules'.

Narrator 2: But those are not laws. Only 'recommendations'.

Narrator 1: But they do say that an arrested person ought to be able to talk to a solicitor privately;

Narrator 2: Ought to be made reasonably comfortable;

Narrator 1:   And (if that person is under seventeen), then the
police ought to tell the parents about the arrest; and the
arrested person should not be interviewed unless a parent or
another adult of the same sex as the arrested person (other than
a police officer) is present.

Sergeant (*with a suitable expression*):   Exactly.

Narrator 1:   And if the police do not obey 'the judges' rules',
they may find the evidence they give in court is not allowed.

Re-enter constable with youth.

Constable: Anyway, thanks for your help. You're free to go
now.

Youth: Thanks for nothing.

*Everyone but the youth leaves, one of the narrators taking the bike while
the youth speaks to the assembly.*

Youth: They mess you about. Waste your time. I don't want
anything more to do with them. Now, where's my bike? (*The
youth looks around.*) My bike! Where's my bike? Someone's
nicked my something bike. (*Calling off stage:*) Oi, police! Police!
(*To the assembly:*) It's times like this when you need the law.

David Self

9: GIVE UP SMOKING!

*This presentation is based on a pamphlet published jointly by the Health
Education Council, the Scottish Health Education Group and ASH
(Action on Smoking and Health).*

*It requires three readers and a 'doctor' or 'biologist' and three
'rehearsed' questioners in the audience. Some of the facts and slogans
included in the presentation might also be displayed as placards or
posters during assembly or around the school after the assembly.*

Enter the 'doctor' or 'biologist'

Doctor: As a doctor (or biologist) I know how much pleasure
and comfort smoking can give and how difficult it can sometimes be to give up. But I also know, only too well, how much
damage cigarette-smoking does to health. I have seen too
many patients suffer from the effects of the habit . . . too many

get bronchitis, heart disease or cancer . . . too many ask for help when it's too late. But it's still not too late for you if you stop smoking now. It's the most important thing you can do to improve your health. That's why I've prescribed this assembly for you.

(Exit)

Reader 1:   There's no easy way to give up smoking. Some people manage it without much trouble, but others find it a bit of a battle. Not only a battle to stop, but also to avoid starting again. Even so, it's a battle that over eight million people in Britain have won.

Reader 2:   But why should you give up smoking?

Reader 1:   Smoking kills. There's no doubt about it. 95,000 people in this country die before their time because of smoking every year.

Reader 3:   Out of every 1000 young people who smoke, six will be killed in traffic accidents and 250 will be killed by smoking.

Reader 1:   The average person killed by smoking loses 10–15 years of life.

Reader 3:   Smokers are much more likely to have a heart attack or be crippled by bronchitis. And their risk of getting lung cancer is up to twenty-five times more than non-smokers.

Reader 1:   The chances are that every cigarette you smoke will shorten your life by 5½ minutes.

Reader 2:   So giving up brings immediate results?

Reader 1:   Your risks of a heart attack, bronchitis and lung cancer will get less.

Reader 3:   You won't be so short of breath.

Reader 1:   You'll help that smoker's cough.

Reader 3:   No more yellow fingers and teeth.

Reader 1:   Your breath, your hair and your clothes stop smelling of stale tobacco.

Reader 3:   If you are pregnant, your baby will stand a better chance of being born healthy.

Reader 1:   Your children will be less likely to start smoking.

Reader 2:   And you'll save money. Later, work out how much you've spent on smoking in the last year.

Reader 1:   Choose a date in the next few days to give up smoking.

Reader 2:   Between now and then, spend some time thinking about your reasons for stopping. If you really make up your mind, you will succeed.

Reader 1:   Tell people you are giving up smoking and tell them when.

Reader 3:   The evening before you give up, smoke your last cigarette and throw the rest away.

Reader 2:   So don't worry about the rest of your life without cigarettes – just take each day as it comes. Keep away from smokers as much as you can. Have a supply of things to nibble, suck or chew. Fruit, nuts, sugarless chewing gum. Anything but cigarettes.

Reader 2:   Remember your reasons for being a non-smoker. Put aside the money you save each day. Watch it grow. Never give in. Not even just one cigarette. Be proud to be a non-smoker.

Reader 1:   And now, question time.

(Re-enter Doctor)

1st Questioner: How long before the craving stops?

Doctor: It depends how much you were addicted to cigarettes. Things usually improve in the second or third week, but it may take longer. Don't make the mistake of thinking it's all right to have a cigarette months later. It isn't.

2nd Questioner: What about my weight?

Doctor: Some people put on weight for a while after they give up. This might be because their appetite is bigger or because they are eating more sweets and fatty things.

3rd Questioner: I've tried and failed.

Doctor: This time you know the reasons and problems. Tell yourself that this time you are really going to give up smoking, for good!

Reader 3:   Remember, out of every 1000 young people, 250 will be killed by smoking.

Reader 1:   That means . . . of you [*indicating assembled pupils*] will be killed by the effects of smoking.

10: THE CRUCIFIXION

In the following passage, arranged for three readers, J. B. Phillips'
version of St Mark's Gospel is interwoven with Canon Phillips' commen-
tary on the gospel.

Reader 1:   They took Jesus to a place called Golgotha (which
means Skull Hill) and they offered him some drugged wine,
but he would not take it. Then they crucified him, and shared
out his garments, drawing lots to see what each of them would
get.

Reader 2:   All executions took place outside the city, possibly at
the roadside so that as many as possible could see what happened to those who set themselves up against the power of
Rome. We do not know why Jesus refused to take their drugged wine that was customarily offered to those who were to
undergo the agony of crucifixion. It may be because of his
promise at the last supper that he would drink no more wine
until he drank it new in the kingdom.

Or it may be that Jesus is prepared to accept the total agony of
crucifixion without alleviation. It was customary for the soldiers to share out the garments of men who were crucified.

Reader 1:   It was nine o'clock in the morning when they nailed
him to the cross. Over his head the placard of his crime read,
'THE KING OF THE JEWS'.

Reader 3:   Of the four gospel writers, Mark alone mentions this
particular time for the crucifixion. Mark was probably using the
Jewish divisions of time. John, who says it was 'about the sixth
hour', was probably using the Roman divisions of time. If this
is so, they would both mean that the crucifixion took place early
in the morning.

Reader 2:   It was usual for the crime of the crucified man to be
nailed over his head and in this case of course the chief crime is
that of making himself out to be King of the Jews.

Reader 1:   They also crucified two bandits at the same time, one
on each side of him. And the passers-by jeered at him, shaking
their heads in mockery, saying, 'Hi, you! You could destroy the
Temple and built it up again in three days, why not come down
from the cross and save yourself?' The chief priests also made
fun of him among themselves and the scribes, and said, 'He

saved others, he cannot save himself. If only this Christ, the king of Israel, would come down from the cross, we should see it and believe!' And even the men who were crucified with him hurled abuse at him.

Reader 3: Two bandits who were crucified at the same time may have been guerrilla fighters, part of Barabbas' party perhaps, or they may have been ordinary highway robbers. The chief priests could not restrain their mockery, even though it was not public. Jesus' fellow-sufferers join in the general derision.

Reader 1: At midday darkness spread over the whole countryside and lasted until three o'clock in the afternoon.

Reader 2: This sudden darkness caused by a sandstorm is not uncommon in some parts of the world and one of the frightening things about it is that one has no knowledge of how long it is going to last.

Reader 1: At three o'clock Jesus cried out in a loud voice, 'My God, my God, why did you forsake me?' Some of the bystanders heard these words which Jesus spoke in Aramaic (*Eloi, Eloi, lama sabachthani?*) and said, 'Listen, he's calling for Elijah!'

Reader 3: The quotation at the end of the period of three hours of darkness is from Psalm 22 and was shouted in a loud voice. The words in Aramaic sound to bystanders roughly like a cry for Elijah.

Reader 1: One man ran off and soaked a sponge in vinegar, put it on a stick, and held it up for Jesus to drink, calling out, 'Let him alone! Let's see if Elijah will come and take him down!' But Jesus let out a great cry, and expired. The curtain of the Temple sanctuary was split in two from the top to the bottom.

Reader 2: One of the peculiar tortures of crucifixion was the appalling thirst which it produced. One of the bystanders held up a sponge soaked in the rough wine of the soldiers for Jesus to drink. Whether it was this man or another of the bystanders who made the next remark we don't know.

But before Jesus could, even if he would, accept such relief he cried out in a loud voice and died. The implication is that this was no feeble whimper of a totally exhausted man but a great shout, possibly even of triumph, and he deliberately handed back his spirit to his Father.

Reader 1: And when the centurion who stood in front of Jesus saw how he died, he said, 'This man was certainly a son of God!'

Reader 3: The centurion had no doubt seen many men die but there was something special in the way Jesus gave up his spirit. Exactly what the centurion's remark meant we do not know. It may well be that the soldier recognized that this was the death of someone extraordinary. Possibly he had read the placard over Jesus' head and felt that the claim that Jesus had made was, in some degree, true.

Reader 2: Other witnesses of the actual death of Jesus were Mary from Magdala, Mary the mother of James (the less or the little) and Joses. There were also other women who had followed Jesus to Jerusalem to be near him at his tragic end.

Reader 1: There were some women there looking on from a distance, among them Mary of Magdala, Mary the mother of the younger James and Joses, and Salome. These were the women who used to follow Jesus as he went about in Galilee and look after him. And there were many other women who had come up to Jerusalem with him.

J. B. Phillips

(See also page 218.)

11: UNWELCOME NEWS

This script was originally written as an introduction to the teaching of the Old Testament prophet, Amos. About 750 BC, he was called to point out to the people of Israel what was wrong with their lives. A somewhat craggy shepherd, he preached in the cities where he took wool (and also fruit) for sale.

It may be used in assembly to introduce a series of readings about Amos or to make the more general point that we are often reluctant to listen to unattractive messages, no matter how wise they are.

It works well in assembly if it is first explained to those present that they are a studio audience present at the recording of a television chat show. A floor manager should be appointed. When he or she puts both hands together above his or her head, the audience should applaud. The moment the floor manager lowers both hands, the applause should stop instantaneously. This should be rehearsed two or three times before the 'recording' begins.

Besides the floor manager, it requires an announcer, the chat show host (Chris Clueless) and the 'prophet', Murdoch MacDonald McDoom. The atmosphere will be helped if it is possible to herald the entry of each character with a cymbal or drum roll or with chords on an electric organ.

Cymbal, drum roll or organ chord

Announcer: . . . And now, from the centre of swinging London *(or local place name)* we present another edition of 'The Clueless Chat Show'.

Fanfare as before.

Announcer: And now here's your host, the man who's never clueless, Chris Clueless.

Floor manager signals for applause; fanfare Enter Chris Clueless.

Clueless: *(Quick patter)* Hi, hullo and howdey! Gr-r-r-eat to be with you. Yes it is, really g-r-r-r-eat! And it's a great, great show tonight, yes, 'cause I've got some great, great guests, and you're just going to love meeting them, yes you really are, but first a Scotsman from one of the distant western isles who's making quite a name for himself as a preacher in, wait for it *(sniggers)*, yes, London's sexy Soho. And if you'd spent all your life up a mountain talking to sheep, you'd want to visit Soho, wouldn't you? *(Pause for laughter)* Seriously though folks, would you put your hands together please for – Murdoch MacDonald McDoom!

Floor manager signals for applause; fanfare. Enter McDoom.

Clueless: Gr-r-r-eat to have you with us, Murdoch.

McDoom: *(Matter-of-fact)* Aye, it is. *(Pause)*

Clueless: It's great to be here, you mean?

McDoom: No. It's great for you to have me here. *(Pause)* It's a chance, d'y' see, for you to hear ma message.

Clueless: Well, that brings me to my first question, Murdoch, and *(sniggers)* I'm sure we're all dying to know, just what is that message?

McDoom: *(Again, very matter-of-fact)* You're doomed. Aye, you're all doomed.

Clueless: Doomed? *(Imitating McDoom)* Doomed? *(Pause)* Why are we doomed?

McDoom: Because of the evil you do. The terrible evil.

Clueless: *(Imitating him)* Terrrrrible evil?

McDoom: I'll tell ye – since I've bin in London *(or . . . . .)* I've seen such things. There's fraud going on, no end of crooked deals; and in the courts, why, if you're rich, you can buy yourself a barrister who'll get you off whether you're innocent or not. And the rich – they nay lift a finger to help the poor –

Clueless: *(Laughing nervously)* This is all getting just a bit heavy –

McDoom: It's the truth. And for this, an' all your evil an' immorality, you're doomed.

Clueless: But life is for living; have a good time, do what you like, enjoy yourself.

McDoom: That way you depart from God's ways and His commandments.

Clueless: Yes well, I mean, I don't go to church myself, but there's plenty who do, and sincerely, I mean, I've nothing against them and well, they're not doomed, surely?

McDoom: Aye. Some o' them, they are. They go to the kirk, and they do no more mean what they say than you do.

Clueless: *(Trying to cheer up the chat)* Yes, well, I mean no. What I mean is, tell us, Murdoch, if we are really so bad, I mean just suppose there is going to be all this doom, tell me, just exactly what will it be like?

McDoom: If we're all so stupid as not to heed God's commands, we'll be destroyed. Simple as that.

Clueless: Oh surely now, come, surely we're not going to be struck by thunderbolts from heaven?

McDoom: Did you nivver hear of yon atomic bomb? And the missiles? And the neutron bomb that'll leave this pretty studio as safe and just destroy the folk in it?

Clueless: *(Uncomfortable pause)* Yes, well. But surely we aren't the ones who'll suffer? We're not the worst, are we audience?

(The audience may respond.)

268

McDoom: Aye well, the Russians are bad.

Clueless: I'm glad to hear it.

McDoom: And the Americans.

Clueless: Yes, well, but I'm –

McDoom: And the Arabs and the Israelis. And the Scots.

Clueless: The Scots? You think you're doomed?

McDoom: Aye. There's sinners enough in Scotland.

Clueless: But you're Scottish.

McDoom: That does na' stop me seeing our faults.

Clueless: Well, we're all very glad to hear that, aren't we?

McDoom: Mind you, we're not as bad as the English.

Clueless: *(Roused)* Oh now, that's –

McDoom: There's many a sinner in England.

Clueless: *(Angry)* Show me one.

McDoom: There's yourself.

Floor manager signals for applause.

McDoom: There's plenty more in yon audience – Especially the teachers. There's plenty o' things wrong in their lives. And the pupils [or students] too. There's many o' them with sins against the Lord. Those who've so-called 'borrowed' things that didna belong to them, those who've let their friends down or enjoyed a bit o' bullying, and those who are sitting there all smugly now, thinking it's nothing to do with them . . .

Clueless: That's quite enough, quite enough, thank you, Murdoch McDoom.

Fanfare. Clueless signals to the Floor manager to hustle McDoom out of the way.

Assembly leader: The trouble with a preacher or prophet, like Murdoch MacDonald McDoom, is to know how to take him. So long as he's not talking to us, directly, it's possible to treat him as just a bit of a laugh; a comic eccentric, out of touch. Maybe a bit of a spoil-sport. But when preachers talk directly to you, then how do we react? As often as not, we become embarrassed and we ignore their message.

David Self

12: EAT TO LIVE!

It is normally a middle-aged preoccupation to be concerned with a diet that might prolong life. In fact, healthy eating habits are best established in one's youth. They are not expensive and may help to counteract both the high consumption of 'junk food' and unhealthy slimming 'fads'.

Reader 1:   Your everyday choice of food can be a key factor in the health of your heart. And if you are choosing food for the family, you've got their hearts in your hands too. So beware of eating the wrong foods and putting on too much weight. The more overweight you are, the more likely you are to get high blood pressure or diabetes, both of which can lead to heart attacks. So take the experts' advice and make an effort to keep your weight down. For most people it's all too easy to put on weight. This might be because it runs in the family – whatever you eat seems to turn straight to fat. Or perhaps you aren't taking enough exercise to burn up the calories in your food.

Reader 2:   But the most likely reason is that you are simply eating far too much of the wrong sorts of food. In other words, too many fatty and sugary foods. These are loaded with calories. Did you know that just one ounce of butter or margarine contains more calories than half a pound of potatoes? And two teaspoons of sugar contain nearly as many calories as a quarter pound of peas. So the best way to keep your weight down is to cut down on the amount of fat and sugar in your daily diet.

Reader 3:   But how do you do that?

Reader 2:   Eat less fat!

Reader 1:   The fat in your food is not only responsible for those extra inches on your waistline. It can also push up your blood cholesterol level. Cholesterol is one of the natural substances in the blood. It is mostly made from the fat in the food we eat. If there's a lot of fat in your diet you may have a high level of cholesterol in your blood.

This can accelerate the build up of atheroma that eventually leads to heart disease. So the higher the level of cholesterol in your blood, the greater the risk of heart trouble. The best thing to do is to cut down on the total amount of fat you eat by up to a quarter.

Reader 3: So I must eat less meat?

Reader 2: Try fish or vegetable dishes. When you do eat meat, choose a leaner cut if you can – it's worth the extra cost. Or eat chicken, which has less fat than other meats and is usually cheaper. Always cut the fatty bits off meat.

Reader 1: Grill, don't fry.

Reader 2: Buy skimmed or semi-skimmed milk instead of full-fat milk. And try yoghurt instead of cream and use less lard or oil in cooking.

Reader 3: You may have heard of *saturated* fats and *unsaturated* fats. The difference between them is their chemical make-up. They are all made up of basic substances called fatty acids. Some of these are saturated fatty acids (or *saturates*). The rest are unsaturated and include a special group called poly-unsaturated fatty acids (or *polyunsaturates*). All the different fats we eat are made up of different combinations of different fatty acids. Most are high in saturates, but some are high in polyunsaturates.

Reader 1: Dietary experts believe that saturates are the main enemy so far as the heart is concerned. Too much fatty food high in saturates can push up your blood cholesterol. And that pushes up your chances of getting heart disease.

About half the fat that most people eat is rich in saturates. Experts believe that we should cut the amount of saturated fats we eat by up to a half.

Reader 2: Remember, whenever you can, choose food *low in saturates* (sometimes labelled *high in polyunsaturates*). Look for margarines and cooking oils labelled 'high in polyunsaturates'.

Reader 3: So what do I eat?

Reader 1: Eat more fibre.

Reader 3: *Fibre* is the name given to a whole range of complex plant substances. They pass right through the intestines without being absorbed into the body. By providing *roughage*, fibre not only aids digestion and helps prevent constipation. It also seems to stop too much fat and sugar getting into the bloodstream too quickly.

And some scientists believe that a high-fibre diet can help keep the blood cholesterol down. What's more, fibre can give satisfying bulk to a meal without adding too many calories.

Fibre comes mainly from bread, cereals, potatoes, peas, leafy vegetables and fruit. All in all, it is the single most important form of food likely to be lacking in your everyday diet.

Reader 2: Remember there is no fibre at all in any food which comes from animals, like meat, eggs and dairy products.

Reader 1: It's not difficult to put fibre in your diet. You simply need to eat more bread, including some wholemeal bread, and potatoes; choose a high-fibre breakfast cereal containing wholegrain or bran; and eat plenty of fruit and vegetables.

Reader 3: Anything else?

Reader 1: Eat less sugar.

Reader 2: Not because sugar is especially harmful to the heart but because it is so tempting that it is difficult not to eat too many calories. Too many calories mean you get fat – and that can be bad for your heart.

Nobody needs sugar. It has no nutritional value other than its energy content. And we can get all the energy (calories) we need from the other food we eat. So try to reduce the amount of sugar you eat by at least a half.

Start by cutting down on sweets, chocolates, soft drinks, jams and other preserves and cakes or pastries. Just have them as an occasional treat. Try drinking your tea and coffee without sugar. Cut down gradually by about half a teaspoon a month. You'll soon get used to not using it.

Reader 3: So that's it?

Reader 2: No, eat less salt.

Reader 1: Most of us eat far more salt than we need. First of all, we buy food that already contains a lot of salt – meat, bacon, sausages, butter, cheese, tinned vegetables, bread and cereals. Then we add more salt when we cook it. And finally we sprinkle more salt on to it when we eat it. Some experts believe that this high intake of salt may be putting up the nation's blood pressure. You can reduce this risk by simply cutting down on the amount of salt you eat.

Reader 3: So that's the way to eat?

Reader 1: If you want to be healthy –

Reader 2: – and fit –

Reader 1: – and not fat –

Reader 2:   – that's the way to eat!

Based on a booklet published by the Health Education Council

13: SELF-SACRIFICE

The dictionary defines self-sacrifice as 'going without things one would like in order to help someone else'.

This sequence of sketches is designed to provoke questions about why some people are prepared to make sacrifices and which sacrifices are worthwhile.

The characters may be altered to suit circumstances. Those suggested are Sebastian and Angela (two 'upper-class' dreamboats, in love with each other; she perhaps wears a stole or fur, he carries a box of chocolates); Ethel and Elsie, two old ladies with shopping; John and Jean, two teachers; and two pupils.

Enter Angela and Sebastian, walking dreamily along, arm in arm.

Angela: Sebastian!

Sebastian: Yes?

Angela: It was a lovely meal. Thank you so much, darling.

Sebastian: *(offering her a chocolate)* Have a Minty-choc.

Angela: A what?

Sebastian: A 'wafer-thin' Minty-choc.

Angela: Oh. No. No. I've given them up. For Lent.

Sebastian: Lent?

Angela: You know. 'Forty days and forty nights'. You have to give up something you like during Lent.

Sebastian: So poor little Angela is depriving herself of Minty-chocs?

Angela: *(quite serious)* Just for Lent. But it's quite a sacrifice, you know.

They walk off.

Enter two old ladies, with shopping baskets.

Elsie: Ethel, you finished your shopping then?

Ethel: *(vaguely)* I think I've got everything.

273

Elsie: Coming for the bus then?

Ethel: No.

Elsie: It'll be dinner time.

Ethel: *(still vague)* Yes.

Elsie: You not going home for your dinner?

Ethel: I'm going to the church hall.

Elsie: For dinner? Is it free?

Ethel: It's a what-d'you-call it.

Elsie: A what?

Ethel: A famine lunch.

Elsie: What's that when it's at home?

Ethel: I think it's soup and a bit of bread.

Elsie: Oh, I couldn't do with that. Meat and two veg, that's what I have. Not a proper meal unless there's a bit of meat. [*Pause*] Is it cheap then?

Ethel: You pay as much as you can.

Elsie: You never!

Ethel: It's for charity.

Elsie: Oh! But you don't have to starve yourself, just to give to charity.

Ethel: It makes you think though. How people in them other countries live. Just a bit of soup. And bread.

Elsie: No one could live on that. Anyway, you'll be hungry.

Ethel: Yes.

Elsie: But what's the point?

Ethel: It makes you think, you know.

They walk off in opposite directions.

Enter two teachers, in conversation.

Jean: I tell you, it was in the paper. This morning.

John: What was?

Jean: Those terrorists. That boy they've got.

John: Oh that. I heard it on the radio.

Jean: Did you hear what his mother said?

John: Mm.

Jean: She wants them to kill her if only they'll let him go.

John: Wonder if she means it.

Jean: I think she does.

John: I must go. The bell'll be going in a minute.

Jean sighs deeply

John: Which lot have you got this afternoon?

Jean: Double history with the Fifth. Then RE with 2M. Don't know what I'm going to do with them.

John: Well, talk about that woman. Offering her life instead of someone else's. And get them to think about being in real danger, and then someone else offering to take their place.

Jean: Selfish lot would just say yes.

John: But would they really?

[*Exeunt*]

A bell rings. Enter two pupils.

Pupil 1: See you at four o'clock?

Pupil 2: Can't today. I'm going round to old Ma Holden.

Pupil 1: Who? That old Ethel woman?

Pupil 2: It's her birthday. I've got her a present.

Pupil 1: But you're hard up.

Pupil 2: She deserves something. Living on her own.

John: [*entering*] Stop gossiping, you lot, into your classes.

Pupil 1: What're you giving her?

Pupil 2: Oh, nothing much. Just a box of Minty-chocs.

[*Exeunt*]

David Self

14: CHRISTIAN AID WEEK

Christian Aid is a division of the British Council of Churches which aims to provide aid for the poorer nations of the world, for refugees and disaster victims. Christian Aid Week is the third week in May. (See page 281.)

This presentation requires a leader and six other readers.

Reader 1: Weary, she stumbles on,
Bearing the grudge of an alien race,
Treading the path where the others have gone,
Regarding the way with a tear-stained face.

The sun shines hot
On the dusty, hard track,
For with the refugees' lot
There is no turning back.

Reader 2: No turning back.

Reader 3: The woman in that poem has left home.

Reader 2: No turning back.

Reader 3: She hasn't packed her bags.

Reader 2: No turning back.

Reader 3: She has no picnic meals with her.

Reader 2: No turning back.

Reader 3: Her husband has been killed.

Reader 2: No turning back.

Reader 3: She must walk now into a new country, a new home, where she hopes she and her children will be free.

Reader 2: No turning back.

Leader: Each year thousands of ordinary people make a decision to leave their home and country. They become refugees. In time of war many thousands become refugees. Whenever there is political unrest many may become refugees. When people move like this to another country, they have an immediate need for food, shelter, clothing and medical care. Listen to some words in the Bible.

Reader 4: When an alien settles in your land you shall not oppress him. He shall be treated as a native born among you, and you shall love him as a man like yourself because you were aliens in Egypt. I am the Lord your God.

(Leviticus 19: 33)

Reader 5: There are many parts of the world where unhappy people, men, women and children, leave everything they have to walk into another country to freedom.

If there have been any recent reports of refugees in the news, use these as illustrations and read one or two short reports from the newspapers.

276

Reader 6: In some parts of the world, countries have guarded their borders so that no one can leave and walk to freedom. Very often people who protest in these countries are shut up in prisons or labour camps.

Leader: Whenever and wherever there are violent struggles in the world, ordinary people leave their homes and are then in desperate need of food, clothing and shelter. Two organisations have long been at work in the world's trouble spots. They are the Red Cross and the United Nations High Commissioner for Refugees. These two organisations plan the programme so that the refugees are fed and some shelter is provided. Clothing, education, medical care and advice on what to do all come at a later stage.

Reader 1: Christian Aid has given help to many refugees throughout the whole of its history. In fact it was first formed to help the thousands of refugees after the Second World War.

Reader 2: Christian Aid gives grants today to many of the churches overseas to help them cope better with the problems faced by refugees.

Reader 3: Christian Aid gives grants to a refugee service in Kenya run by the churches. Many refugees from Rwanda, Uganda and Ethiopia have been helped to settle down, to find jobs and to build a new life for themselves. This is not at all easy in African cities where there are already thousands of un-employed people from the rural areas of the country.

Reader 4: Christian Aid gives grants to a refugee service in Botswana run by the churches. In South Africa, where many political changes are going on, people are constantly on the move. There is an increasing number of school students leaving South Africa to search for a decent education else-where in the world. It is not easy for black children to get a good education in South Africa.

Leader: As long as people hunger,
As long as people thirst,
And ignorance and illness
And warfare do their worst,
As long as there's injustice
In any of God's lands,
I am my brother's keeper
I dare not wash my hands.

John Ferguson

277

That is why during this week many people from the local churches will be out in the streets with tins and delivering envelopes from door to door, collecting money which will go towards several hundreds of projects in many parts of the world. Every project aims at meeting the needs of people who have not been given the same chances as we have of living in a very rich country.

Many Christians use this prayer, the prayer of St Francis:

Lord, help us to work for peace.
Where there is hatred, let us show love;
Where there is injury, pardon;
Where there is discord, union;
Where there is doubt, faith;
Where there is darkness, light;
Where there is sadness, joy;
Where there is despair, hope;
For you and for everyone.   Amen.

15: SUMMERTIME

Parson Woodforde was an eccentric clergyman who lived in the village of Weston Longville in Norfolk in the eighteenth century. He thoroughly enjoyed life but usually remembered to give thanks for the blessings he received.

This presentation is adapted from his famous Diary of a Country Parson *and is arranged for two readers though it could easily be given by one person. It may be used as a reminder that clergymen can enjoy life, as a celebration of holidays and good weather, or as an entertainment in its own right.*

Narrator: June 4th did not begin well for Parson Woodforde.

Woodforde: My tooth had pained me all night, so I got up a little after 5 o'clock this morning, and sent for one Reeves, a man who draws teeth in this parish; and he came about seven. He drew my tooth but shockingly bad indeed. He broke away a great piece of my gum and broke one of the fangs of the tooth. It gave me exquisite pain all the day after, and much pain. I gave the old man that drew it two shillings and sixpence however, but he is too old I think to draw teeth. He can't see very well.

Narrator: Parson Woodforde did not get much rest the next night either.

Woodforde: Very much disturbed in the night by our dog, which was kept within doors tonight. I was obliged to get out of bed naked twice or thrice, to make him quiet. At last I had him into my room, and there he emptied himself all over the floor.

My face is much swelled today, but my tooth is much easier than yesterday.

Narrator: Parson Woodforde never shrank from entertaining his friends and neighbours. Indeed, evenings at Weston Long-ville Parsonage were quite merry affairs, and the Rector saw to it that his guests were well fed, even if they did not always appreciate it.

Woodforde: Mr du Quesne, Mr Donne and sister, Mr Bodham, Mr and Mrs Howes and Mrs Davy came to my house. For dinner, I gave them half a dozen of my own fine tench (taken out of my pond in the yard) stewed, a rump of beef boiled, and a goose roasted, and a pudding.

Mrs Howes found great fault about many things especially the cooking of the fish. Mrs Davy fell downstairs, Miss Donne swallowed a barley corn with its stalk, and many other accidents happened, but none very bad.

Narrator: Parson Woodforde did find time to get on with his job.

Woodforde: I read prayers and preached this morning, at Weston Church.

Narrator: But there were other things to do.

Woodforde: I brewed a vessel of strong beer today. My two large pigs, by drinking some grounds out of the barrell, got so amazingly drunk by it, that they were not able to stand and appeared like dead things almost. I never saw pigs so drunk in my life.

Narrator: Things weren't much better the next day.

Woodforde: My two pigs are still unable to walk yet, but they are better than they were yesterday. They tumble about the yard and can by no means stand at all steady yet.

In the afternoon my two pigs were tolerably sober.

Narrator: In September, Parson Woodforde went on holiday to Yarmouth, taking his nephew, Bill, along with him.

Woodforde: Bill breakfasted with me at Weston today and we are travelling by coach to Yarmouth. We must pay the turnpike one shilling and sixpence.

Narrator: Uncle and nephew seemed to like Yarmouth.

Woodforde: My nephew is highly pleased with the town of Yarmouth. We have taken a walk on the quay and viewed some Dutch vessels. The Dutch are very droll fellows to look at, badly dressed people with monstrous large trousers and many with large wooden shoes. We got on board an English vessel in port, and were well treated with wine and gin, etc.

The sailors behaved very civilly indeed towards us, and I gave them all the silver I had, namely one shilling.

Narrator: When Parson Woodforde's holiday came to an end, he returned to his home at Weston Longville, to give thanks for his holiday.

Woodforde: Reached Weston safely, and found things in decent order. Have never known such fine weather at this season of the year, and I give thanks to God for such glorious weather.

Parson Woodforde (adapted)

ADDRESSES

Age Concern, Bernard Sunley House, 60 Pitcairn Road, Mitcham, Surrey CR4 3LL.

Amnesty International, 5 Roberts Place, off Bowling Green Lane, London EC1 0EJ.

Board of Deputies of British Jews, Woburn House, Upper Woburn Place, London WC1 0EP.

The Buddhist Society, 58 Eccleston Square, London SW1V 1PH.

CND, 11 Goodwin Street, London N4 3HQ.

Catholic Fund for Overseas Development (CAFOD), 21a Soho Square, London W1V 6NR.

Christian Aid, PO Box 1, London SW9 8BH.

Christian Education Movement, 2 Chester House, Pages Lane, Muswell Hill, London N10 1PR.

Commission for Racial Equality, Elliott House, Allington Street, London SW1.

Help the Aged, 157 Waterloo Road, London SE1.

Hindu Centre, 39 Grafton Terrace, London NW5 4JA.

Minaret House, 9 Leslie Park Road, Croydon, Surrey CR0 6TN.

Muslim Educational Trust, 130 Stroud Green Road, London N4 3RZ.

Oxfam, 274 Banbury Road, Oxford OX2 7OZ.

Religious Society of Friends (Quakers), Friends House, Euston Road, London NW1 2BJ.

Save the Children Fund, 157 Clapham Road, London SW9 0PT.

Shelter, 157 Waterloo Road, London SE1 8SF.

Sikh Missionary Society, 10 Featherstone Road, Southall, Middlesex UB2 5AA.

UNICEF, 55 Lincolns Inn Fields, London WC2A 3NB.

War on Want, 467 Caledonian Road, London N7 9BE.

ACKNOWLEDGEMENTS

————•◦•————

The editor and publisher are grateful to the following copyright holders for permission to reproduce copyright material. Every effort has been made to trace owners of copyright material, but in some cases this has not proved possible. The publisher would be glad to hear from any others.

Age Concern for excerpts from *Age Concern at Work* by Niall Dickson; Allison & Busby for 'Uncle Edward's Affliction' from *Selected Poems* by Vernon Scannell; B. T. Batsford Ltd for excerpts from *Through the Year in China* by Frances Wood; *Defence* by Charles Freeman and *Terrorism* by Charles Freeman ('Today's World' series); The Reverend James Bell for excerpts from *Guidance Notes*; The Bodley Head for 'The Duckling' from *Stories and Prose Poems* by Alexander Solzhenitsyn; British Humanist Association for excerpts from *The Humanist Dipper*; The Buddhist Society for excerpts from 'The Way of the Buddha'; Jonathan Cape Limited for 'Perplexity' published in *Thinkers of the East* by Idries Shah; excerpts from *The Human Zoo* by Desmond Morris; CAFOD for excerpt from 'Some Men are Brothers' published in *The World – our Family*; Catholic Truth Society for excerpt from *Ageing in Today's World* by David Hobman; V. C. Chamberlain for excerpt from *Adolescence to Maturity*; Christian Aid for Assembly from 'Day One' from *No Turning Back* and 'A Crusade for Literacy': Christian Aid News for excerpt from 'Women who have Reason to Hope' by John Montagu; excerpt from 'Combating a Cruel Killer' by Derrick Knight; William Collins Sons & Co. Ltd for excerpts from *Discovering Life on Earth* by David Attenborough; Darton Longman & Todd Ltd for excerpt from *Enfolded in Love* edited by Robert Llewelyn, published and copyright 1980; J. M. Dent & Sons Ltd for excerpt from W. A. Steel's translation of

Nathan the Wise by Gotthold Ephraim Lessing, 'Everyman's Library' series; Andre Deutsch Ltd for 'Found Poem' published in *The Ring Around the World* by Jean L'Anselme; Peter Fieldson for excerpt from 'Another Saturday' broadcast by BBC Schools Radio; Victor Gollancz Ltd for excerpts from *Life Ahead* by J. Krishnamurti; excerpts from *The Chocolate War* by Robert Cormier; Gresham Books for excerpt from 'Hymns and their tunes' by Erik Routley published in *Hymns for Church and School*; *The Guardian* for excerpt from Leader article 'The Series 3 Nativity'; Hamish Hamilton Ltd for 'The Bears and the Monkeys' and 'What Happened to Charles' from *Vintage Thurber* by James Thurber, Volumes 1 and 2 edited by Helen Thurber, © the collection 1963 Hamish Hamilton; excerpts from *Human Origins* by Richard E. Leakey; excerpt from *Into Exile* by Joan Lingard; Professor Charles Handy for excerpt from 'The Future of Work' published in *The Listener* 10/3/83; The Health Education Council for excerpts from 'Beating Heart Disease' and 'Give Up Smoking'; William Heinemann Limited for excerpts from *The English Festivals* by Laurence Whistler; excerpts from Gypsies in Britain by F. J. Bryan Long published in *Human Rights*; David Higham Associates Ltd for excerpt from *Mastermind* by Brian Sibley; The Hindu centre, London for excerpt from *Hinduism: Some Basic Facts* by Pandit Usharbudh and Yorke Crompton; Hodder & Stoughton Limited for excerpt from *The Friendship Factor* by Alan Loy McGinnis; excerpts from *Franklin D. Roosevelt* by W. V. Butler; The Hogarth Press for excerpts from *Cider with Rosie* by Laurie Lee; Holt, Rinehart & Winston for excerpts from *Jesus and the Shroud* by Ray Bruce and Ian Wilson; Hulton Educational Publications Ltd for a parable by Brian Wren quoted by David Field in *Christianity in the Modern World*; Hutchinson Publishing Group for excerpt from 'Who Am I?' by Martin Ballard; excerpt from *England in the 17th Century* by Maurice Ashley; The Reverend C. J. Isaacson for excerpt from *Three Norfolk Mystics* by Nicole Marzac-Holland; Longman Group Ltd for excerpts from *A Harvest of Festivals* by Marian Green; excerpt from *Discovering Energy* by Frank Frazer; Lutterworth Press for excerpt from *Thinking About Judaism* by Myer Domnitz; excerpt from *Great Hymns and their Stories* by W. J. Limmer Sheppard; Macdonald & Co. (Publishers) Ltd for excerpt from *The Hindu World* by Patricia Bahree; excerpt from *The Jewish World* by Douglas Charing; excerpt from *The Muslim World* by Richard Tames; Macdonald

Publishers for excerpts from *All About Drinking* by Fiona Foster & Alexander McCall Smith; Julia MacRae Books for excerpts from *Here's the Year* by Peter Watkins and Erica Hughes; the estate of the late Father Robert Manley for 'A Train of Thought' published in *A Motley Miscellany*; Methuen Children's Books for excerpt from *Little House on the Prairie* by Laura Ingalls Wilder; Mitchell Beazley London Ltd for excerpts from *Asthma, Hay Fever and Other Allergies* by Elizabeth Forsythe; National Christian Education Council for excerpt from *Search for Meaning, 5: Image and Imagination* by Ralph Rolls; Norwich Diocesan Committee for Christian Stewardship for excerpts from Christian Stewardship leaflet; Octopus Books Ltd for excerpt from *Esther, the Young Queen* by Geoffrey Marshall-Taylor; Oxfam News for excerpt about the Calcutta Social Project; Oxford University Press for excerpt from *The State of the World's Children 1982–3* by James P. Grant, © United Nations Children's Fund 1982; 'Crucifixion' by Erno Muller from *Every Man Will Shout* compiled by Roger Mansfield and edited by Isobel Armstrong, © Oxford University Press, 1964; Pan Books Ltd for excerpt from *Maggie Philbin's Good-Looking Book* by Maggie Philbin; Penguin Books Ltd for excerpt from *Zadig* by Voltaire from Voltaire: ZADIG/L'INGENU trans. John Butt (Penguin Classics 1964) Copyright © John Butt 1964; excerpts from *The Characters* by Theophrastus from Theophrastus: THE CHARACTERS and Menander: PLAYS AND FRAGMENTS, trans. Philip Vellacott (Penguin Classics 1967) Copyright © Philip Vellacott 1967; 'Ivar's Story' (complete) from *Hrafnkel's Saga and Other Stories*, trans. Herman Pálsson (Penguin Classics 1971) pp. 129–31 Copyright © Herman Pálsson 1970; excerpts from *Utopia* by Sir Thomas More from Thomas More: UTOPIA, trans. Paul Turner (Penguin Classics 1965) Copyright © Paul Turner 1965; A. D. Peters & Co. Ltd for excerpt from *Background to the Long Search* by Professor Ninian Smart; Pickering & Inglis Ltd for excerpts from *I Love Idi Amin* by Bishop Festo Kivengere; Laurence Pollinger Limited for excerpts from *Porpoise Song* by Michael Clegg; Punch Publications Ltd for 'A Chewing Gum Story' by H. A. Field; The Reader's Digest Association Ltd, London for excerpt from 'Getting the Best out of Life' by Harry Emerson Fosdick, © 1955; Religious and Moral Education Press for excerpt from *The Society of Friends* by George Gorman; Routledge & Kegan Paul plc for excerpt from *Jazz and Blues* by Graham Vulliamy; SCM Press Ltd for excerpts from *Five Minutes a Saint* by

John Foster; excerpt from *Listen on Wednesday* by John G. Williams; Shelter for 'Iain's Story' from *Young, Single and Alone*; Carole Smith Literary Agency for 'Convalescent Home' from *The Northern Drift* by Denise Robertson, originally broadcast on BBC Radio; SPCK for excerpts from *Guru Jesus* by Robert Van de Weyer; Stainer & Bell Ltd for one verse from hymn 'My brother's keeper' by John Ferguson; Stanley Thornes (Publishers) Ltd for excerpt from passage on Divali from *Religions of Man* by J. R. S. Whiting; Times Newspapers Ltd for excerpts from 'Blunders of the Crimea; 'First Atomic Bomb on Japan; 'Man Steps on the Moon', all published in *The Times* 11/5/77; United Nations Association for excerpt from 'Human Rights' by Bryan Long; Virago Press Limited for excerpt from *Ordinary Lives* by Carol Adams, published 1982 Copyright © Carol Adams 1982; Ward Lock Educational Co. Ltd for excerpt from *Judaism* by Alan Unterman; excerpt from section on the Khalsa from *Sikhism* by W. Owen Cole and P. S. Sambhi; War on Want for excerpts from leaflets 'Eritrea, a people's survival' and 'Eritrea, born in a war'; A. P. Watt Ltd for excerpt 'When Death Came to Baghdad' from *Tales of the Dervishes* by Idries Shah; Wayland Publishers Ltd for excerpt about glue sniffing from *Addiction in the News* by Vanora Leigh; excerpts from *Freedom from Work* by Barrie Sherman; The Very Reverend Alan Webster for 'William of Norwich' from *Suffering: The Jews of Norwich and Julian of Norwich*.

INDEX